THE HAUGHTONS

PRAISE FOR LONNIE DUSTIN

"La Famiglia—the core of every society. La Famiglia, an impenetrable, unshakable unit when bound together by the sacred threads of integrity and pride. THE FAMILY, vulnerable only to selfish ambition, jealousy, and lies. It is such a family Lonnie Dustin introduces in, The Haughtons: Adoption of Evil. This book promises to stir every emotion as readers join Carrie in her struggle to keep her family's business alive. It is a must-read in 2022!"

— *JOSEPH R. GANNASCOLI, ACTOR, VITO SPATAFORE,*
HBO TV SERIES, THE SOPRANOS

"The Haughtons: Adoption of Evil—A Family Saga Destined for Success!

Lonnie Dustin has created a page-turning saga, bringing much enjoyment to its tale of good and evil. Its characters are either guided by their faith or, in some cases, truly misguided in their actions. So complex are the two characters, Lonnie has written two separate books to reveal what makes them the most unlikeable people they are! The second and third books will be published in the near future. I am certain they will be a must-read!"

"I was fortunate to receive an advanced reader's copy of The Haughtons: Adoption of Evil. It is an excellent, well-written saga. I know Lonnie Dustin. The man is one of the most humble human beings I've met in my entire life. I look forward to reading the rest of the Haughton trilogy and definitely recommend giving this book a read."

"The Haughtons is a compelling story of family dynamics with love, power, deceit, and loss spanning generations. It proves our choices can have lasting consequences felt through the layers of family. Lonnie Dustin captivates the reader by weaving a tale in and out of time."

The Ties that Bind

If you like history, family sagas, a narrative that flips back and forth between generations, and tantalizing descriptions of good food and drink plus long, serious conversations interjected with humor, you'll enjoy The Haughtons: Adoption of Evil."

— *REBECCA CAREY LYLES, AUTHOR OF THE KATE NEILSON SERIES, PRISONERS OF HOPE SERIES, AND CHILDREN OF THE LIGHT SERIES, WWW.BECKYLYLES.COM*

The Haughtons

Adoption of Evil

Lonnie Dustin

For my Family

CONTENTS

PART FOUR
NOT EXACTLY

PART FIVE
TURN OF EVENTS

PART SIX
THE PLAN TAKES SHAPE

PART SEVEN
PLAYING BEN TO THE END

The Haughtons

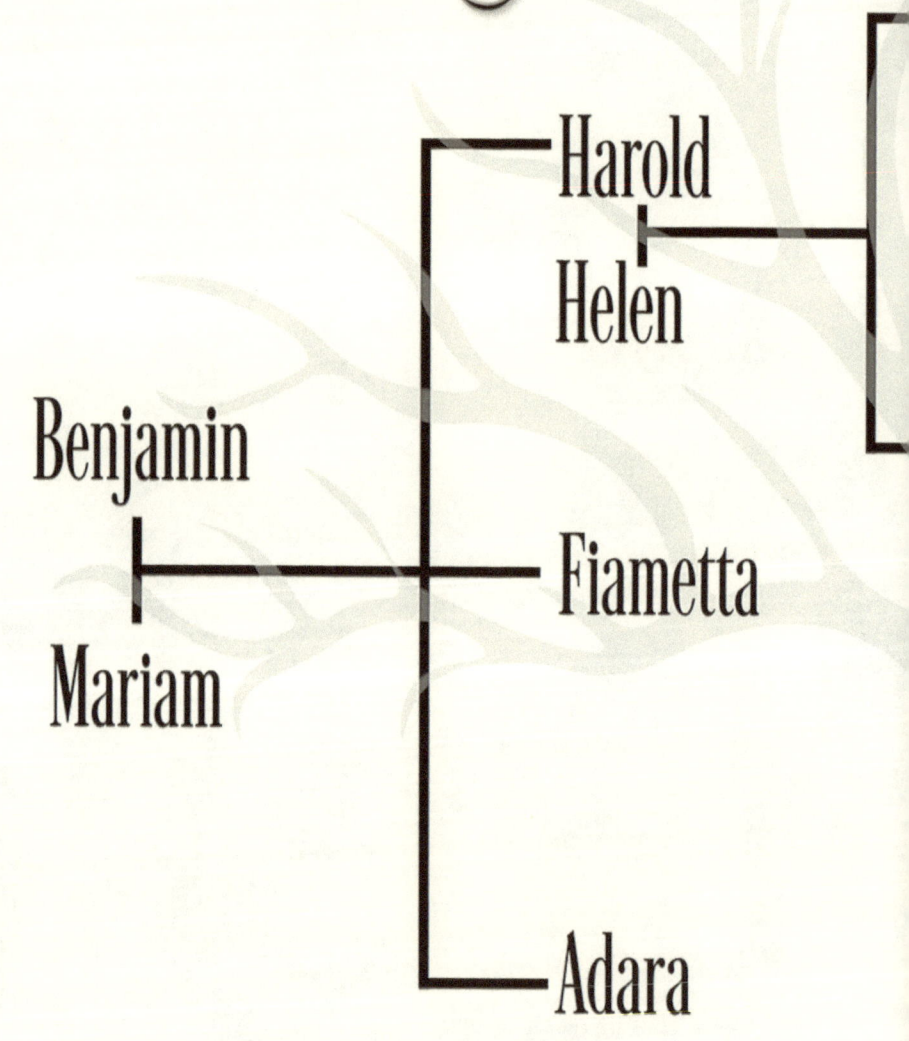

Harold

Helen

Benjamin

Fiametta

Mariam

Adara

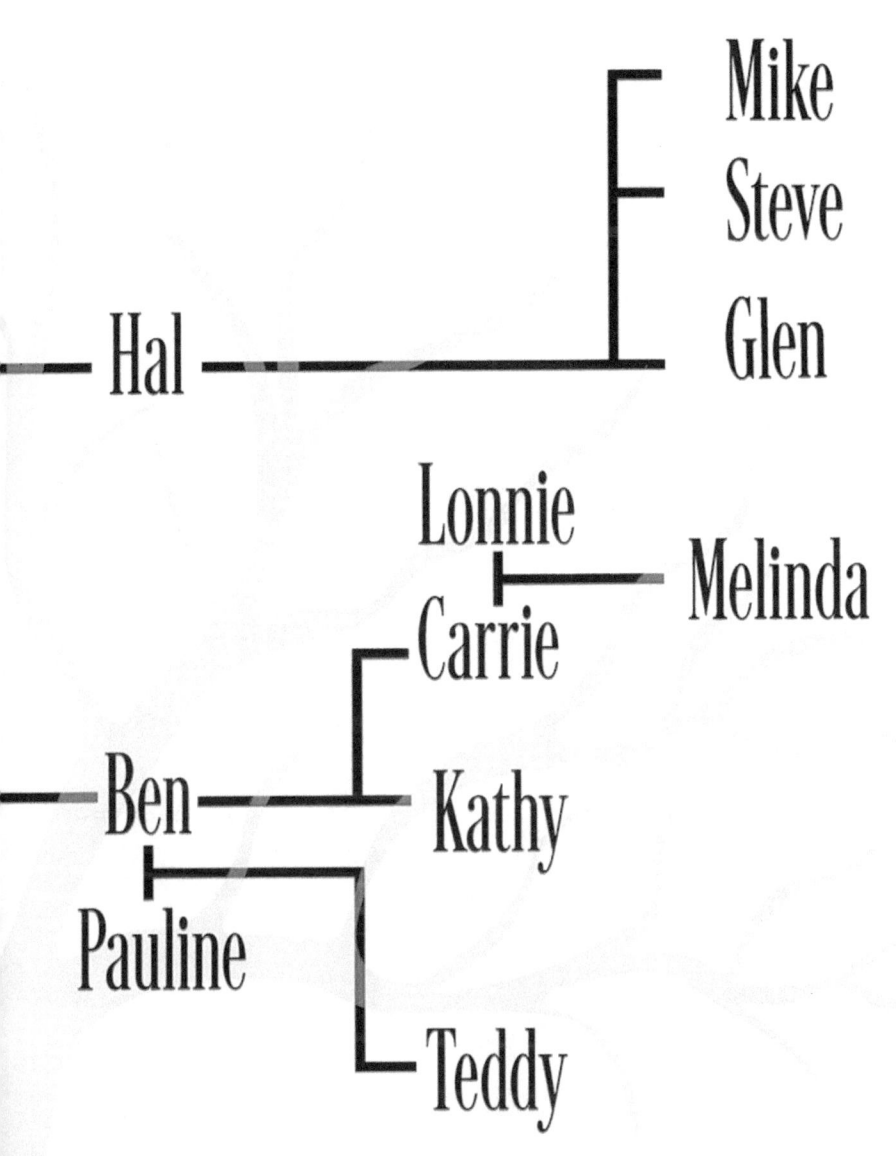

PREFACE

"In every family, there exists a Sacred Thread. When properly woven and maintained, it binds the hearts of family members from generation to generation. It is a thread comprised of faith, integrity, responsibility, commitment, servitude, generosity, humility, and most importantly, love. It is a fragile thread. It often requires mending. Should any one of the components become compromised, the entire thread is weakened. Left unattended, this fragile thread breaks—thus subjecting all that was previously accomplished to loss by the annals of time."

Founder and CEO, Benjamin W. Haughton, spoke these words on February 16, 1903, at the groundbreaking ceremony of the Haughton Manufacturing Corporation. Benjamin Haughton was a man of faith, integrity, and responsibility. By instilling within each employee these principles his corporation's successes would extend far beyond his passing.

Located on the east side of Indianapolis, Indiana, Haughton Manufacturing paid the highest wages of any existing business in the tool & die industry. Consequently, Haughton attracted the most talented employees. Anyone exhibiting a wanton disregard for the Haughton principles was unceremoniously discharged.

"Do right, or do something else!" In Haughton's mind, it was just that simple.

Time has a way of slowly—even inconspicuously—diluting the best-principled families. Years pass, and as individuals "tie the knot" bloodlines intermingle, sometimes creating unintended entanglements. Family bonds are either exponentially strengthened or diabolically weakened by the introduction of twisted strands of twine.

This book chronicles The Haughton's Sacred Thread through three generations. Theirs, however, were no match for the sharpened blades of jealousy, greed, and deception. Pauline and Theodore possessed no regard for the Haughton principles. They were biological outsiders who formed an unholy alliance and waged a winner-take-all battle for the Haughton dynasty.

PART ONE
HAUGHTON
FABRICATION

CHAPTER ONE
THE BEGINNING
JUNE 5, 2017

Carrie's early morning routine required the strategic planning of a military leader. Timing was critical. Once her shower and makeup were completed, Carrie only needed to slip into the business attire she'd positioned precisely in the closet the evening before. A quick glance at her kitchen wall clock brought a sigh of relief —*five minutes to spare*.

The garage door shrieked and groaned as it strained to open. It would have to be serviced. Carrie made a mental note to have it repaired.

Thirty miles away, a long dark driveway gave way to a spacious parking lot awaiting her arrival. The oversized lot had the desired appearance of a blossoming enterprise. Situated deep within what had once been a beautiful garden was the corporate office. It too was once a glorious testimony of success. Now, its paint had faded; its image had withered with neglect. Overgrown shrubs and weeds were all that remained of its once-manicured landscape.

Carrie steered her 2001 Nissan Pathfinder into the empty parking lot. She parked in her assigned space.

She was the first to arrive. For the moment she was safe. It was a quiet morning. She made the disquieting walk from her car, across the parking lot, to the dimly lit glass entry doors. The only sound was the tapping of her heels against the concrete as she walked to the entrance. Such a long walk was not befitting the owner's daughter. The daily repetition had all but eliminated any trace of fear for her safety. Instead, her stomach churned from the prospect of who and what might be awaiting her once inside.

She picked up the *Wall Street Journal* and *USA Today*, unlocked the dimly lit glass doors, and entered the building. The black long-nose tang floated in repose in the cloudy aquarium just as it had for weeks. Carrie hurried up the stairs to her office.

It would be an hour or two before her father arrived. With any luck, Teddy would not arrive.

Carrie meticulously followed the same regimen she'd maintained for 25 years. She situated herself at her desk, turned on her computer, and positioned her coaster where it would await her first cup of coffee. She freed her *Wall Street Journal* from the plastic bag that had protected it from the morning dew, got up from her chair, and proceeded down the hall to her father's office. After powering on his computer, she positioned his coaster just to the left of his telephone and opened his *USA Today*. Carrie returned to the first floor and flipped on the downstairs lights to welcome the packaging division employees who would soon be arriving. She sidled down the narrow hallway lined by archive files and proceeded into the kitchen. Removing precisely three wipes from the dispenser, she thoroughly cleaned the countertops, washed her hands, and proceeded to the next item of business—coffee.

The scent of freshly brewed coffee would be a soothing welcome to everyone.

An hour later, Carrie heard the chime of the front glass doors as the first employees arrived.

Although her office was upstairs and a distance away, Carrie enjoyed setting her work aside and listening to the sounds of their camaraderie. As everyone entered the office and walked to their respective cubical, they were greeted with a round of applause by those who had previously arrived. The gauntlet of welcomes became longer and longer until the last individual entered. When the last person arrived, the entire team would stand and applaud. This early morning welcome had become a Haughton Packaging tradition. Be the last person to arrive, without being late, and start your day receiving an uproarious round of applause!

Once all the employees had settled into their workstations, a few would make their way upstairs to say good morning to Carrie and briefly visit with her. They always took the time to thank her for making coffee.

Carrie would then return to her work. Her job was demanding and difficult. She was filling the shoes of her uncle, who had, for so many years, handled all the finances of the corporation. Carrie felt a tremendous responsibility for the well-being of the company and the well-being of every individual employed by Haughton Fabrication. Their challenges were her challenges, and she would never let an opportunity to personally serve them pass by. She was perfect for the job; it was Carrie's dream job, that is, until Teddy.

Later, Carrie was so focused on the numbers on the screen in front of her she was not aware of the chime from the front glass doors. There was no applause, but the pounding of footsteps coming up the stairs shook her from her work.

When Carrie sensed him standing in her doorway, she would not look up. She continued crunching numbers, any numbers, to avoid eye contact.

"You're going down! Did you hear me? You're going down!"

Another dramatic entrance, another threat. It was another reason to avoid her father's son at all costs.

Teddy pounded his hands on the door frame. His intimidating glare was impossible to avoid. "You are going down. I know everything!" He abruptly turned and made his way back down the stairs. His deep guttural laugh echoed in the stairwell.

From her second-story window, she watched his car leave the parking lot. She'd returned to Indianapolis, Indiana thirty-one years earlier—almost to the day. Now, thirty-one years later, she wondered if she'd made the right decision.

CHAPTER TWO

BEN'S DECISION
JUNE 7, 1986

arrie Haughton received her Bachelor of Arts Degree in 1981 from Swarthmore University in Pennsylvania. Having taught in the Chicago Public School System for three years, she was now celebrating the completion of her academic tenure. She felt secure in her accomplishments and settled in her community, but the phone rang.

"Hello?"

"A... low?"

Carrie immediately recognized the cadence of the greeting. "Hi, Dad! How are you?"

Ben chuckled. "Well, I'm good, good. How ya doing?"

"I'm celebrating! I've completed my tenure! I can finally take a breath." Carrie responded.

"Oh, yea; that's great, great. Hey, listen. I got a little proposal for you."

Carrie's celebration whizzed past Ben without further inquiry or recognition. He had a specific purpose for calling. Carrie's celebration did not fit his purpose, so there was no need to acknowledge it further.

"What's that, Dad?" Carrie inquired.

"Well, ya know, I got this little business over here your great-grandfather started, and it's doing pretty good, pretty good."

Ben was disarmingly humble. It was part of his charm. It was also part of Ben's passive manipulation.

"I was just kind of thinking; I could use some help. I thought perhaps, maybe... well, I'd like you to come back to Indianapolis and give—give me a hand. I mean, I don't want to interrupt your plans or anything, but it would give us a chance to work together, and it might be kinda nice. You'd have a secure job here. I know the owner pretty well." Ben continued to chuckle. "And I can pretty much guarantee a nice income and future with the business." Ben paused, "I'd like to have you here, Carrie. I'd like that a lot."

A myriad of feelings swept over Carrie, too many for her to fully embrace.

She was eleven when her mother and father divorced. She and her sister, Kathy were too young to understand why they were moving from the security of Indianapolis, Indiana, from grandparents, cousins, and the only home they'd ever known.

Kathy, two years Carrie's junior, was quiet and shy. Carrie was boisterous and expressive, while Kathy would quietly comply with changing circumstances. Carrie found no reasonable answers for the divorce, no rationale for her mother's and father's relationship to suddenly come to an end. It went against everything she'd been taught a Haughton represented.

Ben had promised the girls he'd visit them; it was a sincere promise. By air, Chicago was just a little over an hour away. However, those promised visits were soon replaced with Ben's business priorities—he was married to Haughton. His visits became less frequent, and his relationship with his daughters was relegated to occasional obligatory telephone calls.

To minimize the loss, Carrie poured herself into her studies. Her passion to understand, to make sense of the world around her was a driving force in her academic success. She'd thought with the passing of time her feelings, those memories of separation and fear, had passed. Suddenly, they were very present.

"Dad, I wasn't expecting this. You did hear me, didn't you? I just received notification of my tenure here in Chicago. I mean, Dad! This... this is so unexpected. I don't know what to say. I mean—thank you. Thank you for thinking of me, but I am an elementary school teacher. I'm a teacher Dad. I'm not a businessperson."

Ben didn't give it a second thought. He'd made up his mind. "Look, Carrie. You give it some thought. I know it's a big decision, but I think it would be kinda neat to *tighten up some loose ends* and build something together we can be proud of."

"Tighten up some loose ends," well-chosen words. They rekindled conversations she'd had as a little girl with her grandpa Haughton, conversations his father taught him about *the Sacred Thread.*

Carrie was conflicted. It wasn't Haughton Manufacturing that attracted her. It was the opportunity to reunite, and perhaps make up for lost time with her father, as well as participate in the family business.

"Dad, it's, so sudden. I'd have to wrap things up here and, and..." Carrie interrupted her own train of thought and asked, "How soon would you want this to take place?"

Just the question Ben was waiting for. "It shouldn't take you more than a couple of weeks. I'll send the movers next weekend. They can pack up whatever you have. You'll stay with Paul and me until we can find an apartment you like."

"Dad, I don't know what to say. What would I do?"

"Don't you worry about that. There's plenty to do here. You're good with numbers. I'll have you work with Lonnie Dustin. He's the director of our purchasing department. He's a sharp young fella; has a couple of kids. I know he could use some help."

"But, Dad. I need time. I need time to think about all of this."

Ben was stealthily turning Carrie's world upside down. All she did was innocently answer the telephone. Without realizing what was happening, she'd stepped out of her world and into Ben's.

Ben chuckled, "You've got time, Carrie. Look, I don't want to do anything to interrupt your life. I'd like to see you in the family business. I think that's where you belong. That's why your great-grandfather put this thing together, ya know? I think it's a good opportunity, a really good opportunity. Take this week and tie up any loose ends. The movers can be there next Saturday. Do you need anyone to help you pack?"

"Well, no but..."

Ben interrupted, "Super! Look, we'll start clearing out the guest room today. I've got an office already set up for you." Ben paused, "Oh, but you set it up the way you want; you set it up the way you want to have it. Ya know; it's yours, so I want you to be comfortable. Yea, this is super, just super!"

The excitement in her father's voice preyed upon Carrie's deepest emotions. There was no way Carrie Haughton could remain in Chicago. She was moving to Indianapolis, Indiana. In Ben's mind, she'd already arrived.

Lonnie Dustin had just finished matching invoices to bills of lading when his phone rang. It was a call that would also alter the course of his life.

It was Ben. "Hey! Good morning, Lonnie!"

"Good morning, Ben."

"Hey, listen. I want to take you out to lunch today. It will have to be a little later. Are you free at about 1:15?" Ben asked.

"Sure," replied Lonnie, knowing full well he would have to cancel a previously scheduled luncheon with Julie Givens, Representative of 3M Corporation. It wasn't an important luncheon. Their luncheons were more friendly get-togethers. 3M was a good supplier and Julie was attractive—and single.

"That's super, super. I'll see you at about 1:15 then." Ben seemed unusually upbeat.

Lonnie Dustin was originally hired as a line operator. His good nature, honesty, and desire to learn catapulted him from line operator to foreman, from foreman to the director of quality assurance, and now to the director of purchasing, working closely with Ben. Their travels throughout Europe and Asia exposed Lonnie to a broader understanding of the world. The professional friends Ben introduced Lonnie to were, in Lonnie's mind, his graduate school professors. Every meeting, every breakfast, luncheon, and dinner was a master seminar in international business.

He quickly went into the men's room to double-check his attire. Had he shaved close enough? Was his hair too long? Lonnie had to laugh at himself; this was silly—Ben would never audit Lonnie's appearance. When Ben decided, that was it. Although he was a generous man, it was Ben's world, and everyone around him was simply allowed to participate in it. Whatever it was Ben was going to talk about, it was as if it had already happened.

The morning crawled into the early afternoon. If Lonnie had known he would be receiving a late luncheon invitation from Ben, he would have been a bit more judicious in spreading his responsibilities throughout the earlier part of the day instead of finishing them before eleven. Now, all he could do was sit and wait.

Lonnie was astute at surveying situations and forecasting every angle before stepping into a negotiation. He would rehearse every potential question, objection, or restriction and formulate his response well in advance. Suppliers regarded him as a brilliant negotiator, quick to understand complex ideas. They had no idea he'd been rehearsing their meetings for days.

Lonnie believed the luncheon would go one of two ways. First, and most obvious, the tremendous savings the company posted in the third quarter was primarily due to the prudent purchasing practices Lonnie initiated in the first quarter. No doubt, a professional but intimate thank you had been planned by Ben and his brother, Hal.

There was, of course, a second possibility. It was somewhat remote, but it was a possibility to be considered. Ben never wanted to create a challenge for Lonnie and his daughters. He knew it was difficult for Lonnie to maneuver childcare while he was traveling abroad. Perhaps a return to Europe was being planned and Ben wanted Lonnie to have ample time to prepare. Perhaps it was a combination of the two possibilities. Lonnie would receive recognition for the company's savings *and* be invited to travel with Ben to Europe. Either way, it was important for Lonnie to maintain composure and act surprised by Ben's generosity.

At precisely one-fifteen Ben walked through Lonnie's office door.

"Hey, hey, how ya doing, Lon?"

"Super, Ben," Lonnie replied. *Super* was a word Ben often used. Lonnie didn't intend to replicate Ben's idiosyncrasies; it was simply one of those words Lonnie unintentionally adopted because of their closeness.

"So, you got time for a little lunch?" Ben asked as if this was an impromptu offer.

"Sure, Ben. That would be super!" Lonnie replied—capturing the first hint of information haphazardly telegraphed by Ben. Although the luncheon had been planned, Ben was acting like it was a last-minute idea.

The two arrived at St. Elmo and were greeted by Lucien, the maître d. St. Elmo had been Haughton Manufacturing's go-to since Ben's grandfather and namesake began the business. It was known by employees as the 'Tavern of Dreams.' There was always a cause for celebration when Ben or Hal invited a member of the Haughton Team to the Tavern.

"Good afternoon, gentlemen. Where might I sit you, Mr. Haughton?" asked Lucien.

"Let's, uh, let's get something quiet. This is a special luncheon. We've got some great news to discuss."

Quiet; special; great news, Lonnie was adding up Ben's buzzwords with lightning speed.

As they followed Lucien to their table, Lonnie could feel the tension release from his shoulders. He had no reason to continue with calculations. Whatever the reason for their meeting, he knew he was central in its deployment and ready to meet the challenge.

The two men casually visited about the business. Ben mentioned the third-quarter savings but made no mention of Lonnie's contribution.

Odd, thought Lonnie. He immediately calculated the projection of the conversation.

"Yeah. So, Lon, how are the girls doing?"

"Oh, they're super, Ben. Thank you for asking. Divorce is never easy on anyone—especially the kids."

"Yeah, it's tough. It's a tough thing—especially when kids are involved," added Ben. He continued, "When you are dealing with two adults it's different. You have an agreement, cut the checks, and go your separate ways—simple. When you've got kids, it sorta messes things up." Ben seemed reflective.

There was a significantly long pause before Ben continued. "Ya know, I've got two daughters."

Lonnie knew of them only because of their photographs on Ben's desk. Ben never spoke of them; Lonnie knew better than to inquire. Up until that moment, they were simply two photographs of two individuals in a dusty frame.

"My oldest lives in Illinois."

None of this discussion fit the conversation Lonnie had rehearsed. He felt a sudden urge to reel it all back in and direct it to the topic of Haughton Fabrication's third-quarter savings. At least then, Ben would be back on a course Lonnie was prepared to discuss.

"I've made a decision!" Ben announced.

Something told Lonnie, Ben's decision did not involve the dessert menu.

"I'm bringing Carrie, my eldest daughter back to Indiana."

Lonnie responded, "That's great, Ben. I'm happy for you."

"Yea, yea it's going to be super. Listen, I want you to teach her your job."

Ben's statement was firm, proud, and final.

Lonnie sat there. The words repeated in his head, *I want you to teach her your job.*

This wasn't adding up. Lonnie took a deep breath and asked, "My job? My?... Ben, what will I do?"

Ben appeared to be sincerely baffled by Lonnie's question. It was obvious to Ben, "You'll work for her!" Ben exuberantly stated as if he were extending to Lonnie a high honor.

Lonnie sat speechless. His eyes wandered aimlessly around the room. He caught a glimpse of the Coat of Arms hanging on the wall. Until then he'd never paid much attention to it. Underneath was an inscription:

Saint Erasmus of Formia, also known as Saint Elmo. Christian saint and martyr. Born, 3rd century; Died c.303. Venerated as the patron saint of sailors and abdominal pain.

He didn't bother looking at his watch. Instinctively, he knew it was three-o-three. His ship was sinking, and a nauseous feeling made finishing lunch impossible.

With Carrie and Lonnie having been informed, it was now time to tell Pauline.

"She wants to what?" Pauline was incredulous.

"Carrie wants to come back to Indianapolis and work for Haughton Manufacturing," Ben repeated.

"Well, you're not letting her, are you?" Pauline stated matter-of-factly.

"Paul, what was I supposed to say? No? No, I don't want you here—no, I don't want to work with my daughter?"

Pauline immediately elevated the discussion. "No! You were supposed to say the same thing you've always told me, 'The business is no place for a woman. We're supposed to stay home, get pregnant, clean, and cook!'"

"I never said that, Paul. I never said that at all." Ben shook his head as he walked into the family room. Pauline followed in close pursuit.

"Oh, no? Well, you might as well have. You never wanted me to step foot in the plant. Admit it, Haughton. Ever since your father-"

"My father has nothing to do with this!"

Pauline had gone too far. Ben's family's history was too sacred to allow her the convenience of misrepresenting it for her own selfish means. His grandfather and father maintained Haughton Manufacturing through the country's and the family's most difficult years. They were strong people, principled people, and respected contributors to the community.

Pauline enjoyed the lifestyle Haughton Manufacturing afforded her, but she had no regard for the family or its history. Too much of the 'Haughton' personality had been passed down through the generations for Pauline's liking. She didn't like Carrie or Kathy. However, Carrie posed a greater threat. She was strong-willed and determined—difficult in Pauline's eyes. Carrie was a Haughton through and through, and Pauline did not want competition for Ben's attention or his money.

"Carrie is going to work for Haughton Manufacturing, and she is staying here until she can get her own place!" Ben announced as he sat back in his recliner.

"Wait a minute, wait a minute! Staying here? With us? Ben, please!

I never see you as it is. We'll have even less time together if she's around." Pauline's voice softened as she knelt next to his chair. "Sweetheart, I really want us to have more time together." She gently stroked Ben's cheek. "Sweetheart, please? Please tell Carrie no; now is not the time. Now is our time, okay?"

Pauline's pleas fell on deaf ears. "She'll be here in a week."

Pauline bristled, "You're an idiot, Haughton, an idiot! I hate you and your daughter!"

"But you love my money, don't you, Paul? You love my money." Ben calmly replied.

"Yeah? Remember, Haughton, half of it is mine when I divorce you!" Pauline warned.

Ben calmly gazed over his reading glasses directly into Pauline's eyes, "Ya know, Paul, I'd give you half."

CHAPTER THREE
THE MOVE GETS REAL
JUNE 14, 1986

Carrie was surrounded by boxes—boxes hastily filled with elementary school lesson planners, pictures, and crafts. They were momentos of her unfulfilled future. She lamented leaving education before having established any notable memories.

Even though she was expecting the mover's arrival, their knock at her door startled her. Her thoughts were replaced by a sick feeling in the pit of her stomach—she was actually moving. She was leaving Chicago and the stability of her intended career, replacing it with an unknown position within the family's business.

From the time she was a child, Carrie had heard the stories of her family's history. It was a colorful history, a wonderful story—a story of unrivaled success and unimaginable misfortune. The men were strong and the women stronger. How else would they overturn the male-dominated society and enter the world of business, finance, and politics?

A sudden rush of guilt swept over her. Leaving Chicago paled in comparison to the challenges Great-Grandma Miriam and Grandma Helen endured. Stories of their strength and determination inspired Carrie.

What would future generations say about her? Would she uphold the dignity and strength passed down by her grandparents?

CHAPTER FOUR

BENJAMIN & MIRIAM HAUGHTON

AUGUST 26, 1913

I t had been an unusually troublesome morning for Benjamin Haughton. The message penned and left by Miriam, his wife of eight years, was only a footnote to the challenges this man of ascending business influence would endure for the remainder of his life.

A month prior, Miriam would have already prepared Benjamin's melon, sago, vegetable hash, broiled veal cutlets, fried tomatoes, and coffee. She would then be dutifully hanging the sheets and garments on the line to dry. He would finish his breakfast, dab any residue from his thick and bushy handle-bar-mustache, and grab his Crofut & Knapp from the coat rack in the laundry room. He would then wish Miriam a good day, whereupon Miriam would admiringly say, "I love you."

He would respond, *"You are a very good woman,"* and proceed to Haughton Manufacturing. It was, in Benjamin's mind, the way it should be.

This morning, there was only the note:

Dearest.

Fruit is in the icebox. You're a man; you can manage the rest.

Mr. Haughton read Miriam's note once again, then with his glasses perched upon the tip of his nose, a third time. Not a word changed, despite his best efforts.

"A man of means must awake to a healthy breakfast to properly prepare for the bittersweet joy of providing for his family," he begrudgingly muttered to himself.

He rued the day he charged his wife to release the household help and adopt what he felt was the proper domestic call of womanhood.

Benjamin knew where Miriam was without her even saying. What possessed him to give her permission to join the women's club in the first place? Where was the wife he had married who, without question, so dutifully supported his daily political commentary, responding with only a quaint smile and nod? What nonsense was filling her head by this newfound heroine whom Miriam placed such admiration?

And where were his hash browns and veal cutlets?

Miriam would have found the scene amusing—her portly husband fumbling about the kitchen. She might not have found his thoughts quite so humorous.

Dear God, has it come to this? A man starving in his own home whilst his wife is off sipping scandal-water? How can a man run a business with any hope of success when he fails to corral his own wife? A woman's place is in the home!

His frustration mounted as he asked himself, "What is this world coming to?"

He thought for a moment and answered his question aloud, "Certainly not the world of Marie Stuart Edwards; not if the real men of this world have anything to say about it!"

Marie Stuart Edwards may have been shameless in Ben Haughton's world, but to many, she was a charming, brilliant young woman whose education rivaled that of most of the enterprising men in Indiana. A graduate of Smith College, she'd made a name for herself in Michigan where she'd organized a massive movement and won a platform against the dairy industry's abysmal sanitation practices. Having now returned to Indiana, she was bolstered by her newfound acclaim and success. Marie Stuart Edwards was now uniting women's clubs with her gospel of suffrage.

Marie's evangelistic fervor was magnetic. From her youth, she was known as a trailblazer. She was the first girl in Lafayette to ride a bike, the first to attend a women's college, and now the first to decisively impact an entire industry—a man's industry. The time to secure women's equality had arrived. The cause was not new. However, Marie's voice was, and she was positioned to impact the political arena with a fresh and balanced intellectual passion. This drew the ire of many men and the hope of most women.

Benjamin hastily finished his melon. A real meal would have to wait until lunch.

His morning routine usually included a visit with Fil, the Haughton's mare. Benjamin would make his way through the kitchen, the washroom, and then out the door that led to a fence that extended from the side of the house to the garage. He would scoop a handful of oats for the mare and the two would meet across the fence. Each morning Benjamin offered her the oats, tenderly patted her forehead, and bade her adieu until his evening return.

However, this morning Miriam had taken Fil to the women's club meeting. Benjamin would have to forego his normal routine. With a huff, he went directly to the garage, unlocked the double doors, carefully separated them from their center-pin, lifted and then pushed each panel aside to reveal (always as if for the first time) his 1913, Model 30, five-passenger, vertical inline L-head 365.8-cubic inch four-cylinder engine, touring Cadillac. It was breathtakingly beautiful. It was precise in every detail—a quality Benjamin expected in life and in business. Its molded deep blue body and chassis had been meticulously hand-striped, and its upholstery was the finest hand-buffed black leather. Fil was gone—Benjamin tenderly patted the roof of the motor-wagon before taking his place behind the wheel.

Benjamin's motor-wagon would have once been an extravagance. Now it was a business investment. Priced just under the average worker's annual salary, it emanated the trappings of affluence, granting Benjamin Haughton access to the most successful businessmen in the nation. It fit him well and exuded a testimony of success. Haughton Manufacturing was entering the exciting new era of automated manufacturing.

Miriam found the symbolism of Benjamin's motor-wagon far less alluring. The noise of the engine frightened Fil. The nauseating stench of petrol clung to her Paul Poiret. The ride held nothing in common with the smooth lines of its polished body. While Benjamin inexhaustibly praised the attributes of this mechanical marvel, there was by no means the slightest possibility a lady, impeccably coiffured could enter that noisy, smelly, coach and be recognizable upon reaching her destination.

Then there was Fil. Benjamin and Miriam loved Fil. The mare had served the Haughtons for eight years with unfaltering dependability. For Miriam, she represented simplicity and civility. Fil represented a nearly bygone era of quiet when the air was scented by the fragrance of wildflowers instead of the fetor of exhaust. Miriam recalled when Fil became part of the Haughton family eight years earlier. Clayton Brand, a casual friend of the Haughtons had told Benjamin that he could have the irritable, stubborn, and cantankerous filly whom he described as "The most irascible creature God ever had the nerve to create!" On the day Benjamin Haughton arrived to take Fil home, Clayton warned, "I've had my fill of that mare, Haughton! She's yours to contend with!"

When Benjamin brought the mare home, Miriam asked if she had a name.

"Fil," Benjamin declared. "The horse's name is Fil."

It was unthinkable that old Fil, as healthy as she was, would be replaced by Benjamin's motor-wagon, and it troubled Miriam to now see the mare wander the pasture without purpose. Was this to be the price of modern technology?

The Broad Ripple Methodist Church was located on the southeast corner of Morgan and Coil Streets. It was a simple parish church that hummed with daily community activities. The women's club met in the fellowship hall the second Tuesday of every month—more often if special events demanded.

Miriam, like most of the women, arrived reluctantly enthusiastic, seizing upon a glimmer of hope, wondering, *What if it is achievable? What if women in line at the ballot box were within reach?* Her hopes, and theirs, were intermingled with a cautious skepticism: what had not yet been achieved gave them no reasonable foundation to anticipate its accomplishment now.

"Where are our husbands this very moment?" President Alice Wiltshire asked. Her eyes met those of each member of her attentive audience while she let her question hang poignantly before continuing with her well-rehearsed answer:

"Ah, *they* would tell us they are engaged in a most aspiring endeavor to care for the family and eliminate the monkey with a long tail. Ha!"

Alice's boisterous laugh startled Miriam, and she stole a glance to see if those around her had noticed. Instead, she found the others raptly attentive as Alice proceeded. "Fimble-famble!" Alice narrowed her eyes as she earnestly combed the room. "I'll tell you where they are. This very moment they are cursing each one of us for our endeavor to be acknowledged for our intellect, appreciated for our dedication, and applauded for our commitment to complete whatever it is they start—the very things they seldom finish! The right to vote simply allows each of us to be recognized for what we will no doubt end up completing on our own!"

Her statement initiated spontaneous laughter and applause. When they subsided Alice gleefully continued, "My dear ladies. Men are never content. I dare remind you that in the Garden of Eden, Adam walked with God... and he was still not satisfied!"

The ladies erupted with a second volley of laughter. Bolstered hopes now replaced their former restraint.

Abel Walker, the groundskeeper for the Broad Ripple Methodist Episcopal Church and Women's Club, assisted Miriam into her carriage. The gentle and soft-spoken black man patted old Fil on the forehead.

"Now, Miss Miriam, you take good care of Fil. We isn't as spry as we once was." Abel politely remarked.

"Thank you, Mr. Walker. I'll take very good care of her. I will see you soon. Until then, please give Lou Ellen my love. Tell her she is daily in my prayers."

The boyish twinkle in Abel's eyes drew away any attention there might have otherwise been to his withered grin and toothless smile. He tilted his head forward and to the side just a bit as he proudly reached for the tattered brim of his straw hat. The brim crackled as he grasped it between his thumb and forefinger, tipping it as proudly as if it were a fine Stetson.

"Yes ma'am, yes, I'll sure-nuff pass along your love and prayers. If ya'll don't mind, I'll give her a little bit-a' mine too."

Miriam gave a quick flip of the reigns and a click of her tongue to signal Fil they were ready to return home. On the way Miriam's newfound strength began to waiver; would Benjamin approve?

No, no, no, no, NO! I am a woman, and I will accomplish what I need to accomplish—with or without his approval!

Before beginning her half halt onto the long path leading to their garage, Miriam gently pulled on the leather reins bringing a puzzled Fil to a momentary pause. *Still, it might have been wiser to have prepared Benjamin's breakfast,* Miriam thought.

The ladies had all departed. The room was now empty and still. Abel found the stillness unsettling. In the quiet moments, this proud and dedicated servant of the Lord and the Church felt most alone. Left to himself and his thoughts he mourned for Lou Ellen.

Consumption was a death sentence! Hundreds had already died from the waterborne disease carried by the raging current of the flood waters. Although her medical tests were inconclusive, her sudden weight loss, fever, continual coughing, and fatigue indicated the worst. To protect others from the disease Lou Ellen was moved to the Central Indiana Hospital for the Insane. The indignity broke Abel's heart. Methodist Episcopal Church and the Women's Club raised funds that afforded Lou Ellen a residence in a private area of the hospital—an act for which Abel was deeply grateful. Her window overlooked the gardens. Through the thin pane of glass, she could hear the chorus of birds in call and response.

Each morning Abel would walk to the hospital with a single sheet of paper and a pencil. Initially, the receptionist and nursing staff considered him a nuisance—an interruption of their otherwise monotonous routine. As time passed, they welcomed the visits from the man whose faithful love for his dying wife was on unashamed display. He would amble to the front desk, tip his straw hat, bow with a nod, and ask the receptionist to write a note to his wife for him. Each day it was the same message:

"Ain' no disease can sep'rate ah-hearts. I loves you. I'll have breafas' a-wait'n in the mornin'."

In 1910, the motor-wagon was becoming an accepted means of transportation for the aristocratic population of Indianapolis, Indiana. Although many Indianapolis citizens considered these rolling, noisy contraptions a mechanical nuisance, Benjamin Haughton viewed the machines with a prescient clarity that would define his future. A tool and die maker by trade, Mr. Haughton (as his employees respectfully called him), determined a Haughton legacy was possible if he could hitch a ride in this growing industry by stamping parts for the motor-wagon. He had already been stamping parts for the city's interurban train transportation system, Indianapolis Traction & Terminal Company. It was time to capitalize on both.

Contention between streetcar drivers and the ITTC had been brewing for over a year. Untenable working conditions and low pay had prompted drivers in other states to unionize. For the time being, commerce was dependent upon the railways, but employees could foresee the growing impact automobiles would ultimately have upon the supply and delivery chain and, by extension, their job security.

The Haughton Manufacturing employees had been awaiting Mr. Haughton's arrival. They heard the Cadillac as it turned off the street and onto the property. What Benjamin would not hear as he arrived were the pounding steel-upon-steel, leather belt-driven stamping machines of Haughton Manufacturing. Instead, forty-seven normally faithful employees stood out front awaiting his arrival. Al Rankin seemed to be heading up this welcoming committee. His arms were tightly folded with his fist clenched under his upper arms to make his normally average biceps appear unusually large. Al found Mr. Haughton and his Cadillac boorish.

"Gentlemen?" Mr. Haughton's greeting was obviously an inquiry. He remained seated in the Cadillac. He squinted and tilted his head as if attempting to hear something. "It's rather quiet here this morning, don't you think?"

"Mr. Haughton, sir," stammered Walter Sherman. "Sir... well, sir... if the railways go down we'd like to know what's going to happen to us?"

Benjamin evaluated the situation. Except for Al Rankin, the assembly of employees did not appear to be angry. No one appeared to be harboring grievances—but no one was working either!

Through the window of his shiny carriage, Benjamin made a sweeping gesture to the silent machines. He whimsically noted, "Gentleman, I dare say this more immediate situation will most assuredly cause each one of us to go hungry. Come now, there is work to be done!" and he exited his automobile.

Mr. Haughton's unfettered response put Walter at ease. "Sir, if I may. The streetcar workers are growing more and more riled every day. If they stop the lines, how will we manage to get our steel? How will we be able to ship our customer's products? If they bring Marion County and all of Indianapolis to our knees, how will we be able to continue to manufacture? What's gonna happen to our jobs?" As Walter spoke, his fellow employees nodded in agreement.

The purposefulness of his gait as he walked toward the concerned group of men gave them a sense of security. Mr. Haughton had that Haughton glint in his eye. They'd recognized that glint. It was an involuntary response they'd seen whenever Mr. Haughton was about to embark upon something tremendously beneficial to the business. When it was beneficial to the business, it was always beneficial to his employees.

In the early days of Haughton Manufacturing, young Benjamin Haughton's competitors thought him foolish. Who, with any business sense, would post jobs paying wages a third higher than every other tool and die shop? It was folly—a rookie mistake. Exorbitant wages were sure to have a negative impact on his bottom line. It wasn't until every one of their very best tools and die makers lined up at the doors of Benjamin W. Haughton's offices that his rivals realized this young businessman was a force with which to be reckoned.

"Men, we are at a crossroads." He continued, "Surely, it is not the misfortune of the streetcar workers that will cause Haughton Manufacturing to falter." He lent a crescendo of volume and intensity to his words, "No, gentlemen. Such misfortune will fall upon those businesses that decry the well-being of their employees, and their manufacturing families. My concern for your well-being and the concern we have for one another will bolster our business into the automobile industry and far beyond!"

Having reached the climax of his speech, the men cheered; all except Rankin. Al exhibited no emotional commitment, but he remained still and quiet—a response that did not escape Mr. Haughton's trained eye. He had been observing Rankin since hiring him from Prest-O-Lite Company. It had become apparent, Al Rankin took pleasure in stirring trouble. There was no quiet pond he could not disrupt with a carefully tossed stone of contention. Today Rankin had given himself away. Benjamin acted as if his focus was on the cheering group of men. All the while he was sizing up Rankin and considering how best to deal with him. Noting Rankin's measure of influence, Benjamin would not be hasty in addressing this malcontent.

Benjamin Haughton and Carl G. Fisher, President of Prest-O-Lite, were vigorous business competitors. They maintained such an amiable business friendship that should either of the men run low on inventories of steel, tinplate, or raw materials, the other would, without hesitation, loan the same—each repaying the other beyond the value of the original favor.

"Gentlemen!" Mr. Haughton interrupted their cheers of released tension. "If I am not mistaken, there is still work to be done!"

With that and nothing more, Benjamin made his way through the center of the group and into his office. Once at his desk, he turned his attention to the *South Bend Times* earlier placed on his desk by Miss. Rosie.

The whirling of the leather belts and the clanging of metal dies upon tinplate sheets of steel soothed his mind.

CHAPTER FIVE
SOUTH BEND NEWS - TIMES, VOLUME 30 NUMBER 245
AUGUST 26, 1913

How in the world can it be 1913? thought Benjamin as his eyes scanned the front page, he continued his musings. *A means for slowing time must be invented lest we all run out of it without the satisfaction of leaving anything of value to our progeny.*

He made light of the passing of time; nevertheless, it was a concern very close to his heart. "What value was there in toiling if not for the benefit of family and friends? If one toils and has no time for family, they've missed the greatest of blessings. If one prospers while friends persist in their present station, with whom does he enjoy the abundance of his labor? Vanity! It is all vanity. Solomon was right!"

Giving pause to his ruminations provided him time to offer his own commentary.

"Ah, but Solomon was also wealthy!" He chuckled at his resolve. Miss Rosie, seated at her desk just outside Mr. Haughton's office quietly giggled as Mr. Haughton carried on his private conversation.

Benjamin resumed his cursory review of the front page. He quickly assessed lead stories, ignoring common city dribble, and he unconsciously added his own sound effects to each article. Low growls marked his displeasure, an upward hum—curiosity. Conversely, a downward hum signaled resolve. Unbeknownst to him, Rosie enjoyed each morning's virtuosic performance and hid her giggles while quietly guessing which story Mr. Haughton was reading based on his impulsive verbal expressions.

"Ha!" Benjamin exclaimed. "Rosie. Rosie, come in here!"

There was an unusual assertiveness in his voice.

"Rosie, what do you make of this story? I would like a woman's point of view."

LET WOMEN LOOK TO OWN DRESSES
Teaching Daughters to Be Modest and Proper More
Important Than Suffrage, Says Heflin

"Why in heaven's name does a representative of the United States Congress have to be asked to legislate something decent women should be maternally committed to doing?"

Recognizing the familiar rhetorical nature of his inquiry, Rosie listened patiently as Mr. Haughton continued, "Can you tell me that? I must take this home to Miriam. Listen to how the article ends:

'The woman who instills in her daughter the principles of gentleness and modesty and trains her up in
the way she should go has done more for her day and
generation than she can ever hope to do by active
participation in politics.'

"It is an indisputable fact, clear as the print on this page!" Benjamin continued as he held up the paper and flipped it with the back of his hand in a final punctuation.

Rosie could sense this story had personal meaning to Mr. Haughton although the nature of its meaning was not clear.

"That will be all, Rosie. Thank you; thank you. I knew you would understand." He turned his attention back to his paper. The conversation—one-sided as so many others had been—was over.

As Rosie made her way to the door that separated Mr. Haughton's office from her desk, she heard him mutter.

"God help the married men of this nation. Ha! And a double blessing upon any poor soul with a daughter! I don't know how Solomon did it."

The momentary silence was abruptly broken by Mr. Haughton's shout, "Rosie. Come in here; I need you now! Get me Roger Becklund at Republic Sheet and Tube! It appears they've had a serious accident. I want to know if Roger needs help and if this accident might affect our incoming shipments!"

The story was sobering:

FIVE TONS OF MOLTEN METAL POUR OVER MEN YOUNGSTOWN O.

August 26 - Five men were probably fatally burned, and 15 others were seriously hurt when a ladle car at the Republic Sheet & Tube Co. plant overturned Tuesday. The car was carrying five tons of molten metal when it suddenly tipped, the white-hot fluid pouring over the men. As the molten mass struck the floor, it came in contact with a pool of water and exploded, showering workmen many feet away with hot metal.

Republic was one of Haughton Manufacturing's most dependable suppliers. It had two blast furnaces with a total rated capacity of 65 tons of molten steel. The annual production was approximately 80,000 tons, making them the perfect size mill for Haughton Manufacturing, large enough to offer quality production but small enough to appreciate Haughton Manufacturing's orders.

"Mr. Haughton, sir, I'm terribly sorry. Betty Cain at Central says all lines are overloaded. It could be hours or days before we contact Republic. What do you wish me to do?"

The tremor in Rosie's voice gave away her deep sense of concern.

"I see; I see. Well, get Carl Fisher on the line for me, please; thank you, Rosie." Mr. Haughton never wanted his employees harried. He was the boss and as such he was the one to bear the stress.

Moment's later a calmer Rosie peeked around the door and said, "Excuse me, Mr. Haughton? Mr. Fisher is on the line for you." Rosie was relieved to have accomplished his second request so promptly.

"Mr. Fisher."

"Ah, Mr. Haughton," Fisher replied. He knew full well the Republic Sheet and Tube disaster was the most likely reason for Haughton's call, but he asked, "And to what do I attribute the honor of your calling, good sir?"

"Oh, Carl, you know darned well why I am calling. Have you heard from Roger? Has the accident affected you?"

"I'll tell you—we were fortunate. Our director of purchasing convinced me to buy a little more of our large coils than usual—just taking extra precautions. It was our first purchase of raw materials since the flooding. I was against it at first. I don't like tying up dollars in inventory, but it turned out to be a good decision. The larger coils allow me to shear to any of the required dimensions," Carl responded.

The horrific flooding to which Carl referred had taken place earlier that March with rains that began on Easter Sunday morning followed by high winds and cyclones too numerous to number. There was no reprieve from the torrential downpour. Levees failed that were never intended to contain the rushing waters from five major rivers, resulting in ten feet of muddy water covering a five-mile square area. The west side of Indianapolis was particularly devastated. High winds had knocked down all communication lines. Those working and living in that area were never aware of the oncoming danger until it was already upon them. Thirteen states were affected by the storms, leaving 650 dead, innumerable homes and businesses destroyed, and an estimated one million dollars in property damage.

Fortunately, Haughton Manufacturing and Republic Sheet and Tube were located on the east side where the damage was considerably less. But the loss of the Baltimore & Ohio Railroad Main Line and the collapse of bridges across the White River brought shipping to a halt for everyone. Citizens pulled together under the leadership of newly elected Governor Ralston who responded quickly with a dispatch of the National Guard and a volunteer national relief program averting the threat of martial law. President Wilson sent in a small band of Red Cross representatives to the one hundred twelve towns most devastated.

"Benjamin, what's the good word? Is Haughton Manufacturing, okay?" Carl asked. The sincerity in his voice was calming. His willingness to help was what you would expect from a friend.

"Carl," Haughton began with a chuckle of embarrassment in his voice, "I don't really know. I thought God was going to break His promise to us all with that flooding! I've purposely been keeping my inventories low, anticipating it will take the better portion of a year to get commerce running again."

"That's sound business thinking." It was a tongue-in-cheek compliment. "However, you are calling me for something..." chuckled Carl.

"I couldn't reach Republic about our orders. I just wanted to see if you could help in a pinch," Benjamin sheepishly admitted.

With a reassuring laugh, Carl responded, "We're here for you, my friend. I know you would do the same for us."

"Thank you, Carl. Thank you very much; and indeed, we are here to assist if and when you have a need." As he finished his sentence, a thought struck him. "You know, my friend," he continued. "There just might be something more you could do for me."

"And what might that be, Benjamin?"

"Do you remember that sneeze-lurker, Al Rankin?" inquired Haughton.

"Benjamin, Benjamin, Benjamin," Carl laughed uncontrollably. "Forgive me, my friend, for not thanking you earlier. That goldbrick was trouble. I owe you dearly for hiring him out from under me!"

"Well, I've thought of a way to help the both of us," said Benjamin. "I'd like you to hire him back."

"You want me to what?" A shocked Mr. Fisher exclaimed. "I'd *give* you my raw material before I'd hire him!"

"Now, now, Carl. Wait just a minute. I want you to offer him $4.85 per day. That's a good amount more than he is making now. He'll slap me with a resignation. You'll pay him for two weeks. I'll repay you twice the amount you pay him."

Carl was beginning to understand the plan, and he could not help but take pleasure in what he anticipated Benjamin would say next.

"Business is tough these days, Carl," Benjamin continued.

Carl sensed Benjamin's sarcasm, and they both chuckled.

"It will be an unfortunate blow to your company, but you see, in two weeks, the job for which Presto-O-Lite is about to hire Mr. Rankin will be canceled. You'll have no further need of his services, and his employment will be terminated."

Once again, both men chuckled.

Benjamin continued enthusiastically, "Obviously, Mr. Rankin's abrupt departure from Haughton Manufacturing will have caught me totally by surprise. I will have had to modify my production. Ah, yes, my dear friend. Unfortunate as it will be, I will have no openings for the poor man."

The call ended with both men laughing too hard to say goodbye.

Benjamin was still laughing when he hung up the telephone. It took a few minutes for quiet to return and for Benjamin to focus his attention on the current inventory ledger. It detailed the anticipated raw materials to be received and the forecast customer requirements.

With his attention singularly devoted to his inventory quantities, the morning quickly passed.

His office door ajar, Rosie poked her head inside and broke the silence, "I'm sorry, sir. Did you call for me?" she inquired.

Benjamin replied, "No, no, Rosie. I'm afraid what you heard was the bellowing call of an empty stomach," recalling the morning's rather lean breakfast.

Embarrassed, but also humored by the sounds to which her attention had been drawn, Rosie returned to her desk.

He took out his fob, 11:53. He would have precisely seven minutes to arrange his papers, lock his desk, grab his Crofut & Knapp, and make his way to lunch.

"I will be paying a visit to Dr. Stahr today, Rosie," Mr. Haughton called through the door "I do believe he might have something to cure this rambunctious gastric infirmity of mine." Benjamin was referring to Joe Stahr, proprietor of St. Elmo Tavern. He'd opened the tavern eleven years earlier, and it had become a favorite eatery for Indianapolis businessmen and their clients.

Entering St. Elmo, Mr. Haughton was greeted as if he was a personal guest of honor. It was a greeting every patron enjoyed, but Joe made everyone feel it was most sincerely reserved for them.

St. Elmo's hospitality was exceeded only by its epicurean delicacies. That day, the menu featured "Two Heartily Stuffed Pork Chops." Heartily stuffed was precisely what Benjamin wished to be upon finishing his lunch. He continued reviewing the menu. The Schwenker was marinated for three days to infuse the meat with flavor. Juniper berries, garlic, onions, and a splash of German Riesling wine provided guests with an explosion of flavors unequaled by any other eatery. Benjamin ordered the Schwenker, Fladlesuppe, and a side of fried potatoes—German style.

The Fladlesuppe clung to his thick, but neatly groomed, and otherwise impressive, mustache. As was his practice, Joe carefully reviewed his patrons before letting them return to their business rigors. Today,

Joe noted that Mr. Haughton obviously enjoyed his soup since he was transporting a goodly amount on his upper lip.

Once appropriately groomed, he tipped his hat to the waitress, shook hands with Mr. Stahr, and bid them both good day until the next time. The ills of a forsaken breakfast were, for the moment, pardoned until the evening's supper.

Upon his return to Haughton Manufacturing, he was met at the office door by Rosie, who was visibly shaken. "Sir, I have some bad news for you. Mr. Rankin, not fifteen minutes ago, came into the office and declared he was immediately leaving Haughton Manufacturing."

Benjamin could not contain himself. He swooped Rosie in his arms, and kissed her on the cheek, "Thank you, my dear, for the best bad news I've heard today!"

PART TWO
ASHA'S ARRIVAL

CHAPTER SIX

JUNE 5, 2017

C arrie's thoughts were temporarily interrupted by Asha's arrival. Asha's office was adjacent to Carrie's. Asha was Carrie's accounts receivable manager, and as was the case with most Haughton employees, the two of them had become close friends–family.

"Good morning, Carrie," Asha said.

"Good morning, Asha. How was your weekend?"

"What weekend?" Asha replied as she whisked past Carrie's open door and into her office. "Soccer, swimming, cleaning, cooking—I couldn't wait to get back to work to relax!" Asha laughed.

Asha set a small vase of fresh-cut roses on her desk and returned to Carrie's office with a vase and a single yellow rose. Carrie did not allow her eyes to stray from her computer screen. Asha immediately sensed Carrie's uneasiness.

"I brought this for you, Carrie. Is everything all right?"

"I'm not sure." Carrie finally took her eyes off the screen. "Teddy made his hateful existence known. It usually doesn't bother me, but I have a bad feeling about this outburst for some reason."

Why should today's rage be any different? Carrie thought. Intuitively,

Carrie knew her father's son and wife had been plotting—preparing for what—she didn't know.

"Have you had your coffee?" Asha asked.

"Yes, but perhaps a second cup of coffee will get me back on track," Carrie replied. "I'll bring you up a cup."

CHAPTER SEVEN
MISSING
SEPTEMBER 9, 1913

Benjamin awoke to the aroma of freshly ground coffee, sizzling bacon, hash browned potatoes, and freshly baked bread. A smile of anticipation crossed his lips.

"Miriam? Miriam, my lady?"

No doubt, Miriam was in the washroom. Ben made his way down the hall to the kitchen. He was met by the most wondrous culinary cornucopia of delights.

"What a dear heart I've married."

He paused for just a moment to take in all the beautifully displayed muffins, fruits, jellies, and oh, the full olfactory sensation of his freshly brewed coffee.

He passed through the kitchen, through the washroom, and out the back door. His heart was alive with satisfaction.

"I mustn't be the only benefactor of such abundance," he thought to himself, and he grabbed an extra helping of oats for old Fil and patted her on the forehead.

Turning his attention back to the kitchen he called, "Miriam! Where are you?"

There was no response. Fear suddenly replaced Ben's feelings of satisfaction and gratefulness.

"Oh, dear God! Our anniversary! I've missed our anniversary!"

Benjamin rushed back into the house. He had to think fast. "Sweetheart, dearest, where are you? I want to take you into town to... to..." The words faded from his lips. "Wait a minute! It isn't our anniversary. What the devil?"

He ran back into the kitchen and reviewed the calendar hanging on the wall just above the spice rack. Birthday? No. Holiday? No. He'd been so fixated upon the challenges of the potential strike and raw material shortages due to Republic Steel's terrible accident, everything else simply slipped his mind. Surely, he was missing some important celebration. He would have to come up with a plausible excuse for not remembering.

September ninth was the only date circled, "Women's club meeting, 9:00."

"Women's club? Women's club?" Benjamin's jaw clenched as he began to growl. He turned from the calendar and made his way back through the washroom and out the door. He was met by old Fil who appeared to be confused but anxiously awaiting a second handful of oats.

"Fil, there will soon be a very quick conclusion to this women's club nonsense, I assure you!"

He pulled the set pin holding the two garage doors together and pushed the first door open. It squealed as its base ran across the tracks.

One by one the ladies arrived, twenty in total. Heads were uncovered, and a few cigarettes awkwardly dangled from their fingers. Dolly Bettencourt and Margaret Chambers were smoking in public, on church grounds!

These were not the bold expressions of suffrage solidarity Alice had been hoping for. She did appreciate each woman's humble attempt to show their individuality, strength, and commitment. Their actions were not by anyone's accounting giant leaps forward. They were, nevertheless, steps in the right direction. Possibly they were the small steps suffrage would build upon, women's clubs together marching across the nation.

Sadly, Miriam Haughton was missing from the meeting.

"Such a sweet little thing." Alice thought to herself. Alice's keen intuition told her that behind Miriam's prim and proper exterior there resided the heart of a powerful tigress. "Oh that Miriam would one day embrace the true meaning of freedom, of responsibility, of completion as a powerful and free American woman." Alice was about to learn her protégé had tended to her lessons quite well, indeed.

At that precise moment, a deep mechanical grunting and grinding sound interrupted the women's club meeting. The women peered out the window. A few ran to the door and made their way out onto the porch.

At first, she was unrecognizable. Her quiet diminutive stature was replaced by a firm resolute upright posture roaring with the power of a committed heart. She moved with dignity and grace in the 1913, Model 30 five-passenger, vertical, inline L-head 365.8-cubic inch four-cylinder engine touring Cadillac!

Jaws gaping, the women stared in disbelief. Abel Walker abruptly stopped raking leaves along the back side of the building and ran to see what was causing the commotion. The rake he held dropped from his grasp as he shook his head in disbelief. With a second glance, his eyes sparkled with delight. He moved toward the vehicle; his toothless grin betrayed the not-so-well-hidden pride he was feeling.

Upon reaching the beautiful automobile, Abel gallantly tipped his cap and reached for the door.

"No, no, no, my dear man," Miriam calmly said as she patted his hand. "My dear Mr. Walker, would you be so kind as to assist me with the garments?"

The large garment bag was situated in the passenger's seat next to Miriam. "Do be careful not to drop anything, Abel." With that, Miriam stepped from the Cadillac wearing, in public for all to see, her new white bloomers.

The speechless women followed Miriam and Abel into the fellowship hall. Abel walked to the front of the room. Miriam thanked him for his assistance. Miriam then opened the garment bag and revealed thirty newly sewn white bloomers, one for each member of the women's club.

Alice was the first to speak.

"My dear, how? Where?" Alice struggled to formulate the myriad of thoughts going through her mind into one cohesive question. "When did you learn to drive Mr. Haughton's automobile?"

Miriam explained she learned to drive from carefully observing Mr. Haughton shifting from gear to gear. She'd duplicated, her right foot, left foot, right foot, left foot on her Singer Redeye. For the past month, she'd been practicing driving while sewing each of the thirty bloomers she was now proudly presenting to the group.

"Oh, and from now on ladies, it shall be known as the Haughton's automobile!" she exclaimed, raising her chin, closing her eyes in mocked arrogance while posing for her fellow club members with her foot on a stool next to the table where the bloomers were displayed.

The set pin dangled and clanged against the metal trim on the first door as Benjamin pushed the second door open. It seemed unusually difficult and continued to squeal as if registering its reluctance to open completely.

GONE!

The garage was empty. Fil seemed to laugh as she threw her head back and let out a long neigh followed by an even longer toothy whinny.

There was nothing Benjamin could do. The indignity of taking Miriam's carriage to Haughton Manufacturing was almost more than Benjamin could endure, but he had no choice. He opened Fil's gate and walked the mare over to the carriage. After placing the dusty halter on Fil, he attached the lead.

Benjamin turned his attention to the breast collar. He passed the traces over Fil's back and the driving reins through the saddle terrets. After looping the buckled hand ends, he passed them through the back strap. He placed the lead rope around Fil's neck. Benjamin took off the halter and put on the bridle, fastening the reins to it. Dust from the swollen leather straps now lightly covered Benjamin's pinstriped double-breasted suit.

With Fil prepared for the carriage, it was time to attach the traces to the singletree. He released the wrap straps and ran them inside the trace and over the shaft, ahead of the shaft loop, and then under to form a figure eight. The throatlatch and noseband attached, he fastened the traces to the singletree and aligned the shaft to give Fil room to stretch her legs.

Benjamin checked all the fastenings. Everything seemed to be in working order. He took out his fob and checked the time. Twenty-three minutes behind schedule. He became more furious with Miriam for her irresponsible and selfish actions. His lips were pursed, his left eyebrow raised in displeasure as he thought to himself, *There will be words this evening!*

Heads turned as Benjamin journeyed from his home to Haughton Manufacturing. He sat steadfast and resolute. His eyes were fixed straight ahead. He did not acknowledge anyone during the thirty-minute ride. He'd hoped to be as inconspicuous as possible. Fil, on the other hand, neighed, snorted, and whinnied at everyone along the way.

"You women are in this together, I am certain of it!" Benjamin chastised Fil.

Upon arriving at Haughton Manufacturing, he maneuvered Fil and the carriage to the barn area. There, Fil could be watered and fed. Benjamin made his way directly to the main building. He acknowledged no one. He walked past Rosie and into his office without saying a word. There he sat, but only for a moment. Just as abruptly as he arrived, he got up from his chair, made his way back to the door separating his office from Rosie's, and firmly said, "I will not be receiving any calls this morning, Rosie. I do not wish to be interrupted whatsoever!"

Rosie no more wanted to interrupt Mr. Haughton than Mr. Haughton wanted to be interrupted. However, there was a visitor arriving within the hour. Her loyalty to Mr. Haughton overruled her sense of self-preservation. She knocked softly on the door and opened it just a crack. "Excuse me, sir."

"Rosie, did I not just say that I do not want to be interrupted?"

"Sir, you most certainly did."

"And so why is it that I find myself having this conversation?"

"Well, sir, did your request to not be interrupted include the meeting you have scheduled with Mr. Edwards?"

Benjamin's countenance dropped. "Oh, Dear Lord! Rosie, Rosie, please tell me this is all a very bad dream. Tell me this is not the son of the officer and director of the Peru Trust Company and the First National Bank."

"Sir, this is all a very bad dream."

Rosie turned as if to exit but before she made her exit she turned back towards Benjamin, "Oh, and sir? One more thing. Your very bad dream? He will be arriving in about twenty minutes."

Rosie felt quite satisfied with her response. It was seldom Mr. Haughton dropped his guard and showed his vulnerability. It was an even rarer occasion that Rosie left his office with the final word. She fought off any guilt of being flippant deciding instead to enjoy the moment.

Twenty minutes later the office doors opened, and Mr. Edwards entered the room. He was a strikingly good-looking young man. Rosie guessed him to be well over six feet tall. He was dressed to the nines. The double-breasted, dark navy suit fit his slender form as if it were resting upon the shoulders of the mannequin upon which it was tailored. She sat a bit more upright, straightening the wrinkles in her dress as Mr. Edwards approached her desk.

"And you must be Miss Rosie," he said. He was careful not to extend his hand before Rosie extended hers, which she did quite abruptly causing her to blush noticeably.

"Mr. Edwards it is such a pleasure to meet you. Mr. Haughton has been talking about you all morning..."

"Rosie, if I may call you, Rosie."

"By all means, please do," she was quick to respond.

"Rosie, my father wants me to personally meet Mr. Haughton. Is he available?"

"Just one moment, Mr. Edwards..."

"Please, call me Richard. My father is Mr. Edwards."

They both chuckled.

Rosie excused herself to the door that led from Mr. Haughton's office directly into the manufacturing area.

"Sir? Rich-I mean, Mr. Edwards is here to see you."

"And you told him I was still alive?"

"I am so sorry, sir. I was unaware of your passing. I will send my regards to Mrs. Haughton. In the meantime, Mr. Edwards is here to see you."

"I will be right out to greet him, Rosie, thank you." He bowed his head. "Lord? This is Benjamin, Benjamin Haughton. I could use a few moments of your time right now."

Rosie reentered the office.

"Mr. Haughton will be right with you."

Just as Rosie finished her sentence an exuberant, howbeit somewhat dusty and disheveled, Benjamin Haughton threw open his office door.

"Mr. Edwards! I am so happy to welcome you to Haughton Manufacturing. We've been eagerly awaiting your arrival."

"Mr. Haughton, if this meeting is going to progress to a mutually beneficial relationship you are going to have to call me Richard."

Mr. Haughton thrust his hand forward, "Richard, it is!"

"Benjamin, I mean no disrespect, but I can see you've been out with the employees. My father has taught me to be a man who is willing to get his hands dirty! If you own the company, then own it! And that means getting involved with every aspect of the business. I like what I see, Benjamin. I like what I see."

"Well then let me share with you our operation."

As the men exited the office, Mr. Haughton looked back at Rosie. She immediately detected the Haughton glint.

There was no one who could sell an operation like Benjamin W. Haughton. His knowledge and pride were thick with quality and commitment. Haughton Manufacturing needed no warning to prepare for a visit. Haughton Manufacturing was always in pristine condition.

Every worker felt they were Mr. Haughton's friend. Richard could sense this as he followed Benjamin and listened intently to his explanation of each area in the plant. Each employee greeted Mr. Haughton, and Benjamin knew each employee's name. As he walked through the production areas, he would ask how an individual's family was doing, how school was for their youngsters, and how life was outside of Haughton Manufacturing. Richard was impressed. He recognized the sincerity of the communications.

The two men engaged in casual conversation as they toured the manufacturing area. Richard's questions betrayed the casual laissez-faire facade he portrayed. His were the questions of a learned Harvard alumni. Richard was equally impressed with the direct and committed responses Benjamin gave. Benjamin did not know the reason for Richard's visit. He did know that the visit was going very well.

"Benjamin, what do you say we go to lunch?" an enthusiastic Richard Edwards asked.

"Certainly Richard. We can use my-" Benjamin swallowed hard. He thought to himself, *My what? My wife's single-driving carriage?*

"Do you want to use your automobile or mine?" Richard continued.

He immediately took note of Benjamin's hesitation. Benjamin had not hesitated once during their conversation until now. "Benjamin? What are you driving?"

Mr. Haughton's mind was quickly assessing a variety of responses, how to present them in the best light, how to deflect any adversity, and how to apologize for his wife's carriage. "Richard," Benjamin said, with a forthright and unabashed directness. "We will need to ride in your vehicle. I have taken my wife's carriage, seeing as she has driven my automobile to her women's club meeting."

If there was a hint of agitation in his response—Richard did not notice.

"Excuse me?" Richard's shock was immediately evident. "Benjamin, what did you just say?"

"Richard, I apologize. I am unable to take the two of us to lunch because my wife has my automobile, and I am using her carriage. I am dreadfully sorry."

"For what?" exclaimed Richard. "My dear friend, Benjamin! Your bold tenacity, your unashamed recognition of our strong and independent women, is more reassuring to me that my father has made the right choice in presenting options to work together at a much higher level."

Benjamin was unable to respond.

Richard continued, "My dear sir, Marie and I have been wed only nine years. She is like a bridled thoroughbred, with strength under control! You and your wife must join us for supper. I do believe we can accomplish a great deal in business and for the causes of women throughout our nation."

Marie? Marie Edwards? Marie Stuart Edwards? The name rang a bell. *Oh, dear God,* Benjamin thought. *Of course! Marie Stuart Edwards, the woman Miriam was so enamored with! Marie Stuart Edwards, the*

woman causing the upheaval in the Haughton household. Missing break-
fasts every second Tuesday of the month, caused by the influence of Marie
Stuart Edwards! His missing wife and now his missing automobile were all
caused by the influence of Marie Stuart Edwards!

Benjamin searched his mind for a poignant response. All he could muster was, "Wonderful."

"Benjamin, my father thought this might be a pivotal meeting for our two companies. You have done very well. You will continue to do well with or without our collaborative efforts, but we can do much, much more together!"

Having somewhat gathered his composure, Benjamin very frankly answered,

"Richard, I am a businessman. I've enjoyed our meeting today, but I am not long on patience for guessing games. Are you offering a proposal to Haughton Manufacturing of some sort? I have invested the better half of the morning with someone I've just met who speaks as if we are about to become business partners. Tell me, sir, what is your objective?"

"Thank you, Benjamin. Thank you for being direct. We, my father, and I, and all of our holdings, want to be part of your success. We believe you have the tenacity and the determination to make correct, impactful, and enduring decisions. We can learn from you, and you can expand Haughton Manufacturing even further, through acquisition or fiat, for generations to come."

Benjamin carefully considered Richard's response.

"Mr. Edwards, Richard, you must understand that I have never been a man who thinks solely of himself. My decisions, my efforts, and my commitment are indeed for the generations to come. Those genera-tions will only know of me as a picture on a dusty frame—I am, never-theless, accepting responsibility for their welfare to the extent they commit themselves to the welfare of their generation and those to follow. My good man, I do not speak in terms of dreams I speak in terms of responsibility. I mean to instill a personal sense of responsibility into the actions of every employee within Haughton Manufacturing. I will not, I cannot compromise those efforts, nor will I allow anyone or anything to diminish our reputation. It is that reputation that has brought you here today, and it will be that reputation I would ask you to acquire and uphold if we are to take collaborative efforts further."

The words rolled from Benjamin's lips as if they'd been rehearsed. Richard could sense these were not simply the words of an eloquent businessman. Success hinged on Richard's willingness to adopt Benjamin's sense of responsibility. Yes, Richard would have to provide proof of his and his father's good faith through immediate disclosure of business holdings. Yes, Benjamin would need to examine their assets and their proposed plan of action. However, a promising ongoing business relationship, one lasting for generations to come, was dependent upon their mutual core values. Would the intertwining of the two corporations' sacred threads strengthen both?

Richard thoughtfully responded, "Sir, while I cannot at this time provide a specific business plan to accomplish what you have proposed, I can, without hesitation and in good faith, offer an open book to our holdings, our assets, and our liabilities. We entrust you with our proprietary information, fully believing you to be a man of character, a soon-to-be partner our trustees will embrace. Do we have a deal?"

Benjamin paused, not willing to make an immediate commitment. "We have an intention. We have a mutual willingness. We have a foundation upon which irrefragable trust can grow. When there is a deal, I assure you, we will have a deal as well."

With that, Benjamin thrust his open palm forward. It immediately met the grasp of Richard's. The two broadly smiled and congratulated each other. Richard couldn't help but notice a glint in Mr. Haughton's eyes. It was that reassuring look that Richard would depend upon for years to come.

It had been a long day, a proud day, but also an emotionally intense day. It was now time to hitch old Fil and head home. Benjamin knew he had to deal with Miriam. He mentally prepared himself to balance the firmness of a strong man with a willingness to be forgiving. Miriam would have to recognize her fault and pledge to never again overstep her boundaries.

Returning home Ben carefully situated Fil, still attached to Miriam's carriage, directly in front of the garage doors. He strategically positioned a kitchen chair precisely in front of the washroom door that led into the kitchen from the garage—the door Miriam would enter. He did his best to relax his clenched jaw as he heard the Cadillac touring up the long driveway.

His arms were tightly folded—not unlike his last visions of Al Rankin—his eyes focused upon the door. The first thing Miriam would feel when she entered would be his strength—the first thing she would see would be his piercing eyes. His appearance was formidable. Miriam would no doubt recoil in humble submission.

This was it!

Before Benjamin could say a word, he was met by a woman he'd thought he recalled marrying. The forcefulness of her entry caused him to look once more, carefully, to make certain it was Miriam.

"Would you like supper? Yes, or no?" Miriam's voice was threatening as she bolted through the washroom door and directly up to her seated husband.

There are times when firm, strong men—men who consider themselves graciously willing to forgive the improprieties of their wives–are thrust into making decisive decisions. Benjamin now faced one of those times. He suddenly became acutely aware that such a decision could be a matter of life or death.

The heat from the hellfire and brimstone in Miriam's eyes immediately softened Benjamin's jaw. He sat upright in the kitchen chair; his chest rose. He stood to his feet, and with a firm, emphatic, and masculine booming voice he struggled to retort, they were inches apart— nose to nose. Their eyes were fixated upon each other. Time stood still and, in those moments, both mentally recounted the events of their day and the repercussions they had prepared for upon their meeting.

There was nothing to say, no shouting, no arguing. Miriam and Benjamin simply stood there, neither of them willing to back down. Fear melted into love, anger into pride.

Benjamin was the first to move. His outstretched arms welcomed his most beloved prize; they embraced. It was longer than their usual embrace. It was warm and included a loving kiss. They not only physically embraced one another but unselfishly embraced all that each stood for as individuals.

Benjamin softly whispered into Miriam's ear, "My dearest, you have always been free. In your freedom, I am humbly grateful you chose this old baboon with whom to enjoy your freedom. I love you."

Miriam slowly and deliberately lifted her head. With her eyes fixed upon Benjamin's eyes, she affectionately responded, "And you are a very, very good man."

Miriam took Benjamin's hand. They did not stop in the kitchen. Supper would wait.

Twin daughters, Fiametta and Adara, were born precisely nine months later.

CHAPTER EIGHT
A FRESH CUP
JUNE 5, 2017

Carrie poured herself and Asha a fresh cup of coffee. Asha would take hers with cream and sugar. Carrie thought it best to drink her's black.

As she walked back up the stairs, she looked at the stream of company pictures lining the stairwell, the *"Haughton Hall of Fame."* She paid special attention to the picture of her dad and uncle standing with Lonnie and Bud in front of the new production facility. Lonnie had left the company twenty-nine years earlier. She missed those early days when they worked together.

Carrie handed Asha her cup of coffee. "I want you to know I added just the perfect amount of creamer and sugar," Carrie bragged. "I'm taking mine black today! Lord knows what that kid is up to. I need to be alert!"

"What exactly did he do now, Carrie?" Asha asked.

"He slithered up the stairs without a sound and then banged his hands on the door-frames boasting, 'You're going down!' Honestly, Asha, that kid gives me the creeps. Something is not right with him; something is seriously wrong!"

"He scares me, Carrie. I just avoid him. Your dad talks about him as if he was some kind of brilliant child prodigy. What has he ever done —anything?"

"I'll tell you what he has done, and he is not alone. He and Pauline have done everything to ruin my life—and they are so deceptive about it. They create situations; situations that make me the bad guy. Then they bludgeon my dad with their lies until the only source of safety and peace for him is to agree with them. It's awful, Asha."

"How did it all start?" Asha asked.

"How did what start—Teddy?" Carrie asked.

"Well yes—yes Teddy, but what was it like when you first came to Haughton Manufacturing? Weren't you teaching in Chicago? I mean, what made you leave? Did you ever regret your decision—was it the right decision?" Asha's questions were pelting Carrie as if they'd been penned up for years waiting to be released.

"Asha, in the very beginning I thought it would be an opportunity; an opportunity to build a relationship with my dad." Carrie paused for a moment. "I remember my first tour of the facility."

CHAPTER NINE
PLANT TOUR
JUNE 16, 1986

Ben was beaming with pride as he walked Carrie through the production facilities. He too wanted to rekindle the relationship that the divorce unmercifully had blown out. From his upstairs corner office, Lonnie could see Ben and Carrie enter.

"Skinny," Lonnie mumbled to himself when he glanced up from his work. He shook his head in disgust. Ben and Hal had given their approval for Lonnie to venture outside of the United States to purchase Cold Rolled, Tin Mill Black Plate, Stainless, and Galvanized steels for both divisions. Lonnie's distribution of requirements would be divided among four suppliers (two domestic suppliers and two new Asian suppliers). A lot of money rested on this new venture as did Lonnie's reputation.

Lonnie listened to their footsteps coming up the stairs. "Dear Lord, I do not need this right now!"

"Hey, Lonnie; how ya doing? Hey, this is my daughter, Carrie. I'm showing her around all the facilities trying to get her acquainted with everything. She just got in the other day and is ready to get started."

Lonnie politely rose from his chair. "It's nice to meet you." Lonnie was not cold; he was not impolite. He was simply lying through his teeth.

"Hi, Lonnie. It's a pleasure to meet you, too. Dad has told me a lot about you and all the work you do for the company. I'll do my best to assist you. Honestly, this is all very overwhelming for a first-grade teacher..."

Lonnie thought, *Just perfect.*

"Carrie and I are going to catch some lunch over at St. Elmo. Would you like to join us?"

Telling Carrie, it was nice to meet her was like acknowledging the executioner moments before resting his head upon the chopping block. His second lie rolled off his lips more easily than the first. "Ben, I'd love to, but I've got these Genji and Masaki Steel orders to calculate. I want to make certain I've got a backup source of domestic steel in case the foreign doesn't work. I don't want to overbuy and end up with dollars tied up in inventory."

"No, no ya don't want to do that." Ben agreed. "Well, we will have plenty of time to get together now that Carrie is here and ready to get started."

I'm as excited as I can be, Lonnie thought to himself.

"Well, okay, Lon. We'll see you later."

"It was nice to meet you," Carrie added as they turned to leave.

Lonnie appeared to have returned his attention to his work and did not reply.

CHAPTER TEN
TRUTH REVEALED
JUNE 23, 1986

The week passed. Lonnie had all but forgotten Carrie. His attention was focused on first-quarter requirements. Rumors of recession loomed. Stagnant economic growth and a decline in the dollar would affect profit margins. Bud's sales forecasts had to be accurate. It was incumbent upon Lonnie that he understand Bud's numbers and purchase the raw material components accordingly.

"Hi, Lonnie, Dad said he wanted me to meet you in your office this morning. So, what would you like me to do? Where do we start?"

Carrie's sudden appearance startled Lonnie. He was embarrassingly unprepared for her arrival.

I can't believe Ben didn't call me and let me know she would be starting today, he thought to himself. He felt a hopeless sense of abandonment and loss. He'd awakened from his dream of a future with Haughton to the reality that he was just another one of Haughton Manufacturing's many employees.

"Carrie!" Lonnie attempted to compose himself. "I'm sorry, I don't know what to tell you. I'm right in the middle of some very important calculations. I'm really not prepared to train–" Lonnie interrupted himself. His thought process had been broken. Because of Carrie, he would have to go back to the beginning of Bud's forecasts, retrace his own calculations to the point where she'd interrupted, to make certain his numbers were correct. Carrie detected the frustration in his voice "Carrie, I don't have any idea what your father wants you to be doing. I'm sorry, I don't have time right now to be training you, and I have no timeline from him for the transition." There was a forced chuckle in his voice. He looked down and shook his head as he said, "I really don't know what's going on."

Carrie realized instantly she was a threat. Whatever she had done, whatever she had said to make Lonnie uncomfortable was unintended. She wanted to rewind her entrance and make it right.

"Lonnie, I'm sorry I interrupted you. I'm the one who doesn't know what is going on. You must understand, I was a first-grade teacher just a few weeks ago. I'd already established my life. I had no vision of being anything other than that! Family means everything to me. I've been away from my dad since I was eleven years old. I lost him then and simply want to do what I can to bind our relationship. This whole thing is terribly risky for me—but it is also an opportunity to reestablish myself with my family. I just want to know how I can help you."

There was a vulnerability in Carrie's demeanor and a strikingly honest tone in her voice. Lonnie knew Ben. It wasn't difficult to imagine Ben being extremely persuasive with Carrie without really giving her any timeline of his intentions. Nevertheless, Ben had been very clear with Lonnie. This woman would soon replace him, and it was his responsibility to prepare her.

"Look, Carrie. Perhaps we've gotten off on the wrong foot here. I'm going to be perfectly honest with you. I'm having a difficult time with this. It's not your fault. I understand the importance of family. I guess, I guess I just wasn't totally prepared when your father told me he wanted me to train you to take my position."

Carrie's eyes widened, and her jaw dropped, "He what?"

Lonnie observed Carrie's reaction. *Was this the first time Carrie had heard of Ben's intentions or was she putting on a good act?* He concluded it was in his best interest to not drop his guard. There was too much at stake. He would cautiously consider this an act.

"None of this is your problem, Carrie. It's something I must work out. Listen, I have two young daughters. I'm doing all I can to care for them and provide financial security for them."

Lonnie looked down at his desk and once again shook his head. "I don't know why I am telling you all of this. I'm just... I'm, I'm..." Lonnie took a deep breath. There was no use delaying the inevitable. "Carrie, if you are going to take my job, I do not know what my future is. I do not know what my daughters' futures are. I do not know if I can step back into the employee role I was promoted from years ago. This scares me; you scare me!"

He'd said it. There was nothing more to say. Carrie just sat there. Seconds passed. Tears welled in Carrie's eyes as horror emanated from her facial expression. Carrie was in total shock. She shook her head, slowly at first. As she continued to consider what she was hearing, the shaking of her head became more violent, as if to shake off something dark that was clinging to her.

"No! He cannot do this. This isn't right!" Carrie shouted.

There was a sense of determination and strength in Carrie's voice that allayed any previous thoughts Lonnie had about her. There was also a new problem. Lonnie had just unwittingly come between Carrie and her father.

"Lonnie, this just isn't right. I will not be a part of this. You don't understand; you don't understand at all. I'm sorry, but it isn't just you. My sister and I have not been with my father in years. It hasn't been easy for us; it has been a struggle ever since he and my mom divorced. I will not be part of putting your two daughters in harm's way!"

The conversation had changed dramatically. Lonnie was now the one searching for the rewind button. "Okay, look. You and I have put our cards out on the table. Like I said, Carrie, this is your family and your family's business. You deserve to be a part of it. I can't stand in the way of that. If this is what Ben wants, then-"

Carrie interrupted, "Ben isn't going to always get what Ben wants! He wasn't there to make decisions when I was growing up. That might not have been entirely his fault, but I made my own decisions then, and I make my own decisions now! I love my father, but I cannot give up my citizenship in the real world to become an unwilling participant in his!"

It did not take long for Carrie's shock to evolve into anger. Lonnie was baffled. This inner strength was not the makings of a first-grade teacher. Still, he had to calm Carrie down before she vomited the truth of their discussion to Ben.

"Let me try to offer a suggestion," Lonnie began. "Only you and I know the effect your father's plan is having on us. If you go to him angry, you'll put a wedge between you and him—and an end to my employment for being the cause."

Carrie knew that Lonnie was right. He continued. "We've got to faith this one out…"

Carrie interrupted, "What does that mean, 'faith this one out?'"

Lonnie realized he'd taken for granted Carrie's relationship with God. Carrie was looking for tangible, concrete ideas, and he was offering something more spiritual. "Carrie, I'm not making myself clear, I'm sorry. What I mean to say is sometimes we've just got to let God work. We then respond as He allows doors to open and doors to close."

Curiosity temporarily replaced Carrie's anger. "Is that how God works? Opening doors and closing doors? I don't understand much about God, Lonnie." Carrie paused momentarily, considering how to properly communicate her thoughts. She then continued, "But, I sense it is something, God is something, I've always searched for."

Lonnie was now overcome with a feeling of conviction and concern. Carrie was his adversary! However, there was an innocence— a truthfulness in her character. Was it possible God had a plan for him to share the gospel with her? Lonnie's most immediate thought was, *God, please don't make this more confusing than it already is!*

Lonnie responded, "Carrie, this—this is not something—something I would typically talk about at work, much less to the owner's daughter. Have you ever read the Bible?" Carrie detected the hesitancy in Lonnie's voice.

"Lonnie, what's the matter? No, no I have never read the Bible. It just has not been a part of my upbringing. Why do you ask?"

"I just thought perhaps your grandfather might have raised the topic with you at some point when you were growing up," Lonnie replied. Ben and Hal's father—Harold Haughton, was a believer. Lonnie and Mr. Haughton often shared lunch times together discussing the scriptures. They weren't planned meetings, just impromptu times of fellowship.

"Lonnie, you probably know my grandfather better than I know him. Growing up, I lived so far away we seldom saw one another. When we did, religion wasn't a topic that was discussed—especially if Dad or Uncle Hal were around!"

Carrie paused to gather her thoughts. "Lonnie, I've got this—this feeling. I don't know how to explain it. It's like I'm here for a purpose —and I assure you that purpose is not to take your job! I just feel like something is missing in my life. At least in Chicago, I had my teaching career ahead of me. It was mine; I'd worked for it. Now? Now I just feel lost, aimless. I need something to make sense to me. The Bible? I don't know. It just seems so outdated—don't get me wrong. I am not against it or anything. It's just—how can you apply what happened thousands of years ago to today?

"Carrie, there is a book in the Bible, the Book of Proverbs. I think you would be amazed at how applicable it is. Do you have a Bible?" Lonnie asked.

"No, I'm sorry, I don't," Carrie replied.

"Don't worry. I'll bring one in for you." Lonnie returned his thoughts to the business. "Let's not be hasty about Haughton Manufacturing and our discussion today. As long as we are communicating openly, I believe things will find a way of working themselves out."

"I'm telling you, Lonnie, I will not be owned, I will not be controlled!"

Lonnie smiled. "Carrie, I am sensing both of those statements were never more truthfully spoken."

He took the bill of ladings from his desk tray. He then opened his desk file and removed a folder containing invoices.

"I'd like you to match these bills of ladings, we call them BOLs, with the appropriate invoices. Check and see if we received what the shipper and supplier say was sent. You might find situations where things are on backorder. Keep the original invoice and send the BOL you have with a copy of the invoice to accounts payable. We will keep an actual tabulation on the original invoice, along with the dates each shipment was received. That way when everything has been received, we can send the original with the final BOL closing the transaction. I've got a luncheon meeting with 3M. I'll be back after lunch."

"Lonnie, thank you for being honest with me. I look forward to reading the Book of... what was it?"

"Proverbs. The Book of Proverbs," Lonnie stuttered.

CHAPTER ELEVEN
JUNE 5, 2017

"I never realized how much my life would change the day I walked through these doors and told Lonnie I was ready to go to work," Carrie said as she took a chair directly across from Asha's desk. The bitter taste of her coffee overwhelmed her first swallow. "Oh, my goodness that's terrible!" Carrie exclaimed.

Asha laughed. "Carrie, why don't you put some cream and sugar in it?"

"Are you kidding? And ruin what might be the best experience of my day?" Carrie scoffed.

"No, Asha; I never realized what a turning point coming back would be. Was it the right decision? I don't know—it was a decision. I made it and was going to do my best to make the most of it." She paused. "It was either the right decision or God was going to have to shape it into the right decision." Carrie paused once again her face contorted by the bitterness of the coffee. "I just don't know why He allows all the negative. Sometimes I wonder why things can't just go right."

"Keep going, Carrie," Asha encouraged. "What happened next?"

"I remember giving Lonnie a call that Friday. I wanted to reach him before the weekend." Carrie continued.

CHAPTER TWELVE
A BIBLICAL PERSPECTIVE
JUNE 27, 1986

Lonnie was wrapping up the week's work so that he could head into a well-deserved weekend with Melody and Megan, his daughters. His phone rang. It was an internal call from Haughton Manufacturing Packaging.

"Hi, this is Lonnie."

"Hi Lonnie, this is Carrie."

"Hi, Carrie. How can I help you?"

"I just wanted to thank you for giving me that Bible. I want you to know I've read the entire Book of Proverbs."

Lonnie was taken aback to hear Carrie took such an interest in the Old Testament as a study guide for business. *Perhaps I need to go back and read Proverbs myself,* he thought.

"Well, that's super, Carrie. What did you think?"

"Are you kidding me?" She scoffed as Lonnie prepared himself for a tongue-lashing. The audacity! Passing a book in the Bible as a good place to begin learning business. "Unbelievable! It is brilliant; so simple! If you do this, this will happen. If you do that, that will happen. Wise men will do this, unwise will do that. Lonnie, I was on overload trying to take it all in. I mean, sure, there were some parts where I just didn't make the connection; but for the most part, I really enjoyed it!"

"You-you did?" Lonnie stuttered.

"Oh, my gosh! Is there more I should read?" Carrie eagerly inquired.

The innocence of Carrie's question, her vulnerability, and her openness cut deep into Lonnie's heart. He was compelled to share a book in the Bible that would help Carrie understand those connections more easily, more naturally.

"Carrie, I think the Book of John in the New Testament would be the best place to continue. I'd like you to pay close attention to the third chapter."

Lonnie could hear Carrie shuffling papers.

"Hold on a second Lonnie. Ugh! I've got so many notes in front of me, I don't know how I will ever make anything out of them! Okay, okay, I've got a pen and paper. What did you say I should read next?"

Lonnie could not believe this was happening. He was sharing the Bible with Ben Haughton's eldest daughter. Even more astonishing, she was asking him to.

"I suggest you read the first through third chapters of the Book of John. Read the entire Book of John if you wish, but pay attention to the first chapter and the third chapter. The third chapter; that's the one to pay the closest attention to. If you have any questions-" Lonnie swallowed hard, "-just give me a call."

"Well, I won't do that, but I will read the Book of John. I'd like to come by your office on Monday if that is convenient. I'm with my dad in the morning but if you have time after lunch, it would be great. Only if you have time though."

Lonnie looked at his calendar. He could shuffle a few things to clear the afternoon. He appreciated Carrie asking this time and not just showing up unannounced. "We can make that happen. I will be back from lunch between one and one-thirty. Oh, Carrie, before you go, I just realized. There are several Books of John in the Bible. You want to read the fourth book of the New Testament, the Gospel of John."

Carrie responded, "Got it! I can't wait to get home and start reading!"

Lonnie hung up the phone—totally amazed.

The morning of July seventh, Lonnie pulled into the manufacturing facility's parking thinking, "Didn't I just leave here a minute ago?" The weekend was over, and it was time to focus upon second-quarter steel requirements.

The decision to purchase steel from Genji and Masaki Steel was fait accompli. The United States steel manufacturers could not supply high-quality coils. Inclusions resulted in poor quality decorating; pinholes caused the welded sides to explode as they passed through the expander. On the other hand, foreign coils from the continuous casting lines were clean and consistent. Consequently, ordering from Genji and Masaki Steel companies eliminated downtime and raw material losses. Decreasing domestic allocations while increasing foreign allocations, however, it impacted Lonnie's workload. Asia was a long way from Indianapolis. There was no wiggle room for mistakes; his acquisitions had to be correct. Lonnie had committed Haughton Manufacturing to offshore steel. How much to order of the various gauges and SKUs would become Lonnie's top priority.

The manufacturing offices were quite different from the corporate offices. Gears and schematics were spread out on Mike Vagaro's desk, while samples cluttered Bob Padre's Q.A. area. It was an invigorating office where everyone hustled. The team was always creating new methods of increasing quality, decreasing cycle time, and minimizing wear on the machinery. It was Disneyland to master mechanic, Mike Vagaro. He was the best in the business. Mike was hired right out of the Navy by the elder Harold Haughton. Thirty-two years with Haughton

Manufacturing, and Mike would say it seemed like just yesterday he was hired to remove the leather belt drive system and create a modern-day production line.

Lonnie shared a desk with Ben. It allowed both to review one another's schedules and tighten their communications. Lonnie looked at the September first entries. At nine o'clock he and Bud would discuss Bud's sales forecasts through January. Lonnie and Bud allowed two hours for the meeting, but Lonnie knew from experience Bud would be itching to end the meeting sooner. At noon Lonnie would return to the corporate office for a luncheon with corrugate supplier Brown & Pratt.

Ben's schedule was also full. He and Carrie would meet with Cincinnati Milacron at ten o'clock and continue their meeting through lunch at St. Elmo.

The next entry on the schedule confused Lonnie. Carrie had made the entry: "Carrie, Lonnie, John—2:00, Corporate Office."

At two o'clock Lonnie was saying his goodbyes to the Brown & Pratt Representatives when Carrie walked in. Lonnie took a moment to introduce Carrie. The three of them exchanged cards, pleasantries, and polite farewells. Lonnie walked around his desk and took a seat; Carrie took a seat directly across from him.

"How was lunch with your dad?" Lonnie asked.

"It was at St. Elmo. What could go wrong?" Carrie responded.

They both laughed.

"Carrie, there is so much of your family history in that restaurant, personal get-togethers, business decisions; every time I walk through the doors, I imagine your great-grandfather sitting at one of the tables. I think about how many Haughton Manufacturing successes were created from discussions around those tables. It has a romance that only time creates."

"I feel the same way, Lonnie. I don't think I will ever tire of it!"

Lonnie then switched his attention to their meeting. "Carrie, I was at the production office this morning going over my schedule and prepping for my steel orders. I noticed a note you added to today's schedule. Are we expecting someone to join us?" It was obvious, Carrie didn't know what Lonnie was referring to. "John; you made an entry stating that John would be joining us."

"Oh, that," Carrie laughed. "Lonnie, you've forgotten? I promised I would read the verses in John that you gave me on Friday. I made the entry on your and Dad's schedule to remind you that we are supposed to talk more about the Book of John."

Lonnie was embarrassed to have forgotten. Carrie, on the other hand, had placed the utmost importance upon keeping her commitment to read the verses. A wave of conviction washed over Lonnie. How could he have allowed *'things'* to interrupt his focus? All the temporary things that filled his weekend paled at the importance Carrie placed in understanding those verses, and whom those verses referred to. Today, Carrie would minister to Lonnie.

"Lonnie, thank you. Thank you from the bottom of my heart. I've not only found what I have been searching for—I have found *who* I have been searching for. Lonnie, those verses did something to me; in me. I can't explain it. It's like a fog lifted; I understood them, the flow of them. They compelled me to read more. As I read, I felt like pieces of a puzzle were being put together. The Word isn't just an audible sound. The Word is Jesus! Are you kidding me? The Word is Jesus, Lonnie! It even says it clearly, *'and the Word became flesh and lived among us.'* I get it! I get it, Lonnie!"

Lonnie sat there not knowing what to say, how to react.

"Lonnie, this is the most important thing in the world! I need more. I need to understand more. How does it work? There are so many verses. Where do I go from here? Is there a proper order? I have so many questions, Lonnie. I'm going to need help. I'm going to need answers. Will you help me?"

Lonnie was still searching for the right words to say, and he stood in awe of what had just taken place. *Where did this woman get her drive, her unflinching honesty, her strength in vulnerability?* he thought.

"Carrie, of course, I will help you in any way I can. Life doesn't necessarily get any easier, but you never have to feel alone going through it. You now have the indwelling Spirit Who will guide you in all things. Carrie, I cannot express in words how happy I am for you."

"I think I need to find a church. I have so much to learn. Can I visit your church?" Carrie asked enthusiastically.

"Absolutely! Would you like to go Sunday with me and my girls?"

"Are you sure it wouldn't be a problem?"

"No problem at all. We'll pick you up at ten. The service starts with music at ten-thirty."

"Okay then. I'm excited to meet your daughters. What are their names again?"

"Melody and Megan."

"Oh, that's right. What should I wear? Are there any, rituals or words I need to memorize?"

Lonnie laughed. Carrie's spirited questions mingled with her exuberance were a refreshing break from business.

CHAPTER THIRTEEN

JUNE 5, 2017

"Asha, I felt like a fish out of water sitting in that church. I didn't know the songs, I couldn't find the verses, and I felt totally exposed. I thought everyone could see that I was the resident amateur." Carrie chuckled. "When they passed the offering plate, I asked Lonnie how much the service cost!" Asha and Carrie laughed. "And yet, as the service continued, I felt unusually at home."

Carrie attempted another sip of her coffee, grimaced, and said, "Well, I could talk about this all day. We'd better get some work done." Carrie made her way into her adjacent office.

"What? You can't just leave me hanging like that!" Asha called out. "What happened next?"

Carrie just laughed. "We'll go to lunch today. I'll take you to St. Elmo and tell you the whole story—but I promise, you are never going to believe it! Let's get those cash receipts entered and get started on payroll."

"Got it, boss!" Asha said. "Why are family businesses so messy?"

Carrie laughed and from her desk shouted back, "We'll talk about it at lunch."

"Talk about what?" Once again Carrie was startled. Ben was

standing in Carrie's doorway. *I've got to start closing that door!* Carrie thought to herself. "Good morning, Dad. How was your weekend?"

"Oh, I don't want to bug you if you are busy with something."

"No, no it's all right. Dad, Teddy just left minutes ago. He appeared angry with me, and I am not certain what brought it on."

Ben chuckled. He continued chuckling as he was talking. "Well, you know how Ted can be. He's just really, really smart and wants everything to be perfect all the time."

"Dad, he *has* everything perfect!"

Ben laughed. "Well, I guess you're right. It's not too demanding a job when you are running just under capacity and making money. Carrie, He's just so darned smart. It makes it kinda hard to work with him sometimes. I'm telling you; he gets on that computer phone of his and you can ask him anything, anything! In three clicks he has the answer. I mean, it's amazing! I'm not that way; I never was. That's why he is so demanding. He wants everything right now!"

Ben lightly pounded his fist on Carrie's desk as he spoke, chuckling as he imitated Teddy's personality. Carrie knew there was no use discussing the matter further. Explaining to her dad anyone could bring up a number of answers immediately on their cell phone these days would only sound as if she was either competing with Teddy or belittling him.

"Dad, I know you want Teddy to run the business. I just need to be here until I retire. I'll do all that I can to help you train him and help him have a financially healthy company."

"Carrie, you and Kathy will be taken care of. You are the executor of my will. In fact, that reminds me. We need to see Jake Bateman about my will. There are a couple of things I want to change, and I want you to be there with me on Thursday when I change them. Are you free for a couple of hours in the morning?"

Irvin Bateman, Jake's father, had been the Haughton's attorney for over fifty years. He'd worked with Benjamin Haughton, Harold

Haughton, Ben, and Hal Haughton. Irv took a liking to Carrie the moment he was introduced to her.

Jake Batemen was young, energetic, and brilliant. He complimented his father's endeavors in taking over the practice and increasing its growth exponentially.

Ben continued, "I'll give him a call and see when he's got some time."

"Okay, Dad. Just let me know."

Ben turned to walk away. "Hey, Carrie?"

"Yes, Dad?" she heard Ben's footsteps returning to her office.

"Ya wanna go to lunch Thursday since we will be together anyway?"

"Sure, Dad. I'd love to! St. Elmo?"

They both laughed. "Hey! That sounds like a great place! I'll come over and get you and we'll drive down together. I'll let you know what time Jake can see us."

"Okay, I'm looking forward to it!"

"Real good, real good-" His conversation was interrupted by his cell phone ringing.

"A-low? I'm at the office. No, the corporate office. Where are you? Now? Let me just check my messages... Okay, okay I'm coming." Ben turned, walked down the stairs and into the parking lot. Carrie watched from her office window as his car exited the lot.

Asha entered Carrie's office. "What was that all about?"

"I don't know, but do you see what I mean? Something is going on." Carrie replied, still staring out her office window. "I don't know what it is, but something is definitely going on."

"Do you think he heard me?" Asha nervously asked. "Do you think he heard me ask why family businesses are so messy?" Asha was suddenly sickened by the thought Ben had overheard.

"I don't think Dad heard anything. That call bothered him." Carrie turned and continued, "Family business *is* messy, but it doesn't have to be if everyone pulls together. Our family always faced challenges. This company would not exist today if it wasn't for the strength of family."

"Strength of *men*." Asha critically interjected.

"Strength of *family*." Carrie staunchly maintained her point. "The men were strong. They were strong and determined. But think how much stronger the women had to be. My great-grandmother and grandmother not only fought alongside their husbands, but they also had to overcome the societal curse of being women."

CHAPTER FOURTEEN
COURAGE!
SEPTEMBER 23, 1913

U ntil now, the Methodist Episcopal Church Women's Club led a cohesive campaign for suffrage. There was concurrently a movement to yoke temperance with suffrage. Alice was firmly in favor of uniting these two causes, while Miriam believed to do so compromised the potential victory of either. Miriam stood and addressed the women in attendance.

"Ladies, it is only reasonable. If we win the right to vote, we hold in our hands the opportunity to attain the Temperance Initiative and many other worthy causes. If, however, we dilute our mission by attaching additional worthy causes to our quest for suffrage, we willfully defeat our core endeavor and achieve neither of the intended objectives. This is what the opposition wants! Let us be singular in our endeavor. Let us speak with one voice. Let us take careful steps to accomplish the greater value so that we might, with God's help, achieve those things that benefit all children, women, and men alike in our great nation."

The applause was boisterous and immediate.

Alice banged her gavel against the podium. While she had a deep love for Miriam and while she was proud of the transformation she had witnessed in Miriam's maturity and strength, she could not contain her disapproval of Miriam's statement.

"Mrs. Haughton; Miriam. While I respect your enthusiasm, I cannot disagree with you more. How is it that you and others here applauding feel it is appropriate to compromise what is spiritually and socially right, for the selfish endeavor of gaining our right to vote? If we chose to move in the direction, you suggest and we lose, have we not lost the opportunity for any influence upon the morals of our society? I say we fight for both! Both are right! Ladies, we must not relegate one above the other. Either we are strong and move forward together, or we capitulate to play our male counterpart's long and exhausting games of give and take. We have for too long given! It is time for us and for all women to take!"

The applause was once again impulsive, albeit somewhat muted by confusion.

"Alice, we are so close to an agreement. Women throughout our nation are setting aside their individual goals, delaying their private gratifications, to unite in formulating an unshakable foundation. A foundation upon which our nation, for the first time, sees and hears the heart of America not simply the business of keeping her wheels of industrial enterprise turning."

"No! With all due respect, Miriam, we cannot tiptoe into the waters we rightfully, collaboratively own! If we dare wade into the river politic, we expose ourselves to the men who have been controlling its flow. Do we not have a cause? Do we not agree upon the evils of liquor, of lives broken because of its evil influence? Are we to say that the safety and stability of the home are any less important than our quest for suffrage? Are you willing to unequivocally make that statement?"

"Alice, no! I am not in opposition to the endeavors to which you refer. But if we do not win the right to vote, what good is our cry for these other causes? Have your cries for temperance changed anything? No!" Turning her attention to the women in attendance Miriam asked,

"Ladies, have any of you influenced our local governing bodies with your cries for social change?"

Miriam took time to intently gaze into the eyes of every woman seated before her. This was not a cursory perusal of an audience. Miriam was searching into the depths of each woman's soul.

"No ladies; no! As sincere as we might be, we will only remain the bothersome gnat flying in the ears of our male masters if we do not first establish our equality with our vote!"

Gone was any endeavor to be polite. If this argument could not be won within the walls of women's clubs across America, the war for equality would never become a cohesive issue for a public vote.

"Miriam, you are beginning to whine."

"Alice, listen to yourself! You are now drumming the accusations of a man!"

With that, Alice slammed her gavel against the podium, breaking its handle and causing the head of the wooden mallet to fly into the center of the group of women.

"This meeting is adjourned!"

Miriam exited the hall. Dolly Bettencourt and Margaret Chambers pursued her. They'd heard her argument and wanted to console her with their vote of approval.

"Miriam, Miriam, please wait," Dolly begged.

Miriam appeared not to hear their call, but instead, she walked purposefully to the Haughton automobile. Abel was awaiting her and opened the driver-side door as she arrived. She took his hand for assistance as the ladies caught up. To their surprise, they did not find Miriam in need of consoling. Quite the contrary, Miriam had a broad and confident smile as she gave a nod and a wink.

"Ladies, I will wait for nothing. I will press forward; however, I will do so for the primary cause, which has been my endeavor from the beginning, suffrage! We will win! Courage ladies, courage!" The ladies applauded as the Haughton Cadillac coughed to life and Miriam headed homeward.

Alice approached the two. "And what is it that has each of you celebrating?"

The ladies noted the disgust in Alice's voice. This was not the time
to back down. Dolly was first to respond. "Alice, we are fighting for
suffrage. Do you remember? Suffrage. Once we win, and we will win,
we will fight for every endeavor affecting the lives of women and children throughout the country. It takes leadership, Alice. Your display of
anger is not leadership. It is what the men expect. You must not divide
the cause and minimize our primary purpose!"

Alice began, "But I-"

She was immediately interrupted by Margaret. "No, Alice! There
are no 'buts.' We are in this together and we need you to join arms with
Miriam. Alice, she is gifted. She exudes an inner strength that inspires.
You see it too; you fear it—we understand. Do not let your fear derail
us. It is her inner strength, bolstered by our support, that which will
gain the respect of anyone in opposition to our cause. Courage!"

CHAPTER FIFTEEN

THE MARCH

A bel began his morning earlier than usual; this was not a usual day. The women's club's first suffrage march would begin promptly at noon. Abel would prepare light refreshments for the ladies on Tuesdays, but today, he would be preparing a full breakfast, complete with eggs, hash browns, biscuits, and gravy. There would be fresh-cut flowers at each table and the best fresh-roasted coffee in town.

Abel would attend to the needs of the sanctuary and fellowship hall before preparing breakfast. He had never been given a formal job description; there was no need. Abel was a quiet, selfless, and loving man who, without hesitation, was committed to caring for the Lord's house and the needs of the parishioners attending.

Both of Abel's grandparents, on his mother's side, had been young slaves on the very grounds the Methodist Episcopal Church now stood. In 1820, an Indiana Supreme Court freed all remaining slaves in the state. His parents met one another on these grounds. Young Abel made a commitment to his mama and pa—he would dedicate himself to caring for their family's sacred grounds of freedom.

Today Abel had a rigorous schedule:

- Up at 5:00 AM
- Clean the sanctuary by 6:30 AM
- Clean the fellowship hall for the women's club breakfast by 7:30 AM
- Set up tables and chairs, meal prep for breakfast by 9:00 AM
- Leave a note for Lou Ellen 9:30 AM
- Begin cooking at 10:00 AM
- Serve breakfast at 10:45 AM
- Cleanup by 1:00 PM

It was now 8:45 AM. Abel had only to peel a few more russets before walking to the Central Indiana Hospital to leave his love note for Lou Ellen.

Abel's pace was quick, but he had hardly broken a sweat as he walked through the doors of Central. It was a scene that had been repeated every day for the past seven months. As he entered the hospital, Abel noticed an unfamiliar nurse seated at the front desk.

"Good morning, you must be Mr. Walker."

"Morn'n ma'am. Yes'm I is. Pleased to meet you." Abel politely tipped his hat. "I'd likes to have a note sent to Lou Ellen Walker, if ya'll don't mind." There was an uncomfortable pause. Not a pause of indecision, but a decisive pause. Instinctively, Abel knew something had happened. "Ma'am, is, is there sump'n wrong?"

"I am so very sorry, Mr. Walker. We will not be able to deliver your note."

Tears welled in Abel's eyes as an involuntary deep breath, shaking him to his core, overcame him. A hand gently touched his shoulder. His head dropped awaiting the news from the doctor. He'd mustered as much strength as the moment would allow. Abel turned and found himself looking directly into the eyes of his beautiful bride, Lou Ellen.

As all the nurses converged on the scene, the receptionist behind the desk warmly said, "Mr. Walker, you'll have to deliver your love personally from now on. Lou Ellen is being released; she is well."

There was not a dry eye in the room.

Dr. Warner Brystol approached Abel and Lou Ellen. "Abel, Lou Ellen has a pulmonary issue, but it is not life-threatening. We had to take every precaution. It so closely mirrors tuberculosis we had to error to the possibility that it was. Your wife is a fighter. Lou Ellen, congratulations. I'd like to see you in three months. I believe the best medicine I can give to you is to send you home."

Lou Ellen looked into Abel's eyes. "Old man, you gotta breakfast to cook for me. You've promised it to me every day for seven months. I'm fix'n to enjoy it with you!"

They once again embraced.

"Oh, my Lawd!" Abel shouted. "I gots to fix breafas' for the ladies! We gots to get back to the church!"

Dr. Bristol interrupted, "That won't be a problem, Mr. Walker. I will be happy to take you."

Broad Ripple Methodist Episcopal Church was teeming with excitement! "Ladies? Ladies, please! May I have your attention?" The veins in Alice's neck budged as she strained her voice to bring the raucous group under control.

"Mr. Walker should be here any moment, and we will begin serving breakfast. In the meantime, I would like to go over the route we will take and the objectives we wish to achieve along the way."

One by one, conversations concluded, and the ladies took their seats.

"We will begin our march on Coil Street and turn right onto Logans Port Avenue. We will pass our leaflets along the way encouraging women to join our cause and our club. We will then turn right onto Riverview Drive distributing leaflets to those congregating along the White River. Continuing south on Riverview, where it becomes Washington Boulevard, we will turn left where Washington Boulevard intersects 62nd Street. I do hope we will have a respectful number of ladies join our march as we turn left onto 62nd Street just a short way to Central. We will turn right onto Central and continue until we turn left onto 59th Street."

Betty Thomas interrupted, "Alice, my dear. When are you expecting Mr. Walker to arrive? Shouldn't he be here by now?"

"Alice, let's eat. You can give us the directions while we are eating," continued Delores Miller.

"Please, ladies. Mr. Walker will be here momentarily, please! It is important to know where our greatest opportunities will be during our march. When we arrive at the corners of 59th Street and 62nd Street, we will be joined by Grace Clarke, a leading suffrage activist and journalist. You've read her column in the *Indianapolis Star*. Grace will be accompanied by representatives from the Woman's Franchise League."

Alice's announcement recaptured the ladies' attention. Grace Julian Clarke's joining them in their march for suffrage was, to this humble group of twenty women, validation. It solidified their commitment to the vision of suffrage and to one another.

Their excitement was suddenly interrupted by a familiar voice coming from the back of the room.

"Excuse me, ladies." Abel Walker interjected, "I's sorry to be so late." There was immediate applause at the sound of Abel Walker's voice. "I hates to impose upon all-ya'll but I gots a guest I'd like to have joined us for breafas'. You see, for seven months I been promising her I'd have it ready."

Abel stepped aside. His chest once again raised with an involuntary deep and emotional breath as Lou Ellen stepped into the doorway. No one moved; no one made a sound. It was as if God held their tongues so that their hearts could take in the miracle they were witnessing.

With unshakable determination, Lou Ellen spoke, "Sisters we has work to do. We has a mission that cannot be denied. We has new life, new hope, and new opportunities await us just round the corner. Today, I walk with you grateful for my new freedom, and I am ready to fight for the freedom of all women across dis nation."

Cheers, tears, and praises echoed throughout the halls of the church.

Miriam, rising from her chair, implored the ladies, "Ladies, we must take this energy to the streets. Our praises will be a precursor to the power we are about to attain. Our joy will be in the justification of our cause. Our victory will be the fulfillment of the visions of Susan B. Anthony, Alice Stone Blackwell, Carrie Chapman Catt, Paula Wright Davis, Julia Ward Howe—and although Julia recently went to be with the Lord herself, 'Battle Hymn of the Republic' shall be our battle cry: glory, glory, hallelujah! And there are many more who have gone before us. Let us carry their banner into the promised land of true freedom."

Lou Ellen walked up to Miriam. "Mrs. Haughton, may I give you a hug?"

"Mrs. Walker, it would be my honor. Please, dear, You and Mr. Walker sit here with me. Today we will walk together! We'll join arms and show the world this is a walk for the freedom of all women."

Following breakfast and prayer, with Lou Ellen by her side, Miriam led the Marion County Women's Club Suffrage March.

"Miriam, Lou Ellen, Miriam, Lou Ellen; please wait!" Miriam could hear Alice's call. Alice made her way from the back of the group and approached Miriam. "I would be honored if you would allow me to walk with the two of you ladies." Alice paused for a moment to emphasize her change of heart. "To proudly walk with you ladies—for suffrage!" Alice turned and addressed their fellow marchers, "Ladies, Miriam is correct. Our first steps together shall be for suffrage!"

Once again, the ladies enthusiastically chanted, "Cour-age! Cour-age! Cour-age!" They marched down Coil Street, chanting as they marched. Turning right onto Logans Port Avenue, they were met by twelve armed police officers. Miriam bristled. "Sir! I see absolutely no reason for such a show of force against our small group of women!"

One of the officers stepped forward, "Ma'am, we're not in opposition. We have been ordered by the city to maintain crowd control."

"Crowd control? Ha!" chided Alice.

Miriam pushed forward, and the officers flanked the ladies on either side.

The women approached Riverview Drive and could hear what sounded to be voices in the distance. The sound swelled into a thundering surge as they turned onto Riverview Drive. The humble group was met with cheers and applause as they came into view. Hundreds of women lined the street awaiting their arrival. Many held signs demanding equality. Every woman proudly waved an American flag. In a matter of seconds, this little band of determined women grew to a force of over one hundred suffragists.

Their celebration of force was short-lived as a group of angry men awaited the ladies on the corner of Washington Boulevard and 62nd Street. Reaching the corner, the women were assailed with demeaning slurs and insults.

Rage surged from deep within Miriam's soul. She'd never stood before such a pitiful assembly. She raised her hand and brought the ladies to a temporary halt. Stepping away from Lou Ellen and Alice, she walked directly up to the man who seemed to be the leader of the protest. He shoved a hastily scribbled, butcher-paper sign ladened with vulgar epithets in Miriam's face. Without a moment's hesitation, she reached forward, grabbed the top of the sign, and tore it from top to bottom.

"You, and the likes of you, will no longer hide behind your filthy signs and slurs. You will no longer be allowed to organize against us in the shadows. I stand before you, not your band of pitiful miscreants." Miriam moved closer to the man. "I do not fear you." She paused, looking over the man's shoulder at those standing behind him. She stared every man in the eye. Brushing past the leader of the group, she walked toward those following. "I do not hate you. No, I would not waste such emotion. I despise your narrow-minded, self-centered disregard for your wives and daughters—for all women!" She turned her attention back to the man. She glared at him for a moment as her emotional courage once again swelled and she met him face to face. She could smell the stench of chewing tobacco as he breathed rapidly. "I am standing before you! What have *you* to say? I ask *you*. Not your assembly. Speak!" Fear had paralyzed the man. Never had he faced a woman who spoke with such threatening power.

Recognizing this man had been neutralized, Miriam turned her attention to the band of men who followed him.

"I ask any one of you; no, I challenge you; come out from the crowd and stand for what you believe. You men, hear me out! Bold outbursts and passionate oratory do not establish the truth. Chaotic frenzy is not inspiration. Treading upon the sacred altar of another's beliefs is not evangelism. Words of condemnation are not proof of power." She looked back at the man pitifully standing alone with the torn sign at his feet. Miriam continued, "Inciting an uprising against another's freedom is not evidence of leadership." Facing the group of men, Miriam motioned with her right hand to their leader. "I ask you. Who blindly authorized this man's display to be honored as evidence of a worthy cause? What validates your willful abuse of our honor, our character, and our beliefs? Who would follow this tyrant's noise?" Miriam wagged her finger in the faces of the men. "I warn you, each one of you! Watch closely, you who would wade into this man's rapids, lest you be misled to think you govern the course!"

No one said a word. The corner of Washington Boulevard and 62nd Street had never been more still. Miriam returned to the center of the boulevard, and she forcefully locked arms with Lou Ellen and Alice.

"Ladies, we march!"

Onlookers continued to join in the march, increasing the suffragist's numbers with every step they took. By the time they reached Broad Ripple Park, over 350 women were added to the original band of 22. The rally at Broad Ripple was a celebration of confidence. Women would no longer be denied. Suffrage was within their grasp.

CHAPTER SIXTEEN
COLLABORATION
NOVEMBER 1913

The guard's outstretched palm brought Richard's and Benjamin's pace to a halt. "I am sorry, gentlemen. No one is allowed to enter the statehouse without approval from the governor."

Richard's polite but authoritative response to the guard caught Benjamin by surprise. "Officer, we appreciate the gravity of the situation; however, we are here with the full authority of the Chamber of Commerce to participate in confidential business negotiations."

We are? thought Benjamin. *I was under the impression we were simply here submitting a request to bid on future State contracts.*

A month earlier Richard was hovering nervously outside Benjamin's office door

"Benjamin, we've got to take action!" There was an unmistakable urgency in Richard's voice.

Benjamin was never one to express business concerns outwardly. He maintained his calm and controlled demeanor. "Come in, Richard. Let's talk."

"Benjamin, I believe that, between now and mid-November, Amalgamated will organize with Traction and Terminal Company drivers."

"And?" urged Benjamin.

"And," Richard continued, "When they do, they'll shut down Indianapolis. Amalgamated Street Railway Employees can be very persuasive. Things could become dangerous."

"Coffee?" Benjamin calmly asked.

"Please," answered Richard.

Haughton's office door had remained open just enough that Rosie overheard Mr. Haughton's offer. Without prompting, Rosie prepared and set two cups of coffee in front of the men. "Thank you, Rosie," responded Haughton.

Benjamin caught the pleasant aroma from his cup, took a sip, then held the cup in his hands as he leaned back in his chair. His breath was as easy as if he were reading the Sunday edition of the *Times*. "Come now, Richard," he said with a smile. "No one is going to sit back and watch the hub of the United States transportation be brought to its knees."

Edwards went on with the same insistency, "Benjamin, remember ATU has already been successful in their efforts. It has been twenty years since *The Motorman and Conductor* were printed. That is twenty years of dedicated refinement in organizing street railway employees. This is not a rehearsal; they mean business!"

Benjamin could sense his financial partner's concern. This issue was going to require his full attention. "All right, all right," he said as if a solution was already forming in his mind. "Let's discuss what actions, if any, that Haughton Manufacturing should take to prepare for a slowdown of the rails."

Richard shifted to the edge of his chair and leaned toward Benjamin.

"I've been giving it a good deal of thought, Benjamin," he said. "We have to be totally open and transparent with our employees. It is better they get their news from us than from rabble-rousers who have their own agendas. That's first, Benjamin." This caught Benjamin's attention. He'd stopped stirring his coffee and was now listening intently.

"Second, we have to make certain we have enough raw material to continue stamping."

"Ideally, yes," Benjamin offered.

"And third, Benjamin, let's contact all of our customers; tell them we are fully prepared to complete their orders, and that we'll be running around the clock to protect their businesses from any disruption in transportation."

Richard had never seen Benjamin look more incredulous. With a tone of disbelief, Benjamin asked, "Around the clock?" His brow furrowed, "How in the name of... Richard, my friend, how do you propose we accomplish non-stop production with our present labor force?"

Richard settled back in his chair, crossed his right leg over his left, took a sip of coffee, and said confidently, "We will introduce twelve-hour shifts." With that Benjamin tightly closed his eyes trying desperately to align his thoughts with Richard's. Richard continued, "Employees will only work three days a week. With their overtime pay, they will still be making as much if not more than their current wages. We will have a day shift and a night shift, from seven to seven with ample maintenance to repair problems and reduce downtime."

"Three days a week? Overtime pay?" There was a glint in Haughton's eye. "Edwards, that just might work! I like the idea. If it does work, it just might be something we want to think about keeping."

With one month under their belts, Richard and Benjamin were prepared to be aggressive, pursuing more business rather than preparing for less.

The guard asked Richard and Benjamin for their identifications, where their meeting was to take place and the time of their scheduled meeting. Finding both Richard Edwards and Benjamin Haughton on the schedule (howbeit not for his presumed purpose), the men were allowed to enter.

"I am very sorry to have delayed you, gentlemen. We have our orders."

"Nonsense, my good man. We are grateful for your service. Could you please direct Mr. Haughton and me to the Chamber of Commerce Department?"

"Yes, sir. Take the stairs to the third floor. Turn right and then take an immediate left. Chairman DeHority's office is the third door down. He has been notified of your arrival."

Richard and Benjamin walked through the anteroom into the spacious lobby and across to the massive central marble staircase. As they reached the third floor, they were met by a very distressed W.A. DeHority, Chairman of the Municipal Expenditures Committee in the Chamber of Commerce.

"Haughton? Edwards?"

"Yes, sir, Chairman DeHority?"

"Yes, of course. Come now, we must not be late for the meeting."

Chairman DeHority led the way. Benjamin grabbed Richard's arm. "Richard, does it appear to you that we are no longer controlling our purpose for being here?"

Richard raised an index finger to his lips, "Shh."

The strikers were more organized, more determined, and more volatile than Richard had predicted. Indianapolis was at war. Strikebreakers attempted to restart the rails. This led to four days of rioting. Businesses were brought to a halt with over ten-thousand protesters taking to the streets. Violence led to the deaths of four union members and two strikebreakers. Police could not contain the mob. Fearing for their own lives, the police disregarded their orders to engage.

All the while Haughton Manufacturing continued filling orders and building its finished goods inventory. Their 24-hour split schedule was working. However, employees feared retribution from strikers. Many of the employees chose to remain within the Haughton facilities around the clock rather than risk leaving and facing an angry mob.

Benjamin and Richard provided cots, blankets, and food. No one knew how long this battle of the wills would last.

The warehouse quickly filled with finished orders. Benjamin decided to build a backlog of finished goods for their larger customers. These items were inventoried in the lithography room. Work-in-process was stacked in the coil room. As coils were pulled for slitting, the space was filled with work-in-process.

Richard and Benjamin shuttled products along back roads to grateful customers. Orders, however, could not keep up with the product continuing to fill Haughton Manufacturing's facilities. Benjamin decided to reduce the night shift's production by 50 percent. Employees displaced by the reduction took on maintenance responsibilities in shipping and receiving, slitting, blanking, deburring, painting, die setting, punching, coating, and packaging areas. It was an opportunity to upgrade processes and motivate the workforce by preparing for expansion.

On November 5, Governor Ralston ordered the city to be prepared for martial law. A sundown curfew was initiated, and the Indiana National Guard was ordered to make itself visible on the streets. At noon, on November 6th, the Indiana Statehouse was besieged by thousands of protesters. Governor Ralston's cabinet members warned him against addressing the angry crowd, but Samuel Ralston did not hesitate to make his way to the statehouse steps.

"On January 13, 1913, I took a solemn oath to see that the laws of my state would be executed. I am confronted with serious conditions. I have seen lives sacrificed on our streets, and it is not for me to debate who was at fault. I know that life was not secure and that we must make life secure everywhere in our state. Whatever steps may be taken in the future, I hope you will uphold the enforcement of the law. I give you my word. As your governor, I will personally lead the efforts for arbitration. Make no mistake about it, we will come to an agreement, and we will establish protocols to address future grievances for all workers in our great state. Future arbitrations will be achieved in a safe and equitable manner."

His words were emphatic. The citizens were confident. If he said it, it would be done. Governor Ralston's first eleven months in office were tumultuous. His resolve to address issues for the benefit of every citizen in Indiana had won the hearts of his constituents and the respect of his rivals.

"Benjamin. I haven't a clue as to what we are about to engage in— but let's keep that just between us." Richard quietly whispered.

"Um, right!" Benjamin replied.

They followed Chairman DeHority into the governor's chamber. Governor Ralston greeted them as they walked in. Chairman DeHority made the introductions.

"Governor Ralston, this is," DeHority paused as he looked at his morning roster. It occurred to him he had no idea who the two men were he was about to introduce Governor Ralson to. "Er, Mr. Richard Edwards and Mr. Benjamin Haughton." Governor Ralston greeted both men with a handshake, purposefully walked past them, and entered an adjacent conference room.

"Gentlemen! Come in, come in! Take a seat, gentlemen. We are about to embark upon a very serious task. I have promised our citizens a quick and equitable resolution to the present labor conditions and that is exactly what we are going to provide them. Thank you for volunteering in this endeavor."

Richard quickly jotted down a note and passed it along to Benjamin. It read:

Please carefully and inconspicuously, pick your jaw up off the floor.

Richard gave a quiet chuckle as Benjamin read the note. Benjamin closed his eyes, ever so slightly, and shook his head in disbelief.

It surprised Richard that Benjamin was the first to speak.

"Governor Ralston, sir. Your speech on the steps was powerful. Thank you, I am inspired and motivated to quickly address the situation in such a way that we impact not only these circumstances but the way we do business in the future throughout Indiana."

"Well thank you, Mr. Haugh-"

"If I may continue, sir. It is imperative we do not leave this table without deconstructing the current events and identifying the genesis of this strike. Today, this moment determines the course of action the four of us will take to appropriately and conclusively respond to employee demands. And we must do so without weakening the underpinning of the transit industry."

Richard caught the tempo of Benjamin's comments.

"Mr. Haughton is correct, sir. For us to expedite future resolve we must, for the moment, step away from focusing our attentions solely upon immediate solutions and focus our attention upon those procedures that will be appropriate for any future uprisings."

Governor Ralston was pleased and reassured by what he was hearing. He turned to Chairman DeHority. "W., I don't know how you did it but thank you for bringing together these two men. They obviously grasp the gravity of the situation and appear to possess the ability and experience to help us resolve the issue."

"Sir, to be perfectly frank, I'm not certain how it all came together myself."

Their initial meeting lasted four hours. Benjamin Haughton was brilliant. By suggesting a deconstruction of all events leading to the moment, he encouraged Governor Ralston to openly bring him and Richard up to date without exposing their bewilderment as to why they were even there.

Governor Ralston explained the first attempts to unionize had failed. However, those attempts did manage to seize the attention of the Terminal and Traction Company leadership.

Richard interjected, "Gentlemen, our transit employees are fighting for a sense of security! They and their families are still reeling from the devastation caused by the floods. Security, security! And they do not see security in a wage. Wages are temporal; they can end. No, gentlemen. They have now experienced security in numbers! If one or two of them leave, they will be replaced in a moment. But by collaborating, by joining forces for a defined common cause they create mass work stoppage and bring industries to a grinding halt!"

Governor Ralston was frustrated. "Confound it; that is exactly what we are experiencing at this very moment! I know what has happened and I want to know what we are going to do about it!"

Benjamin offered, "We design employee securities and initiate their perceived power to be utilized only when all other forms of negotiations have failed. We eliminate the element of surprises by initiating monthly meetings with a representative of our employees and a representative of the union."

Governor Ralston immediately rejected the suggestion. "What? We cannot have unions running our businesses!"

Richard had anticipated the objections Governor Ralston might raise. He knew Ralston would object to any more power given to labor unions. In numerous speeches, Ralston had expressed concern that unions would soon hold the reins of businesses throughout the state. "No, sir," Richard argued. "Not running them, advising them. We can either treat the union as an adversary or we can relegate them to an advisory position. Their primary responsibility will be to oversee our actions in light of employees' demands."

Ralston responded more aggressively. "No! No that cannot work. What is the safeguard for industry? What? Do we just roll over for every dissatisfied individual? That is a weakness, Edwards! Weakness!"

Richard continued, "Sir, with all due respect. Suppose you control the steps in arbitration. If you control the money and control the hours, you are by no means in a position of weakness. You see, we design a method of arbitration before grievances escalate. Everyone knows in advance the steps agreed upon to voice grievances and resolve issues, and those methods do not always involve money. They can and should be more personal. Give employees sick leave. Give them time off to grieve the loss of a loved one. These are incremental costs, controlled costs, that we establish within our businesses. They do not happen every day, and we will agree with the employees and their union representative on the parameters required to apply for those benefits. Let us not forget. We pay the employees. The union takes their dues. That is a strength that we must not abuse, but we also must not let the employees forget."

"Hmmm, I see. So, by offering them future securities we create present stability within our workforce."

Benjamin interjected, "Not only stability, productivity! We make certain employees are paid a fair wage and, in addition, assign incremental increases for high-quality, high-yield productivity. We set goals, and quotas, based on the history we have already established. When employees exceed those goals without compromising the quality of products or services, they immediately share in the financial benefit to the company. We have regular riders; they provide our base income. They will be there day in and day out. But let's consider our workers who increase their ridership and therefore their till. By offering a percentage of the increase, the employee is motivated to provide a greater service to our citizens. He benefits, the company benefits, and the public benefits."

"How do we provide protection for the industry?" DeHority interjected.

Benjamin continued, "Open communication. We must keep our workforce and the public informed. Once again, we control the information—we control the perception. Gentlemen, do not forget, our employees want their jobs. Ultimately, the bargaining chip remains in the dealer's hand. And we, gentlemen, remain the dealer. As we anticipate future growth, we make commitments to our employees based on those forecasts. The employee is the first to notice an increase or decrease in orders or, in this case, ridership. They will not collaboratively attempt to squeeze blood out of a turnip. Certainly, one or two individuals might push back, but that is the power we hold. We steer the ship, and everyone on board knows that if the ship sinks, we all drown. Furthermore, we must maintain the right to stay afloat! In the direst of situations, the industry must maintain the right to hire non-union employees, and unions will not be allowed to solicit membership on company property."

Richard concluded, "By establishing a monthly minimum wage, employees can budget their costs of living. By increasing their productivity, employees control their income and increase their standard of living. Our plan considers the current situation but focuses on future variables. By treating our employees fairly and communicating with them openly, the union becomes the least of our concerns. They serve only to offer alternatives to the employee—most of which the employee will already be enjoying. If the industry is for any reason disrupted, employees will be the first to know about it. In those circumstances, employees, union representatives, and industry leaders will work together to arbitrate resolve. By that time, we will have already proven our trustworthiness and our commitment."

Governor Ralston was now on board. "Gentlemen, let's put this to paper. I believe we are heading in the right direction. I want Amalgamated contacted immediately. Let's get John Thorpe in this meeting."

John J. Thorpe was the vice president of the Amalgamated Association of Steel and Electrical Railway Employees of America. He'd been leading the efforts to unionize in Indianapolis. Ralston thought the plan sound enough that parading AASEREA's vice president would solidify a sense of well-being with angry strikers.

"Let's get Ethelbert Stewart in here too. He mediated the coal mining dispute in Colorado. If he can successfully negotiate between those employees and the Rockefeller's interests, he will be a bonus to our team. I want to call a special session of the Indiana General Assembly following our meetings with them."

Governor Ralston turned his attention back to Richard and Benjamin. "Gentlemen, you of course will be in those meetings. I rely heavily upon your experience and sound reasoning. I need that on my team. Left on my own, I tend to dismantle the building to fix a leaky roof!"

Benjamin laughed and responded, "Of course we will be in those meetings and will, to the best of our abilities, serve to facilitate a mutually agreed-upon course of action."

Religious leaders had proven to be ineffective in previous attempts to quell the violence. Twenty-nine police officers, fearing for their own safety, walked off their jobs, leaving the citizens without protection. Two men were already dead from wounds suffered during the melee, and hundreds more were injured.

For three long days and nights, Governor Ralston, Mayor Lew Shank, Chairman DeHority, John J. Thorpe, Ethelbert Stewart, Benjamin Haughton, and Richard Edwards pounded out a proposal.

Haughton and Edwards were resolute. The proposal had to be accomplished in two steps. The present situation had to be addressed and subjugated. First, all strikebreakers brought in from Chicago would immediately vacate. The Traction and Terminal Company would initiate an open-door policy for all employees. They would furthermore agree to take back, without retribution, all strikers who had not participated in the violence. Leaflets would be distributed, informing employees that they would have twelve hours from the signing of the proposal to return to their stations or forfeit their positions. All grievances would be heard within five days of the employees returning to their positions. Mutually acceptable terms would be negotiated and implemented.

In the second phase, the employees would be given a general forecast describing the Traction and Terminal Company's intentions for the next three years. Employee representatives would participate in a monthly review of those intentions as they pertain to the well-being of the employees. Employees would agree that there would be no stoppage of work during this period.

On November ninth, the initial proposal was accepted. For the next three months, grievances would be heard. The Public Service Commission would arbitrate any disputes during this period, and negotiations would be brought to a conclusion.

Benjamin Haughton and Richard Edwards were exhausted. It was late. Days had passed since they'd been home, and Benjamin felt out of touch with the rest of the world. His thoughts returned immediately to Haughton Manufacturing. Although they'd accomplished much, would their efforts impact its success?

Benjamin and Richard walked down the marble staircase of the state building. Benjamin broke the silence. "Give me a sheet of steel, Richard. I'll bend it and shape it. I'll form it into anything you want. It's far more malleable than pig-headed politicians!"

Richard patted Benjamin on the back. "My dear friend, I'm sorry our meeting went a bit longer than I'd originally expected..."

The two men stopped about midway down the steps, turned towards one another, and gave each other a hearty handshake. As they turned to continue down the steps, they were both startled by the call of William DeHority. His voice echoed throughout the empty rotunda.

"Gentlemen, gentlemen wait! You forgot this."

Benjamin and Richard looked at one another. Overcoat, and hat, Benjamin patted his chest, pen, and pocketbook. Richard pulled back his overcoat and checked for his fob and watch.

Chairman DeHority ran up to them. "Gentlemen," Benjamin looked at the envelope Chairman DeHority was handing him. "I'm glad I caught you. You almost forgot this. I believe it is what you came for."

DeHority stood there as proud as a schoolboy, handing in a perfect paper. A puzzled Benjamin slowly released the flap on the envelope to reveal its contents.

"The State of Indiana hereby gives exclusive contract to Haughton

Manufacturing for the manufacturing of all state, city and municipal signs, and license plates."

The contract was the first and largest state contract ever awarded to any private business. It would be followed by contracts from Illinois, Michigan, and Ohio. Haughton Manufacturing had become the primary manufacturer of license plates, signs, stamped, and fabricated products throughout the eastern states.

The three men hugged one another. Benjamin threw his arm over the shoulder of William DeHority. "William, I suggest Haughton Manufacturing take the three of us out to the finest dinners and drinks in Indianapolis. Have you eaten at St. Elmo?"

PART THREE
ST. ELMO

PART THREE
STUDENTS

CHAPTER SEVENTEEN
JUNE 5, 2017

"Good afternoon, ladies. Welcome to St. Elmo. Shall I prepare the Haughton Table for you, Ms. Carrie?" asked the Maître D.

A sudden shiver went down Carrie's spine. "By any chance has my father made a reservation here today?"

"He and your brother left just moments ago. They were here quite early. Were you intending to meet with them?"

"Not hardly," Carrie's words escaped her lips before she gave them a thought.

The Maître D was quick to pick up tension in Carrie's response. Defusing what he felt might be a sensitive subject he responded, "Well then, you shall have our undivided attention for as long as you wish. Our special today is warm hospitality and will be served with every dish on the menu; bon appétite!"

It only took a moment, and the Haughton Table was prepared for Carrie and Asha. "Ladies, if you would please follow me." The Maître D led them to their table and pulled out a chair for Carrie.

"If you don't mind, I'd like to sit facing the front today. Asha, why don't you sit here?" Carrie suggested.

"Ha! Are you kidding? I'm at St. Elmo. I'll sit anywhere you tell me to sit!" Asha gratefully responded.

"I feel sick, Asha. Can you imagine if we'd have run into Dad and Teddy?" Carrie whispered.

"Enough about them. I want to know more about you. What it was like when you first came. I want to know the real history of this company." Asha paused for a moment. "Carrie, I'm sorry. I'm being way too nosey. I don't want to pry. I want you to tell me everything, willingly." Both ladies laughed at Asha's unabated honesty.

"If I'm going to tell you everything, you're going to need a drink!" Carrie said through her laughter.

"Good afternoon, ladies. Welcome to St. Elmo. My name is Alexander, and I will be your server this afternoon. May I start you out with something other than water to drink?"

Asha waited for Carrie to order. "I would like a gin and tonic." She looked at Asha and continued, "A bottomless gin and tonic, please!"

Alexander chuckled, "One of those mornings?"

"One of those *lives*!" Carrie replied.

"I will have the same, light on the tonic." Asha laughed.

"Wonderful, ladies. I will have those ready for you right away and will advise the bar to be prepared for multiple refills!" Alexander smiled as he turned to get their drinks.

"Okay, start with you working for Lonnie. What was that like? I heard he and your dad were really close. I've got to tell you. There were a lot of rumors going around about why he left. Come on, give me the scoop."

Carrie once again chuckled. "Lonnie did everything he could to train me. I probably frustrated him with my questions. He once told me training me was like teaching a two-year-old who kept asking, 'why?' The time Lonnie and I spent together was strictly business." Carrie's words were interrupted by Asha's chiding laughter. "No, really, Asha. It really was. That is, until—well until it wasn't!"

CHAPTER EIGHTEEN
THE PARK
MAY 26, 1988

It did not take long for Lonnie to recognize Carrie was an extremely capable woman. Working together, the two implemented numerous improvements in Haughton Fabrication's procurement processes. Lonnie found Carrie inquisitive, honest, and highly intelligent with an analytical mind to coordinate facts and figures far beyond Lonnie's more creative and communicative talents.

There was little Lonnie could do to retain his position if, in Ben's world, Carrie was to be the director. She was more than qualified to do so. Carrie never gave Lonnie a reason for concern. She was amiable, polite, and thoughtful; Carrie was fun to be around. She was certainly not the self-serving corporate climber Lonnie had originally assumed her to be. Carrie was, in every sense of the word, a lady. Lonnie faced a new challenge. It was a challenge he knew he would be unable to overcome. He was falling in love.

"Ya want to take a ride with me? I'm going over to Everitt's to pick up an order for the tool shop."

"Sure, Lon. Let me just finish attaching these receiving and BOL's to the invoices. They've got to go in today's mail run. The sooner we get them to accounting the sooner we'll get paid."

"No problem, Carrie. I'll run out to the tool shop and see if they need anything other than the carbides they ordered."

Things were going just as Lonnie had hoped. They would be alone, away from the office and the manufacturing plant. Lonnie could then approach Carrie on a more personal level. He was compelled to lay his cards on the table. He had developed unintended feelings for her, and he wouldn't be able to hide them any longer. Lonnie could think of no reason to hesitate—that is, no reason other than total exposure, potential embarrassment, and probable unemployment.

The ride to Everitt's was like a playful vacation. Lonnie and Carrie continually switched radio stations back and forth. He'd push the presets to country western, and Carrie would turn the dial to disco and rock & roll. Carrie knew the names of every band, every recording artist, every one of their albums, and the lyrics to every song. What else didn't he know about this woman?

"I grew up in this area," Lonnie commented. "Our church youth group spent a lot of time in Washington Park. Want to take a ride over there?"

"Sure!" Carrie responded.

Lonnie turned on North Rural Street, towards the basketball courts. He parked the car and asked Carrie to join him for a walk.

Washington Park was no longer a sweeping carpet of plush lawns framed by the beauty of manicured gardens. It had become overgrown with wild oat and sprangletop. The basketball courts were nestled in an area adjacent to a large open field. Lonnie led Carrie across the field to the bordering trees on the opposite side of the park. He shared his memories of playing capture the flag and flag football on that field. They were good memories, innocent memories.

Carrie had only fleeting memories of her early childhood years. "When my mom and dad divorced, I was eleven years old. Mom moved Kathy and me to Lake Tippecanoe for a short while. Mom remarried, and we moved to Illinois. It seems we were always on the move. There was no time to make real friendships."

"I'm very sorry you lost that part of your life, Carrie."

"Huh, so am I. I thank God for my grandparents and my mom. They were our stability."

Lonnie and Carrie sat on a park bench just under a tulip tree.

"How did you know tulip trees were my favorite?"

Of course, it was only coincidental, but Lonnie replied, "In my line of business it pays to know everything." Carrie playfully slapped his shoulder and laughed. Moments passed. Lonnie took a deep breath, "Carrie, you know I've grown very fond of you. I haven't really done much to hide it—that is except from the other employees."

"Yes, I know. Evidently, I'm better at keeping secrets." Carrie responded.

"What do you mean?" Lonnie had not expected Carrie to admit she'd so abruptly been aware of his growing feelings for her.

"Lonnie, I've obviously kept my feelings for you from you!" A soft smile began to form as Carrie's eyes penetrated his heart.

The light breeze carried crisp cool air. Lonnie felt his palms moisten. "Okay, look, I'm going to come right out and say it and let whatever happens happen. Carrie, I believe we've been brought together. I believe we will always be together."

Carrie didn't let her eyes stray from Lonnie's gaze. There was a moment of silence. Carrie responded, "And?"

Lonnie, now totally caught off guard, thought to himself, *and? And? What do you mean, and?* Lonnie had not prepared for that question. "Well, I suppose I, uh, well, I just thought if you're willing to go along with such a crazy idea... you should have some say in how it all plays out!"

"Lonnie, we do pretty well working together at the office. I think we will do even better working together—forever."

It was their first kiss.

For the next three months, Lonnie and Carrie would drive to Muldoon's in Carmel. The late-night rendezvous gave them time to enjoy one another's company. They'd order loaded potato skins and

Irish coffees and openly shared, unabated, their hearts with one another. It was late enough in the evening, and Carmel was just remote enough to allow them the privacy they desired. It was as if they had always known each other. Their lives were complete.

August 27, 1988. Tonight, there would be a change of venue. This evening's rendezvous was not slated for Muldoon's. Lonnie made reservations in the heart of Indianapolis at the Hyatt Regency's Eagle's Nest.

"Lonnie, this goes against everything we've been trying to do. What if someone sees us?"

Lonnie chuckled, "Carrie this is a long-term relationship. We are at the very beginning. Someone is bound to find out sometime, somewhere. I just thought it would be nice to enjoy a romantic evening without being on the run."

"Okay. But you better have a good story to tell if someone finds out!" Carrie warned.

"Don't worry, honey. I've got it covered." Lonnie assured her.

They arrived at the Hyatt and made their way to the rooftop.

"Good evening, Mr. Dustin. We have a comfortable window table for you just as you requested. Is this a special occasion?"

"Every day that I am with the love of my life is a special occasion," Lonnie responded.

Carrie smiled, and without hesitation, she took Lonnie's hand as they walked to the table. She noticed the delicious entrée that was being served and whispered in his ear, "Lonnie, look at this food! I am going to apologize in advance—I am definitely not ordering potato skins tonight!"

Lonnie smiled.

The view was magnificent. How could it not be? Atop the Hyatt Regency, The Eagle's Nest makes a complete three-hundred and sixty degrees rotation every forty-five minutes. Lonnie and Carrie could see all of Indianapolis. Carrie was a bit concerned that all of Indianapolis could also see them.

They'd just finished their appetizers when Carrie remarked, "Lonnie it felt so good to take your hand when we walked to our table. We held hands right in front of God and all creation! It just felt right! I am tired of hiding in the shadows."

Lonnie wiped his lips and got up from his chair. Carrie was still looking out the window and did not notice the change in Lonnie's position until she turned back from the window to comment on the sunset. Lonnie was now at her side.

"Carrie, I'm tired of hiding in the shadows, too. I'm tired of hiding my love for you. I am tired of minimizing the most wonderful blessing I have ever received." As Lonnie kneeled, he reached into his coat pocket to reveal a very special box. He held it out to Carrie. Opening the lid, he said, "No more shadows. Carrie, I love you. Will you marry me?"

Carrie could not hold back her tears. "Yes, yes, YES!" She emphatically responded. Her enthusiasm caught the attention of everyone seated around them. As patrons realized what they were witnessing, they immediately broke into applause and congratulations.

Lonnie looked around, "This is the way it should be, Carrie. This is the way it will be for the rest of our lives. Let's always celebrate finding one another!"

Leaving the Eagle's Nest, Lonnie and Carrie discovered their fame preceded them. Congratulations were extended from everyone they passed. Walking through the lobby, total strangers came up to them and offered their congratulations. Carrie wondered if the Eagle's Nest had notified the lobby that they were coming down the elevator.

"Honey, your hand has been fully extended and you've been staring at your finger since we entered the elevator. It just might be the reason for all the attention!"

An older couple approached them, "Congratulations, my dears. Charles and I have been happily married for forty-four years."

The woman's husband corrected her. "You mean fifty-four years, my dear."

In a sharp retort, the woman replied, "I said *happily* married."

All four of them laughed. Lonnie thanked them for their kindness and told them their brief encounter would be a memorable inspiration for years to come.

On the way back to Carrie's apartment, Carrie asked, "How are you going to tell my father?"

"Well," Lonnie appeared to be considering Carrie's question for the first time. He'd given it a good deal of thought. "He seems to like having lunch at St. Elmo when there is important business to discuss. I've got some important business. I think Ben and I will be having lunch this coming week."

CHAPTER NINETEEN
IT'S A GOOD THING
AUGUST 29, 1988

Carrie had concerns about Lonnie's lunch with her father. Lonnie didn't give it a second thought. "Honey, let's be reasonable about this. Your dad and I have traveled the world together. He knows me. I have never given him any reason to question my integrity or character. The luncheon will be fine. I love you. Isn't that what is most important?"

"Lonnie, I'll be glad when this luncheon is over. Just remember, you are a guest in his world."

Lonnie interrupted, "No, no, babe. That's where you are wrong. I don't live in his world. I will make it my ambition to never live in his world. If we start out that way, we are committing ourselves to the whims of your dad. No. This is our world, and he can accept it or reject it. Regardless, it has absolutely no effect on my love for you and the future we are planning together."

"I'll be waiting for your call. I love you," Carrie nervously responded.

Lonnie reassured Carrie, "Well there you go! What else really matters? Talk with you in a couple of hours."

Carrie's concern was amusing. Lonnie had rehearsed the luncheon numerous times and was prepared to enjoy the afternoon with his future father-in-law.

"A-low?"

"Hi, Ben. It's Lonnie."

"Oh yeah, yeah. How ya doin', Lonnie?"

"Super, Ben. Ben, I'd like to take you to lunch today. We can eat at a new restaurant. Ever heard of St. Elmo?"

Ben laughed. "Yeah, ya know, I think I've heard of that place."

They both laughed.

"Sure, I'm open. What are we meeting about?"

"Well, I want to update you on how Carrie and I are doing–"

Ben interrupted, "Oh super, super. I've been meaning to get together about that. That's super. Yeah, let's do it. Let's do it. I'll drive."

"Super, Ben. Let's say about eleven-thirty?"

"Eleven-thirty. Super. That will give me enough time to digest my McDonald's apple pie before drinking!"

They both laughed again. Things were going very well. "Okay, I'll see you then."

This was going even better than Lonnie had anticipated. He was doing all he could to contain himself and the excitement of telling Ben about his love for Carrie and their love for each other. The burden of hiding the truth was about to be lifted, and Lonnie could feel the weight being released.

Ben knocked on Lonnie's door and then entered. "Hey, Lon. What's doing?"

"Ah, just cleaning up some inventory corrections. Ya know, after nine years it still irks me the way these auditors dig into our numbers! Heck, I'm the one hiring them to review the inventory, but they always make me feel like I'm being interrogated. They probe and probe and probe. I give them an answer or an explanation and it is never quite enough. I get a 'Well, all right I suppose' attitude from them. All that's missing are the bright lights and cattle prods!"

"Ha ha, ha. Yeah, I know. That's why you're good at that stuff. I'd never keep a good auditor. They'd ask me how I got the numbers; I'd tell them. They'd probe further, and I'd fire them!"

"Ha. Well, they are doing their job and our results are always spot on. It's just that some of these young kids forget who is signing their checks. I mean, come on—they're working for us. It's not the other way around."

"Well, like I said, That's why you do it and not me. Hey, let's get some lunch, Lon. Where's this new place we're going?"

Once again, they both laughed.

They jumped into Ben's Cadillac and headed to St. Elmo. There was general conversation along the way—sports mostly.

"So Schmidt retired, huh?" Ben asked.

"That's what I heard," Lonnie responded. "One of the best third basemen ever to play the game."

"Yeah, Philadelphia is going to miss him. He's hall-of-fame material—no doubt about it." Ben added.

"I think you're right." Lonnie could feel his expression transform into a smile.

Upon entering St. Elmo, Lonnie, and Ben went directly to their usual table. After a few pleasantries with their server, Sadie, Ben abruptly declared, "It's time to get something to drink! Lonnie, what are you having?"

"Ya know, Ben, it's a special day. Sadie, I think I'll have a gin martini, Tanqueray, please. Oh, and can I have three olives?"

"Tanqueray martini, three olives. Absolutely, sir. And for you, Mr. Haughton?"

"Ya know..." Ben chuckled. "I think I'll try something new. I'll have a double Harveys Bristol Cream on the rocks."

Ben had that Haughton glint in his eye. Everyone knew he always ordered Harveys.

"Yes, sir. I'll get those right away. Would you like to look at the menu or would you like a little time to visit?"

"We'll go ahead and order," Ben said. "I think we both know what we want."

"Very well, sir. What will you be having?"

"I'm going to start with a shrimp cocktail and can you get me the lamb chops? Oh, do you have a little mint jelly you could put on the side?"

"Of course, Mr. Haughton. Can I bring you a salad?"

"Oh, no, no. I don't want to fill up too much. I've gotta save room for dessert!"

"All right, sir." Sadie turned to Lonnie.

"And for you?"

"What's the fresh fish today?"

"Today, we are serving pan-fried sanddabs, prepared with a light butter and panko, garnished with capers and a light sprinkle of parsley."

"That sounds super," Lonnie responded. "I'll have that."

Ben interrupted, "Wait a minute, wait a minute! Is that going to be better than my lamb? I don't want him getting anything better than me."

Sadie chuckled.

"Mr. Haughton, I am sure you will enjoy your lamb. I'll ask the chef to prepare it extra-special so there will be no competition whatsoever."

The three of them laughed, and Sadie left to attend to her duties.

"Ya know, Lonnie. My grandfather started coming here in 1902, just after it opened. As a matter of fact, my dad would bring Hal and me here just to make certain the tradition was kept alive. They went through some tough times, tough times. Ya know it's funny. I always thought my dad was all goofed up when it came to running the business. Now that it is my responsibility, I realize how smart the old man really is."

"I really enjoy him, Ben. He is at the office, without fail, every morning."

"Yep, every morning, at six o'clock sharp! He unlocks the door, hangs up his overcoat, takes out the flag, and runs it up the flagpole. Ha! Then he goes into his office, closes the door, and no one has any idea what he does until three!"

Ben let out a big laugh. Lonnie joined him, but he was careful. He did not want to be mistaken for laughing at the elder Mr. Haughton.

Lunch was served. The presentation was beautiful. It was beautiful enough to turn the heads of patrons seated at the bar as Sadie brought the dishes to the Haughton table.

It was time. Lonnie was surprised by his level of calm. What might otherwise have been the reason for anxiety was, in Lonnie's mind, cause for celebration.

"Ben, Carrie, and I have been seeing a lot of each other."

"Yea, that's super, super. You've done a heck of a job training her, a heck of a job. And I really appreciate it. Ya know, anyone else might have felt threatened to train the boss's daughter. You know, we'll never change your salary. We really appreciate the job you've done."

"Ben, I appreciate that very much. What I want you to know is Carrie, and I have been seeing each other after work hours and–"

Ben interrupted. "Listen, you have a very important job; a difficult job. I'm sure you've had to work overtime often—maybe even weekends. Don't you worry. You'll be compensated for every minute you've taken after hours."

"Well, I also appreciate that, Ben, but the truth is, we've been seeing each other socially."

Ben still had absolutely no idea what Lonnie was trying to communicate; his brow furrowed.

Lonnie continued, "Ben, what I am trying to tell you is that Carrie and I have fallen in love, and we want your blessing on our marriage."

At that moment, Ben's world came to a screeching halt. He just sat there staring at his plate. Lonnie suddenly became aware of the sweat accumulating on his own upper lip. There was no movement, no show of emotion; there were no words spoken. This was not what Lonnie had planned.

An eternity of suspended animation seemed to pass. Ben glanced towards the servers' station and motioned Sadie to come over to the table.

"Yes, Mr. Haughton?"

"Get me a scotch, straight up."

"Right away, sir."

He then returned to his stoic posture; his eyes were fixed upon his half-consumed lamb chop. Lonnie had never seen Ben order scotch; no one ever saw Ben order scotch!

Sadie returned with Ben's scotch, which, without a moment's hesitation, he drank.

Ben then turned his attention directly to Lonnie.

"Lonnie, I think it is a good thing for a man and woman to fall in love and get married, a good thing. You have my blessing—and you're fired." He then, matter-of-factly, dabbed his lips, got up from the table, and exited. Lonnie sat there for a moment, pondering what had just taken place. He watched out the window as Ben's Cadillac left St. Elmo.

That went well. Lonnie sarcastically thought to himself. *All there is left for me to do now is call a cab so that I can get back to the office, call Carrie with the good news—and begin cleaning out my desk!*

Lonnie paid the bill and got up from the table.

No problem at all, he thought.

CHAPTER TWENTY
CARRIE'S RESPONSE
AUGUST 29, 1988

"He what? Lonnie don't say that! Don't you dare say that! No!"

Lonnie could sense confused terror in Carrie's voice. He tried to calm her with his own nervous snicker. "Yea, it didn't go exactly the way I'd hoped. I'm still in a bit of a shock."

Carrie's voice was amplified, "Lonnie, you are not kidding! This is the truth; this really happened? This is terrible! What are we going to do?"

Lonnie, hoping to calm Carrie and add some level of composure to the discussion responded, "Well, first of all, we are not going to panic. We found each other out of adversity. We've grown together out of adversity. Carrie, the two of us will be tested all our lives—it's just the way it's been, it's just the way it will be. But with both of us, committed to God and to each other, we'll conquer any adversary—bring it on!"

"Oh Lonnie, please don't say 'bring it on.' We don't need to invite challenges. They seem to appear on their own all too easily!"

"Babe, let's give it some time. I'm going to act as if I am finished with Haughton Fabrication. I don't think your dad's decision will be reversed. Perhaps he'll think about it and give me a grace period to find another job. Let's pray for that. Carrie, we are in this together. With God, we are invincible!"

"Yeah, but Lonnie, God's not out of a job! I'm new at this faith stuff; it's scary."

Lonnie could sense Carrie was acclimating to the reality. "Ha! I'm old at this and it is still scary! Let's hold hands and see what God is going to do."

A calmer Carrie asked, "Where are you now?"

Lonnie responded, "I took a cab back to the office. His car is not here. He probably went home."

Returning to her original level of angst Carrie asked, "What do you mean you took a cab?"

Lonnie hesitantly responded, "Carrie when he got up from the table, I think he forgot we took the same car—at least, I hope he forgot."

"Lonnie, this is unbelievable!"

Once again, Lonnie attempted to put a positive spin on the situation. "It's crazy. On the flip side, we don't have to hide our feelings any longer."

Anger replaced Carrie's fears. "Do you mean our feelings for each other or our feelings for my Dad?"

Lonnie urged Carrie, "Wait a minute. One of us has to stay employed! I'll see you later. I think I could use a drink."

"Do you want to meet somewhere?" Carrie asked.

"Absolutely not. I'll pick you up at your apartment. From here on out we are together forever!" Lonnie replied.

"Forever!" Carrie echoed Lonnie's comment and continued, "I'll see you at the apartment. Oh my God, this really happened!"

CHAPTER TWENTY-ONE
JUNE 5, 2017

Alexander returned with their drinks. "Here you are, ladies. Have you had time to look at the menu?"

"Actually, I know what I want," Carrie replied. "Asha? Asha, Alexander is ready to take your order."

Asha's jaw dangled from her otherwise attractive features. "I don't believe it!" Asha finally said.

"Oh, it's really nothing," Alexander replied. "I take orders throughout the afternoon and into the early evening."

"Oh my gosh, I'm sorry. I'll have the strip with the Béarnaise sauce, please." Asha was embarrassed at being caught off guard.

"Will there be a starter, perhaps a small Caesar with that?" Alexander asked.

"That would be wonderful, thank you."

"And for you?" Alexander turned his attention to Carrie.

"I'll have the Sashimi please; just the Sashimi-" Carrie was interrupted by Asha, "-And much more gin and tonic!"

Alexander smiled, "Of course!"

"Carrie, What did Lonnie do? What did you say to your dad? How can you still have a relationship with him?"

CHAPTER TWENTY-TWO
BEN'S EXPLANATION
AUGUST 30, 1988

I t was Tuesday morning. Lonnie didn't know what to do. If he went to work and Ben didn't want him there, it could lead to an awkward confrontation. If he didn't go and Ben expected to see him, he would only add to Ben's anger for being AWOL. Considering the two options, Lonnie decided the best compromise was to go to the production office. He would begin closing open items of business and clearing out his personal items. If Ben expected to see Lonnie at the corporate office, he would ultimately search for him at Production.

At precisely nine o'clock, Carrie got a call. "Hi Carrie, it's Dad. Is Lonnie there by any chance?"

"Sure, Dad. Let me get him for you."

"Well, if he's busy with something just have him call me back."

"Well, to be perfectly honest with you, he's cleaning out his desk."

"Oh, yeah, yeah-" Ben interrupted himself with nervous laughter. "Listen, I don't want him to do that just yet. Why don't the two of you come down here for lunch today? I think it might be a good thing for us to talk."

"Dad, I love you, but lunch and conflict aren't appealing to me. This whole thing has me very upset..."

Ben interrupted, "No, no, no. I understand, I understand. No, I don't want a conflict. I just needed some time to think this thing through. Lonnie hit me with quite a blow yesterday."

"No, Dad. Lonnie honorably asked for your blessing on our marriage." Carrie's voice was firm and resolute. "You hit us with quite a blow!"

"No—I understand, I understand. Look, that's what we need to talk about. I, I kind of overreacted because of some other things that are going on that you two are unaware of. I just want to explain to you what was going through my mind when, when Lonnie asked."

"Hold on just a minute, Dad. Let me ask Lonnie."

Carrie put her dad on hold and asked Lonnie if he wanted to take a chance on going to lunch.

"Sure, as long as he's not driving!" Lonnie replied.

Lonnie was never one to let someone else be his go-between. He picked up the phone and spoke freely as if nothing had ever happened.

"Ben! What's the plan?"

"Hi, Lon, How ya doing? Hey, listen. I want to get together with you two kids for lunch today. Let's talk this thing through. I, I was not on my best game yesterday, and I want to clear the air. Can we do that?"

"Ben, not a problem. I look forward to it! Where should we meet you?"

"Ah heck, Lon. Let's meet at St. Elmo. I don't think I finished my lunch from yesterday!"

Lonnie was careful to give a lighthearted chuckle to set Ben's mind at ease; the meeting would be peaceful.

"You bet! See you at noon?" Lonnie asked.

"Noon. Yeah, yeah noon will be great. I'll see you at noon. You and Carrie will be coming in together?"

"Yes, Ben. We will be together." Lonnie replied.

The conversation ended leaving Lonnie in the same state of mind he'd begun the day. He was at work, but was he supposed to be?

Carrie was a nervous wreck for the next three hours. How was she to respond to her father after he'd fired her fiancé the previous day?

At eleven-thirty, Lonnie and Carrie left for lunch. They arrived ten minutes early and were surprised to find Ben's car already in the parking lot.

"Lonnie, this can't be good!" Carrie argued.

"Carrie, he fired me yesterday. There are far too many witnesses here for him to shoot me today!"

"Lonnie, I'm serious! I just don't trust him now. I don't know what he will do."

"Look Carrie, I've known your dad a very long time. When all is said and done, he will try to do what is right."

"Yeah, what's right in *Ben's* world," Carrie said under her breath.

They entered St. Elmo. Ben was seated at the Haughton Table. Ben got up from his seat. Carrie immediately grabbed Lonnie's hand. Lonnie was a bit hesitant about Carrie's timing, but he took her hand as they walked to the table.

"Hey, hey, hey! Glad you two could come. Thank you, thanks a lot for coming. What do ya say we order some drinks?"

"That would be super, Ben. Thanks so much for inviting us." Lonnie said as he loosened his grip on Carrie's hand and extended it to Ben. The two men shook hands, and the three sat down to order drinks.

To Carrie's and Lonnie's surprise, Ben raised his glass and said proudly, "Well, here's to the happy couple. But I want you to know, I'm not paying overtime anymore for after-hours work!"

Everyone appeared to relax.

"Listen, kids. I owe you an explanation. For the last several weeks, Hal and I have been in discussions about his boys and your and Kathy's involvement with the business. We want the family line to continue, but we are very concerned about spouses becoming involved. We don't think that's such a good thing. It's not good for the business and not good for family life. Last week, we signed a written agreement that no spouses would ever be employed by either of us. Lonnie, when you told me you and Carrie wanted to get married, I realized I'd just lost my top employee! Hal feels the same way. We hate to see you go, but we've got no choice. If you stay, when Kathy marries, her husband might want a job, as will the boy's wives. We can't set that precedent; it just won't work. We've got to protect the integrity of the corporation."

Lonnie thought it was a plausible explanation. Carrie thought it was a decision to make certain the wives would never hold a place of leadership in the corporation. Ben continued. "Lon, here's what Hal and I want to do. We want you to stay with Haughton Fabrication till the end of the year. That gives you seven months to secure another position. You take all the time you need to secure a good position. Leave during the day for interviews, whatever you need. We'll give you the highest recommendation to anyone who asks."

Lonnie reached across the table. The two men gripped one another's hands a bit more firmly than a casual handshake. It was a gentleman's contract of peace.

Carrie never said a word. Although not intended, her placidity was a formidable non-response to her father's explanation. It told him that she was steadfast and immovable in her decision.

"So, have you set a date, a location?"

Carrie broke her silence, "It will be before the end of the year. Dad, I don't want to have a wedding. We intend to take our pastor and his wife to a quiet location and share our vows privately. In November, we'll host Thanksgiving so both sides of the family will have an opportunity to get to know each other better."

"That sounds super. So will you be living in your place, Lonnie?"

"Actually, Ben, I'm putting my place up for sale as soon as Carrie and I make some modifications to it. I don't plan on doing anything expensive. A fresh coat of paint does wonders. When we sell it, I think we'll have enough to purchase a home Carrie can call her own."

Ben became quiet. Lonnie and Carrie were concerned about the break in the flow of conversation. Neither felt the least bit compelled to fill the silence. Ben nodded his head as if agreeing with what he was thinking. "Well," Ben's shoulders shook as he quietly laughed at his thought. "I'm getting off kind of easy on this wedding. Perhaps, if you'll let me, I could help to make certain you have enough to purchase that home you two want."

Carrie knew her dad better than anyone. This was not the time to be proud; it was the time to be grateful. Accepting Ben's offer was another way of letting him know she was accepting him.

"Dad, we will keep you posted on what we are seeing in the market. When we find something, we are interested in, we will let you know. Thank you for your offer. I love you."

It was the correct response at precisely the right time. In January, Lonnie and Carrie purchased their first home.

CHAPTER TWENTY-THREE
JUNE 5, 2017

"Here are your meals, ladies. Be careful these plates are very hot. Is there anything else? Perhaps more bread?" Alexander paused as Asha tapped her empty glass. "Oh, my goodness! I apologize I will be right back with those refills!"

"Thank you," Carrie replied. "This looks yummy!"

Alexander hurried over to the bar as Carrie turned her attention back to Asha. "Asha, our family history reads like a fictional novel. Each experience seemed to build upon the next until... Well, until now. I'm living it and still can't believe it is happening!"

"What about your grandfather? There have been a lot of stories about him. I heard he didn't really own the company. I heard-" Asha hesitated, "I heard some pretty terrible stories about him. Are they true?"

"Asha, my grandpa Haughton was the kindest, warmest man alive. He was the youngest of the three, the only boy." Carrie paused to enjoy another bite of Sashimi. "This is absolutely wonderful, Asha. Would you like a bite?"

"Absolutely not!" Asha refused. "You'll want a bite of my steak, and

I'm not sharing with anyone!" The ladies clinked their glasses together, sipped their drinks and Carrie continued with the story.

CHAPTER TWENTY-FOUR
FAITH AND HOPE
JUNE 5, 1915

I t was the girls' first birthday. Fia and Addie each wore the finest dresses money could buy. Their daisy-printed white lingerie dresses with white ruffles and accent yellow bows betrayed any attempt the Haughtons might have had to hide the success of Haughton Manufacturing.

Benjamin and Miriam planned a quiet evening, enjoying the girls at home. It had been an unusually cool day. They sat in front of the family room fireplace. It brought back memories of their first years together. Benjamin popped popcorn in the fireplace and gave the girls their gifts. Fia and Addie loved their Teddy bears, but the two hand-made sock dolls Miriam made were their favorites.

Miriam carefully constructed each doll. She'd made a pledge from the time of their birth, Fia and Addie would be raised with strong back-bones and warm hearts capable of carrying and caring for the weight of the world. Her sock dolls emulated the foundational truths she would instill in her daughters.

Miriam embroidered the name, "Faith" on the collar of the white sock doll. Miriam recalled the Bible verse in Hebrews 11:1, '*Now faith is the substance of things hoped for, the evidence of things not seen.*'

There was much to do within the suffrage movement, but it would be useless if Miriam could not pass along faith and hope to her young daughters and to future generations.

Miriam embroidered the name, "Hope" on the collar of the black sock doll. She recalled the Bible verse found in the Old Testament. Jeremiah 29:11,

'For I know the thoughts that I think toward you, saith the Lord, thoughts of peace, and not of evil, to give you an expected end.'

Benjamin took a handful of popcorn and asked Miriam, "Which one gets the black doll?"

Before there was a moment even to begin to determine the proper response, Miriam smiled and asked, "What black doll? These socks are a pair, my dear. One cannot do without the other. Prejudice is a matter of the heart, not the skin. It is the value of a human being, their potential, and their freedom, to express their potential through opportunity and productivity that will one day change the course of our nation."

Benjamin did not immediately respond. He sat quietly. Miriam's message demanded respect and careful consideration. His heart swelled with pride as he contemplated the power of Miriam's words.

"Dearest, I see a pair of beautiful sock dolls. They will continue to bring happiness to our daughters because they were given in love and deep devotion. They have meaning beyond stitches and buttons. I thank you for the beautiful gift you have given to them, and to me."

Benjamin turned the logs on the fire. There was a sudden roar of flames. He held Miriam closely under the goose-down comforter. She was as happy and content as she'd ever been. The fresh burst of heat between them was something to which the fireplace contributed little, and neither of them would have predicted how quickly their world would change.

CHAPTER TWENTY-FIVE

HOW COULD YOU?
JULY 3, 1915

"Benjamin! BENJAMIN!" On the opposite end of their home, Benjamin could detect the strain in Miriam's voice. He came at a run.

"What is it, dearest?" he asked.

"Oh, dear God," her eyes were brimming with tears, but he sensed alarm—not sadness. "Benjamin, how could you do this to me?"

Looking at his wife, the bedroom, and its furnishings, he was at a loss to offer any kind of response. "What in heaven's name are you talking about?"

Miriam raised her eyes to her husband. Tears had slowly cascaded down her cheeks. "Benjamin! I am PREGNANT!" she punctuated each word.

"I'm pregnant." Her voice momentarily softened as the truth sank in. Her lips kept forming the words, "Pregnant, pregnant, I'm pregnant," but she made no sound. She lowered her head; a tear fell from her cheek onto her lap. She wiped her cheeks and again directed her pleading gaze to Benjamin's eyes; "How could you do this to me?"

Benjamin's chin met his chest. The thick folds of skin around his neck rested over his starched collar. He focused on a scuff on the toe of his right shoe as her question hung in the air. There was silence; not a word was spoken between them. Miriam awaited his response. Slowly, wrinkles formed on the outside edges of Benjamin's eyes. He raised his head and with a wry smile he said, rather matter-of-factly, "Well now; I will consider that a rhetorical question."

"Benjamin! This is no joking matter. Do you understand? I'm pregnant." She looked away for the first time.

He moved closer to her side, closing the gap between them. Taking her hands in his, he whispered, "Miriam, this is wonderful news! We should be rejoicing! Remember the good book says, *'Children are a gift from the Lord. They are a reward from Him.'*"

Miriam was resolute. "Do not quote scripture to me right now!"

"But—"

"How could you do this to me?" she asked imploringly, returning her eyes to meet his.

With a grin, he answered, "Well, I must admit, my dearest, the frequency of your comings and goings required quite a bit of talent on my part."

She ignored his lighthearted response. Instead, she looked beyond the ceiling and cried out, "Oh, dear God. Why this? Why now? I feel You are leading me. Why then put such a stumbling block in my path?"

Benjamin gathered his wife in his arms. "Miriam," he began, "This need not be a stumbling block. It may not be part of our plans, but we certainly cannot diminish the fact that it is most obviously part of His."

Miriam remained rigid in his embrace and unmoved by his words.

"Oh, dear God, why?" she begged.

Benjamin held her close. "Dearest, let us be grateful; let us be grateful together. We can do anything together," he said in his most encouraging voice. He went on, "We always have, we always will. We are Haughtons! Be strong, my dearest!"

He felt the resistance in her body soften. Meeting his admiring stare with a twinkle of her own, she asked, "And what if this baby is another girl?"

That thought had not crossed Benjamin's mind. Eyes that had been so intent on buoying his wife's mood now stared some place upward, beyond her, and his familiar twinkle had—for the moment at least—disappeared as he uttered his own brief prayer, "Oh, dear God... WHY?"

Had his attention not been directed heavenward, Benjamin would have recognized an unfamiliar glint in Miriam's eyes. She rested her forehead on his slumping shoulder.

CHAPTER TWENTY-SIX
DAFFODILS
MARCH 4, 1916

"Congratulations Mr. Haughton, you have a son!"

The world was introduced to Harold Warren Haughton, born March 4, 1916, weighing seven pounds six ounces, and measuring twenty-two inches in length.

Benjamin Haughton was a strong man, unaccustomed to expressions of emotion. Today, he simply bowed his head into his cupped hands and wept. "A son!" the thought escaped his lips. Upon realizing he'd actually vocalized his heart, he continued, "Oh, God. You know how I adore my two daughters. If you would have given Miriam another daughter, I would have considered myself equally blessed. But oh, dear God, how grateful I am that you have given me a son!"

It was an awkward prayer—nevertheless, it was sincere gratitude coming from the depths of Benjamin Haughton's soul. Hearing the doctor's pronouncement, meant Harold Warren Haughton would carry the family name. It made the success of Haughton Manufacturing purposeful not only for the moment but for generations to come.

"How is my wife? How is Miriam?"

"You have a very strong woman, Mr. Haughton," the nurse responded.

"May I see her? I must see her."

"She will be ready for you in just a few minutes."

"Flowers! I must bring her flowers. Do you have daffodils? Where can I purchase flowers?"

"Mr. Haughton, please, calm down. You can purchase flowers at–"

"Daffodils, they must be daffodils!" Benjamin interrupted.

"Yes sir, daffodils, just around the corner at Bertermann Brothers. They have a beautiful selection of–"

"Yes, yes. Thank you! Thank you very much. A son! Oh, my goodness! A son!"

Benjamin recognized his exuberance and attempted to gain control.

"Mind you, my dear, I would have been equally happy had Miriam given me a daughter," he paused momentarily and said, "Another daughter."

The realization hit him, "Oh, dear Lord, another daughter?"

The nurse could see the glazed look in Benjamin's eyes as the image of a third daughter passed briefly through his mind.

"Certainly, Mr. Haughton. Certainly, you would have."

"Yes, yes indeed. Daffodils. Tell Miriam I will return shortly. No! No, don't tell her anything. I will be right back. Where did you say the shop is?"

"It is right around the corner. Go out the front door and turn to the right. Bertermann's is on Massachusetts Avenue."

At thirty-six years of age, Benjamin sprinted down the stairs like a youngster. As he made it to the first floor, the nurse could hear him shout, "Thank God, a son!"

Twenty minutes later, Benjamin quietly entered the private room. Miriam's bed was angled towards the window and elevated so that she could gaze into the garden. He quietly approached the bed. Miriam felt his presence.

"You're welcome, husband."

Benjamin was overcome by the power he felt emanating from his wife, the mother of his children. He walked around the corner of the bed. His eyes welled with tears of joy and gratefulness; he could not speak. He sat the daffodils on the table and simply knelt by the bed placing his head on Miriam's lap. She lovingly stroked his forehead and smiled.

"Daffodils, a thing of beauty."

As Miriam stroked his forehead, she softly recited John Keats's poem:

> A thing of beauty is a joy forever:
> Its loveliness increases; it will never
> Pass into nothingness, but still will keep
> A bower quiet for us, and a sleep
> Full of sweet dreams, health, and quiet breathing.

Miriam continued, "My dear, we have a son. One who will carry the Haughton name and the Haughton values. He will uphold the Haughton drive and the Haughton perseverance and carry them into the next generation. We must be mindful to teach him the beauties of nature for it is there he will understand the hand of God. Harold will learn to depend upon Him in all his endeavors."

Tears flowed unabated from Benjamin's eyes. The enormity of raising a son was beginning to sink in. Business must never replace the joy of living, greed must never replace the fulfillment of giving, success must never diminish the power and unity of family.

Benjamin said nothing. Miriam instinctively knew her words had affected Benjamin's thoughts.

"I suppose I now have two men to care for."

CHAPTER TWENTY-SEVEN
NANNY NEEDS
APRIL 10, 1917

Miriam would not let the ladies down. The woman's club depended upon her leadership and her persuasive skills as an orator. Not only had she become the new president of the Broad Ripple Methodist Episcopal Church Women's Club, but she also now sat on the advisory boards of eight additional women's clubs.

Benjamin invested the bulk of his time with the exclusive contract Haughton Manufacturing had been awarded by the state of Indiana. He felt extremely uncomfortable, even vulnerable with one client now controlling 70 percent of Haughton Manufacturing's business. Richard, on the other hand, believed that they could easily expand Haughton Manufacturing through acquisitions, thereby offsetting any long-term damage should the state ever decide to pull their business or open it up to additional bidding. None of it made sense to Benjamin. He knew how to manufacture. He was not a politician. Buying other businesses simply meant growing too large, too fast, in areas he knew too little about. It was, in his opinion, a recipe for disaster.

Fia and Addie were now two years old, and Harold had just reached his first birthday. The energy level within the Haughton home had risen to a fever pitch. No question about it; the Haughton had to hire at least one full-time nanny.

Miriam assumed the responsibility of interviewing and hiring. She announced the job opportunity at all nine of the women's clubs. The person she would hire had to be willing to move into the Haughton's home as a permanent resident. She had to possess a spotless reputation, numerous references, and extensive experience working with children.

"Dear, what other requirements should there be?" Miriam asked Benjamin.

"Did you clearly state part-time lion-tamer? That, above all else, would be a benefit." Benjamin responded.

"Really, Benjamin! Sometimes you can be so difficult!"

"It's my job," Benjamin chuckled.

Miriam was not prepared for the large number of responses she received. Unfortunately, most of the applicants were looking for housing. They either had no experience as a nanny, and therefore did not want the responsibility, or, they had a tremendous experience as a nanny, and therefore did not want the responsibility!

The whole process was overwhelming.

"Benjamin, there has to be someone." Miriam groaned. "She must be looking for us, but we just haven't found each other."

"My dear, it would be beneficial if our paths cross before the children graduate."

"Oh, you're no help. Honestly, Benjamin. I'm doing the best I can."

"Miriam, please don't be offended. I know you are doing everything possible to find our children the perfect nanny. I too believe she is out there. We just need to keep looking, keep praying and keep expecting. Come here dear, let me give you a hug."

"Absolutely not! Your hugs are what got us into this predicament!"

They both laughed and embraced—but not too tightly and not too long.

CHAPTER TWENTY-EIGHT

LEOLA JONES

JULY 19, 1917

"Your name?" inquired Mr. Haughton.

"Leola, Leola Jones, sir."

"Former occupation?"

"I was an assistant elementary school teacher in Chicago, sir. I worked under Superintendent Ella Young. Before that, I was a cook. I'm a very good cook, sir."

"What was your reason for leaving education?"

"I am an educated woman, sir. I wanted to become the first negro woman to teach in the elementary school system. That opportunity isn't open to negro women, yet. I have no family in Chicago. I have no family here for that matter, but I felt I needed a new beginning. Indianapolis seemed to be a place of opportunity and so, until the good Lord leads me elsewhere, I am here."

Benjamin set his pen down and rolled his chair back from the desk. He remained seated. Folding his hands in his lap he asked, "Where are you currently staying?"

"Excuse me?" Leola asked.

"Where is your current residence?" Benjamin repeated his question.

"I'm staying in a boarding house on the east side."

"Is it safe?"

"I beg your pardon, sir. Forgive me for saying this, but these are somewhat odd questions to ask in an interview. Yes, yes, I trust it will be safe enough."

Mr. Haughton unfolded his hands, rolled his chair to its original position, and said, "Miss Leola Jones, I have no openings for you at Haughton Manufacturing."

Rising Leola politely responded. "Well, I thank you very much for your time, sir. I–"

Mr. Haughton moved his chair forward further. His belly was now resting against his desk. Motioning Leola to remain seated he said, "You didn't allow me to finish Miss. Jones. I have no openings for you here, but I would like you to meet Mrs. Haughton, my wife. I believe you two have been looking for each other."

Leola's expression revealed her uncomfortable confusion. "Sir, I don't understand."

Mr. Haughton explained, "Miss Jones, I want you to come to my home tomorrow morning, let's say around eleven o'clock. I know this seems a bit odd, but I believe you and Mrs. Haughton meeting is a divine appointment."

Leola stood and responded, "Sir, I will see you and Mrs. Haughton tomorrow morning at eleven o'clock."

Mr. Haughton stood as Leola rose from her chair. Walking past Leola to the door leading into the main office, he said, "Rosie? Rosie, please give Miss Jones directions to my home."

Rosie smiled and replied, "Yes sir, Mr. Haughton."

Turning his attention back to Leola, Mr. Haughton smiled and said, "Miss Jones, it is an honor to find—I'm sorry, to meet you."

A bewildered Leola Jones stepped outside Mr. Haughton's office and stood in front of Rosie's desk. She was doing her best to resist smiling as Leola asked, "Excuse me, Miss Rosie?"

"Yes?" Rosie responded.

"Can you explain to me what just happened?"

Rosie finished writing Haughton's address on a piece of paper. Handing the paper to Leola, Rosie lovingly patted Leola's hand.

"Certainly, dear. I believe you have just met your new family."

CHAPTER TWENTY-NINE
CHANGE
NOVEMBER 1921

The ratification of the 19th Amendment to the Constitution, on August 18, 1920, and the special election vote in September 1921, granted women the right to vote on a state level. This, however, was not the end of Miriam's commitment; this was the beginning. With an even greater fervor, Miriam poured herself into protecting and expanding women's rights and influence. She feared, without total and unwavering commitment, what women worked so diligently to gain could easily be lost. She vowed to never submit herself or the cause to her male counterparts.

"Ladies, we must be strong. We must be vigilant. Do not think for a moment the rights we now have are etched in stone. Our status is fragile. We must live our lives as if every man is looking for our weaknesses —and we must not have any weaknesses! Never lower your integrity for the purpose of edifying a man. Their egos are insatiable and untamed."

While Miriam's message had not changed, Miriam had changed, changed dramatically. Benjamin realized the change, but he could do nothing to alter the course his wife was blazing. He refused to give in to his emotions but quietly felt he'd lost his best friend.

St. Elmo was where the men of Marion County would gather to commiserate. Benjamin felt a sense of responsibility for the marriage upheavals his friends were experiencing. After all, Miriam was his wife. She'd led the suffrage effort and showed no signs of relaxing her commitment to total equality.

Benjamin attempted to make light of the situation by participating in his friend's misery. "Gentlemen, perhaps one of you could assist me. When I leave home for work, I am at a loss for the appropriate valediction. This morning, I wished Miriam a nice day. She immediately retorted, 'Don't tell me what kind of day to have!'" The men laughed and extended their drinks across the table toasting one another's mutual circumstances.

That year, the Haughtons lost old Fil. The loss was difficult for the entire family. Fil had been a faithful companion, a friend. Old Fil was family. Ginger was a beautiful filly, and the children loved her dearly, but Benjamin knew she could never replace the memory of old Fil.

Benjamin Haughton found himself longing for the simplicity of the past.

CHAPTER THIRTY
RAISING THE YOUNG HAUGHTON'S

Miriam was strict about two house rules:

1.The girls must never have boys in the house.

2.Harold must always take care of the girls. However, he was to do so in such a manner that it did not draw attention to their need for his protection. After all, they were Miriam Haughton's daughters and must always be seen as self-sufficient young women.

Miriam explained, "Harold is to care for his sisters. Certainly not for sake of their need. It is chivalry, purely chivalry. Mind you, chivalry is far less the need of the female gender as it is a necessary discipline for the male. Never forget that, Leola."

To which Leola would always reply, "Yes, Mrs. Haughton. I'll do exactly as you wish."

Mr. Haughton was less eloquent and much more to the point:

1.If the girls bring boys home, stay in the room and keep your eyes on them!

2.If the girls are ever taken advantage of, let Harold whoop 'em!

To which Leola would always reply, "Harold can have whatever is left after I'm through with them!"

As for discipline, Leola had full reign to do whatever she deemed necessary. Leola was strict. She made it a point to initiate what she called "memorable discipline." This dissuaded the children from soon repeating the same offense. There were occasions when reminders were in order, especially for Harold.

The Haughton children were well aware of who they were. Benjamin and Miriam made certain of it. They were Haughtons, children of Marion County's leading suffragist and most noteworthy businessman. Continually under the watchful eyes of their community, they had fewer freedoms than most children their age.

When not at home with Leola, Fiametta and Adara were with their mother at the women's club. They were cute. They were adored by the women at the club, and their presence gave Miriam the temporal satisfaction of motherhood.

Fiametta was resentful. She longed for social interaction with other children. She could see them playing, riding bikes, and making chalk drawings on the street from the window of the Haughton Cadillac as they passed on their way to the women's club.

On those few occasions when they did intermingle with other children, Fia felt awkward and uncomfortable. It was not at all what she'd imagined. "They are silly, mother, silly and quite naughty. I prefer not to be with them. And they are very rude to Addie, Mother—not at all welcoming."

Adara, the second born of the twins, was not aware of the other children's behaviors. Forever smiling, she lived in her own whimsical world of fantasy. She was a very special child. Addie blessed the Haughton family with her simplicity and gentle spirit.

Harold, on the other hand, was precocious, a young boy whose inquisitive nature was far beyond the limitations his mother deemed appropriate. Benjamin took pride in his son's curiosity and probing questions. Harold's dispensary of endless energy provided Benjamin with constant amusement. Miriam found such delinquency intolerable.

Miriam continued her war against anyone who would forestall

suffrage and women's rights. Her fight engendered a rigid determination but an unintended bitterness towards men. Leola could see Miriam's cause beginning to overwhelm Miriam's relationship with Benjamin and Harold.

Benjamin was fully submerged in a growing business and took her aggression with a grain of salt. To young Harold, Miriam's words stung like salt in a wound.

Try as she may to be a positive influence, Leola could only watch the distance between mother and son widen as their animosity continued to swell. To Harold's ear, every word spewing from his mother's lips was a political indictment of the male species and another speech extolling women's rights. Harold grew weary of the guilt he felt being her son.

However, there was one occasion—one time when Harold would recall feeling his mother's love—or something similar to love.

Harold and his mother were ordered to Irvington High School to meet in Mr. Winebury's office.

Mr. Winebury was the headmaster at Irvington High School. It was Harold's first year at Irvington. Harold had been implicated for placing a tack on the chair of his unsuspecting history teacher, Mr. Enos.

Oddly, on this occasion, Harold was innocent of the indiscretion.

The headmaster was more reluctant about the meeting than Harold. He knew he would be facing Miriam Haughton.

"Good morning, ma'am. Please take a seat."

"I will stand thank you. This should not take long at all."

"The reason we are here is because your son has been accused of placing a tack on Mr. Enos's chair–"

Miriam interrupted, "He didn't do it. Now, is there anything else that you find so pressing that you would interrupt my day and my son's education?"

Even though the headmaster expected a confrontation, Miriam's overt aggression took him by surprise causing him to temporarily dismiss his self-restraint. "Woman, it is about time someone put you in your place!"

"I have a proper name, and I expect to be addressed by it!"

"That is no way for a woman to talk to a man!"

"Do forgive me. I didn't recognize I was addressing one!"

Although entertained by the exchange, Harold rolled his eyes as his mother began her speech:

"Women did not merely seek a document that venerates our equality. Our equality was a matter of fact. Do not be mistaken. It has always been a matter of fact. What we sought was the reasonable opportunity to share in those processes that govern our lives. We sought emancipation from laws dictated to us while seeking the event to participate in the making of such laws that govern all of us. May I remind you, sir, we have won!"

The headmaster sat dumbfounded. He struggled to recall the purpose of the meeting. Miriam took advantage of his momentary lapse.

"Do not for a moment believe your gender or title gives you the right to belittle me or my son. He did not do it, period! Good day!"

With that, Miriam and Harold left the office.

Later that afternoon, Mr. Enos visited the office. Mr. Winebury was at his desk reviewing the days' attendance records.

"Excuse me, Mr. Winebury?" Mr. Winebury did not look up from his work but acknowledged Mr. Enos's presence with a hum. Mr. Enos was emphatic, "Did you have your meeting with Mrs. Haughton concerning Harold's actions, my pain, and the disruption of my class?"

Mr. Winebury casually continued his review of the attendance records but responded, "Yes, Mr. Enos. I did."

Mr. Enos was more forceful, "And, sir, what was the outcome of that meeting—if I may ask?"

Mr. Winebury looked up from the roster, smiled, and matter-of-factly responded, "He didn't do it."

CHAPTER THIRTY-ONE

BONDING

Benjamin assumed the responsibility of raising Harold. Father and son created a bond that would never be broken. Harold worshiped his father. His feelings were bolstered by the community's love and respect for Mr. Haughton. Benjamin's and Harold's long talks were a welcomed education, and if they came across a question Benjamin could not answer, they would research the answer together.

Above all else, Benjamin instilled in Harold the importance of the Sacred Thread. The young man's heart was seared with the repetitive words of his father. "Son, you must remember those things that are most important in life, faith, integrity, responsibility, commitment, servitude, generosity, humility, and most importantly, love. Instill them in your heart and give them freely to all you meet."

His father's words were magnetic. Benjamin offered them; he never forced them upon his children. They were, if accepted, a pathway—the American dream, a path for generations to come. Harold embraced their importance, and he followed his father's admonition—with one exception, humility. After all, he was a Haughton. Harold was the product of two distinct, strong personalities. Benjamin quietly observed the influence Miriam's exuberance created in Harold's development.

Harold's boisterous self-confidence was a source of stability for some of the people who knew him and an annoyance for others. Privately, Benjamin wished his son had known his mother prior to her life commitment to suffrage. He perceived a potential weakness occurring in the Sacred Thread. It motivated him to more purposefully groom Harold to appreciate life while at the same time taking full advantage of the opportunities life had to offer.

"My boy, the good book says, '*When pride comes, then comes disgrace, but with the humble is wisdom.*'"

"Father," Harold confidently responded, "I will honor the values you have instilled in me. I will carry them forward to the next generations. However, I will cautiously endeavor to remain humble. The world is changing. You must understand, Father, if a man exhibits too much humility, the world will conclude he has too much to be humble about!"

Benjamin shook his head as he twirled the tip of his bushy mustache. Harold gave him a sense of pride and wonder. He chuckled to himself as he could only imagine the experiences yet to befall his young, precocious son.

Harold began working at Haughton Manufacturing on his sixteenth birthday. His father handed him his first tool. Benjamin carefully removed it from the steel cabinet. He explained in detail how it was to be treated with respect. Harold stood transfixed as his father explained every component, the brushes, the cap, the shaft, and the handle. After a thorough explanation, Benjamin handed Harold—a broom.

"My boy, if you cannot operate this piece of equipment, you will never be able to operate the machinery you see before you."

It was a beautiful manufacturing facility, state-of-the-art. The machinery glistened as if it had just been purchased. There was pride in every detail of the manufacturing process. Benjamin and Richard had taken a little tool shop, expanded its influence, secured the Indiana state contract, which was the first and largest contract awarded to Haughton Manufacturing, and continued expanding its product line.

Harold took his responsibilities seriously. During his high school years, he would keep his father's plant glistening. Haughton Manufacturing was his future. One day it would be his company.

CHAPTER THIRTY-TWO
KEROTHEN PHIL AEI!
JUNE 17, 1932

T he dean of boys called out the next name, "Harold Warren Haughton."

Harold walked across the stage and, at sixteen years of age, proudly received his high school diploma. He adjusted the tassel of his mortar board to the opposite side, representing passage into higher education. For Harold Warren Haughton, it would mean an immediate move to Cambridge, Massachusetts, Harvard University, and the newly constructed Lowell House.

Benjamin urged Harold to immediately join one of the fraternities on campus. There, Harold would be thrust into a brotherhood of like-minded, success-oriented young men whose friendships he would carry throughout his life.

Harold and his father independently reached the same conclusion. Delta Kappa Epsilon, DKE, would be the fraternity best suited for Harold. Its open motto, *"Kerothen Philoi Aei"* or "Friends from the Heart, Forever," encouraged each young man to be forward thinkers committed to personal development, while networking with their brothers to secure their mutual merits in whatever pursuits their journey would reveal.

Maintaining membership within the fraternity was no easy task. There were time commitments, financial commitments, academic requirements, and required community and social involvements.

And there were the parties. Benjamin was firm with Harold about the prospect of fraternity parties. "You are attending one of the most prestigious universities in the United States of America. You will become a member of one of the leading fraternities. You are a Haughton. I expect you to bring honor to your family, your university, and the principles set forth by your fraternity!"

While his words were firm, he knew Harold was entering the best times of his life. He had a modicum of envy, imagining the experiences that were now awaiting his son.

"I intend for you to come back refreshed and prepared to enter the next chapter of your life, young man," Benjamin said.

"Mother, Father, when I return, I will be more than prepared to fulfill your dreams and, with God's help, the dreams of future generations. Thank you!"

CHAPTER THIRTY-THREE
A "DATE" TO REMEMBER
FEBRUARY 11, 1933

They met at a party. Barbara Louise McCleary stood all of four feet ten inches and was disarmingly beautiful. She needed no makeup—nor did she wear any. Long, thick red hair framed her porcelain face. A hint of freckles was divinely positioned across her nose and onto her soft cheeks. Her eyes were a bold turquoise, shaded by long lashes and brows that turned slightly up just above her nose, giving her a perpetual look of wonderment and innocence. A few moments after an introduction, her fighting Irish heritage diminished any thought of her being a demure, naïve young woman. She was as fiery as her fiery red hair.

Not being one to conform to the status quo, Barbara and three of her classmates sought to establish Harvard's first fraternity for women. It raised the ire of existing fraternities and sororities. Although she was not successful in her endeavor, Barbara Louise McCleary established a name for herself as a strong and, at times, ruthless leader. She was just the type of challenging woman Harold was attracted to—at least until the conquest.

Likewise, Barbara was attracted to Harold. His personality seemed to dare anyone to break through its polished veneer. To Barbara, it was magnetic. She would accept the dare and be ever so stealthy in penetrating this young man's emotions. Was she looking for a suitor? Absolutely not. It was all about Barbara. It was about the thrill of the hunt and the pride of the victor.

To the casual observer, they might have seemed the perfect couple. However, Harold's and Barbara's relationship was far from perfect. Neither was particularly invested in the relationship. In essence, they were egocentric—each using the other for his and her personal gain. They were the spoils of conquest. Harold's and Barbara's relationship was far from what it appeared to be.

Harold fueled Barbara's fiery jealousy, acting as if his continued attraction to other young women was naive and innocent. It was, in reality, solely meant to get under Barbara's skin. On the other hand, Barbara did nothing to hide her vengeful scorn for any girl who dare give Harold a flirtatious glance. Harold found it temporarily fulfilling until he realized his social circle was slowly eroding.

He was not the least bit sensitive about the breakup. Barbara wouldn't be impressed with sensitivity, anyway. Without discussion or warning, he left one morning and simply did not return. It was over in his mind, and he moved on. Barbara's only feeling was vengeance. She didn't care about the relationship and needed no consoling. No one treated Barbara McCleary that way and got away with it. Harold Haughton would be a name she would not forget.

CHAPTER THIRTY-FOUR
GRADUATION GIFT
MAY 28, 1935

Harold graduated early from Harvard University on May 24, 1935, having received his business degree with honors and his "most eligible bachelor degree" from every sorority on campus, also with honors.

He arrived home four days later to be greeted by Benjamin, Miriam, Fiametta, Adara, and Leola. Benjamin looked forward to Harold taking the helm of Haughton Manufacturing. Miriam looked forward to finding a wife for Harold, and of course, being blessed with beautiful granddaughters.

Adara simply looked forward to being together. With her hands clasped just below her chin, a broad smile, and a slight bounce of anticipation, Adara asked, "Will we have a big dinner tonight, Leola? Will we have a big dinner—just like it used to be?"

"My dear, we will have a dinner that will rival a dinner fit for a king and queen!" Leola replied.

"Wonderful!" Adara exclaimed as she threw both arms high over her head, and in an instant hugged herself with delight twisting back and forth in total satisfaction.

When Harold left for college, and the girls moved into their own home, Leola's responsibilities were completed. Mr. and Mrs. Haughton were not ready to return to a totally empty house, and they had grown fond of Leola. She was truly family. They asked her if she would consider staying. Miriam needed someone to care for the house and prepare meals. Benjamin needed someone to occasionally take his place listening to Miriam.

Leola agreed to stay with Mr. and Mrs. Haughton on a month-to-month trial basis. They were now well into their thirty-eighth *trial* month together. Leola would remain a permanent fixture in the Haughton family.

Adara carefully set the table with what had always been her childhood favorite, Minton fine bone China. She'd worked carefully with Leola to create a warm menu that would be everything Leola had promised.

Harold's first meal would be baked stuffed pork chops with savory bread stuffing. Accenting the main course was sesame-ginger roasted broccoli, parmesan pesto, and roasted potatoes. Leola's freshly baked bread would continually circle the table, followed by her honey-whipped butter.

As dinner drew to a close, Addie could hardly contain herself. She knew what the dessert was; she'd helped Leola prepare it. It was Harold's favorite. Addie was agonizing in her attempt to keep the secret.

"Addie, would you like to bring dessert to the table?" Asked Leola.

There was no answer. In a flash, Addie disappeared through the swinging door and into the kitchen. The family could hear her giggles as she opened the large walk-in refrigerator door. Moments later, Addie reappeared, carefully backing into the dining room, shielding, until the very last moment, the treasure she was carrying. As she turned, everyone accentuated her thrill with their own oohs and aahs.

Buttercream stuffed chocolate eclairs! At this point, Harold threw his arms into the air mimicking Addie's show of approval, "Wonderful!" Harold exclaimed. Everyone applauded. Harold took the tray from his sister and set it on the table.

He turned to Addie. "Addie, my love. This is the best homecoming any brother could have ever imagined." He hugged her, and as he did, he thanked everyone for making the evening special.

The last of the eclairs had met their intended fate. It was time to present Harold with a graduation gift. Benjamin and Miriam stood together as they handed him the sealed envelope.

"What's this?" Harold asked.

"Go ahead and open it, son." Miriam proudly responded.

Harold opened the envelope. There was a card and yet another sealed envelope.

Dearest Son,
You have been a blessing to the two of us since your birth. You've worked hard to be the young man we are so proud of. You've carried the Haughton family name with honor.
You've earned some time to relax, to enjoy the beauty and the vastness of nature. It is there you will see the hand of God and you will grow to depend upon His leading.
We are proud, beyond measure, of the man you have become.
God's richest blessings upon you and those you are blessed to touch.
Remember to always mind the Thread.

Mother and Father.

The second envelope contained an all-expense paid cruise throughout the Mediterranean on the *Conte di Savoia*.

"Father, Mother, this is far too much to spend on me for having graduated. You knew when I started Harvard I would finish. Spending this much on me is unnecessary."

Benjamin laughed. He laughed so hard he could hardly speak.

"Ha! Spend? Spend you say? Ha! Miriam, did you hear your son?

Spend! Ha!" He turned his attention back to Harold. "Spend on you, you say. My dear boy, did you not just graduate from Harvard University with a degree in business? And yet you cannot clearly determine the difference between a gift and an investment?"

Harold began to see the picture more clearly.

"This is our security payment. It is solely intended to assure your mother and me a very happy retirement while you take over the operations at Haughton Manufacturing!"

Harold glanced back and forth at them—as if he was pondering a very difficult decision. In a most theatrical tone of voice, Harold responded, "I don't know, Father. There are certain risk assessments I must consider before accepting such a proposition. Who knows what the two of you might do left to your own devices? Is it wise for me to commit my efforts to your undetermined future? What do you have for me as security?"

Miriam interjected, "I have a swift kick in the pants for you if you don't just accept the ticket and say thank you! You may become the next 'Mr. Haughton,' but I will always be your mother!"

They all laughed.

"Then I gratefully accept! The first thing we learned in business was that if your mother says to do it, do it!"

There were abundant hugs of congratulations and thankfulness.

CHAPTER THIRTY-FIVE
GRANDMA HELEN'S BIRTH
OCTOBER 21, 1914

I t was year four of the Great War. Eight hundred and seventy-six thousand souls were lost since the first shots fired in 1914. It was beginning to look as if this horrible world war would soon be over, but an even more devastating worldwide plague was about to emerge.

While optimism was on the rise, a sinister epidemic was beginning to spread. It started within military ranks but soon swept throughout the population of New London, Connecticut, with influenza. This was not to be the usual yearly wave of illness. This would escalate into one of the worst epidemics to strike the northeastern states. In Connecticut alone, there were 105,056 cases of influenza and 2,256 cases of pneumonia, resulting in 10,593 deaths.

In the midst of such a human tragedy, on October 21, Helen Bernadette Cannon entered the world of Lyda and Dalton Cannon. Born by midwife in the family home, Helen was protected from the ravages of the epidemic.

The Cannons were a prominent family in Waterbury. Helen's great-grandfather, Augustus Reginald Cannon, was a successful businessman in the screw and fastener industry. Like so many men of his time, Augustus worked hard to provide opportunities for his children and for their future generations. Every Cannon family member was at one time, or another, employed by Cannon Metal Works And Fasteners.

Helen was the youngest of five children. The Cannons were wealthy but lived in modest accommodations choosing rather to enjoy extravagant world travels. The variety of cultures, foods, and architecture inspired young Helen to pursue higher education in international relations. Encouraged by the quality of leadership exhibited by President Professor Katharine Blunt, Helen attended Connecticut College for Women. Blunt enhanced the curriculum and the accreditation at Connecticut College, providing female graduates with a more level playing field with their male counterparts.

President Blunt felt strongly that education should not be bound by the walls of a campus classroom. She encouraged her students to pursue study abroad and initiated college credit for independent study. Helen took full advantage of the program and in her junior year advanced her international studies and world experience in Paris, France.

Following her graduation in 1935, Helen set out on a three-month European tour.

CONTE DI SAVOIA

While cruising Italy on the *Conte di Savoia*, relaxing on the lido deck at the main pool bar, Helen noticed a distinguished, handsome young man. There were numerous older men at the pool, but this younger gentleman caught her attention. Helen attempted to inconspicuously keep an eye on him while occasionally glancing down at her *Fortune Magazine* and sipping her William Larue Weller on the rocks. The man appeared to be alone.

After several minutes, the man wrote something on a piece of paper and handed it to the bartender.

He was on, what appeared to Helen to be, his second martini when the porter walked through the deck holding a sign with the name paging,

"HAUGHTON."

The young man Helen had been watching also noticed the porter and the message. He abruptly finished his martini and left his place at the bar. He walked briskly past Helen. She noticed his Rolex wristwatch, a very good sign. "Haughton!"

After an hour in the warm Italian sun, Helen returned to her suite. She was surprised to find a bouquet of daisies, a plate with two Luisa Spagnoli, Baci Perugina chocolates, and an invitation to the Captain's Dinner on her bed. Helen was thrilled to receive the invitation and would spend the next several hours prepping herself for the occasion.

She arrived in the first-class dining room. Its honey-colored panels of travertine marble, gold leaf ceilings, and tall silver leather columns were breathtaking. She presented the host with her invitation and was escorted to her table.

The service was remarkable. A centerpiece of fresh daisies and two chocolates once again greeted her.

Remarkable! She thought.

"Good evening, miss. My name is Vittorio. I am pleased to be your server this evening. Is there anything the lady wishes in addition to her William Larue Weller?"

Absolutely remarkable! There was a moment of uneasiness. *How in the world do they know my drink? I must be more discrete about what I do here. They most certainly are watching!* She smiled at Vittorio, "No, no thank you. For the moment I'd like to just sit here and enjoy everything I am experiencing."

"As you wish, miss. I will return at your convenience."

"Thank you, thank you very much."

"It is my pleasure."

A few moments later, Helen heard a voice coming from just to the right of her. The person speaking had positioned himself so that she could not actually see to whom the voice belonged.

"I find the Pierce-Arrow one of the most beautiful motorcars on the road."

As Helen was attempting to put the abrupt comment into context, the voice continued. "I couldn't help noticing, while we were at the pool today, you seemed to be on that page of your magazine for quite some time."

With that, a note was dropped over Helen's shoulder. It fluttered directly in front of her and came to rest on her napkin. On the note was written the following message:

"There is an attractive young lady sunning to my left. I would like to know her drink of choice. Also, if she remains there, in ten minutes please have me paged; Haughton."

Harold stepped from behind Helen's chair.

"Please allow me to introduce myself. My name is Harold Haughton. May I ask whom I have the pleasure of meeting?"

"Well, I, well yes, please. I mean, yes. My name is Helen Conner, Mr. Haughton. How do you do?"

"Miss Conner. It is Miss, is it not?"

"Why, yes, yes it is."

Helen was becoming more uncomfortable by the second. She could feel her cheeks flush. Harold could see this and wanted to set her mind at ease.

"Miss Conner. I hope the daisies I sent to your suite are a flower you approve of. They symbolize innocence and purity. I assure you, while I find you most attractive, I wish to bring you no discomfort. I will reluctantly excuse myself if you wish, but I would be honored if you would allow me to join you for dinner."

Harold's comment had allowed just enough time for Helen to regain her composure.

"Mr. Haughton I would enjoy that. I would enjoy that very much."

Helen reached her hand forward. Harold politely took it and bowed in thanks.

"I would like it if you would call me Harold."

Helen wanted to respond, *and I would like it if you would call me anytime you want.* She restrained herself and responded, "Thank you, uh. Thank you, Harold. Please call me Helen."

There was a glint in Harold's eyes. "Ah, Helen; the shining light. It is a pleasure to meet you."

He'd done his homework.

CHAPTER THIRTY-SIX
FIAMETTA'S LAMENT
SEPTEMBER 1935

"Mother? What are we to do with ourselves?" There was a tone of desperation in Fiametta's voice.

"Whatever do you mean, Fiametta?" Miriam inquired.

Fiametta continued, her volume increased. "Harold has finished college and is traveling around the world. He will no doubt take over Haughton Manufacturing when Daddy passes. All we do is sit at the women's club. What are we to do with our lives?"

With a flip of her wrist, Miriam dismissed the notion that Fiametta should have any cause for such concern. "Oh, fiddle-faddle. You and Adara have endless opportunities before you. Look how far women have come. I dare say when I was your age there were no choices. There were no opportunities. Women were to submit to the man's world. She bore his children, fed, and cared for him in his old age, and then buried him along with any chance of having a future of her own once he'd died."

"Mother, that's dreadful!" Fiametta scolded.

Ignoring Fiametta's response, Miriam continued. "It need not be for you and Adara how it was when I was growing up. Look at what you have before you. You are Haughtons. Your father is successful in business, and I have paved a way for you and your sister to enjoy whatever endeavors you choose."

Fiametta was not backing down. "What does Daddy really do these days? Does he run the machinery? Does he repair the machinery? Does he actually manufacture anything himself?" she asked, knowing the answer.

Unaware her daughter was stealthily using her words against her, Miriam gave a sniffy retort, "Oh my goodness, no child. He hires others to do those things. He makes important decisions about the business. He directs its manufacturing, its marketing, its sales, and acquisitions. He decides the future of Haughton Manufacturing, and he is highly respected for his ability to do so."

Fiametta was nimble with her questioning. "But he doesn't *actually do* any of the work. He makes decisions based upon information others give him, right?"

Miriam was suddenly confused by the direction the conversation was taking. How was it that she found herself now agreeing with Fiametta's point of view? Miriam hesitated as she answered, "I, I suppose so. He makes his decisions by listening to the information he is given and by his personal experience." Miriam became stern as she recognized an opportunity to take back control of the conversation. "Remember, he poured his heart into Haughton Manufacturing. It wasn't always successful. It was a struggle, but your father persevered."

Fiametta, sensing her mother had taken the bait, pointed an accusing finger toward her mother. Through a clenched jaw, she slowly and deliberately announced, "And then he will die, and you will bury him!"

"Fiametta!" Miriam was shocked. Never had Fiametta spoken such harsh words to her.

Fiametta was not finished. Like an attorney setting up the defendant for final arguments, Fiametta paced directly in front of Miriam, not three feet away. She never took her eyes off Miriam's shocked gaze. Then she paused. In a subdued tone of voice resolved, "Mother, what is the difference? You'll still end up caring for him. What happens when he can no longer make the decisions for Haughton Manufacturing?"

Miriam just stood there, her mouth trembling with emotion.

Fiametta would not give her time to respond. "No! No, let me answer my own question." She glanced momentarily, but thoughtfully at the floor, and then her eyes returned, piercing directly into her mother's soul. "Harold will run it—won't he?" She threw back her shoulders and puffed out her chest in a mocking display of testosterone and privilege. "Harold is the man." Having made her point, Fiametta returned to her questioning. "Again, I ask, what is the difference, Mother? What have you really accomplished?" Fiametta shook her head. "No," she said in a whisper. "No!" Her volume increased as did the violence of her head wagging. "It is still a man's world, Mother! And it will remain a man's world until we are making the final decisions!"

"Fiametta, you govern your words carefully. You are my daughter, my daughter, and I am Miriam Haughton!"

"Yes, Haughton," Fiametta turned as if to walk away. She then once again paused. Without turning back towards her mother, she slowly spoke. There was satisfaction in her voice, a stinging satisfaction. It was the satisfaction of an attorney who had orchestrated the case perfectly and was about to bring it to a successful conclusion. "Yes, Mother, and you even willingly gave up your name!" She didn't turn to see her mother's reaction. She'd made her point and continued walking to her room. Miriam followed, but Fia's words cut deep. Miriam stopped and slowly walked to her office. What had she really accomplished if even her own daughters questioned their futures? While she'd invested so much time preparing a future, what had she accomplished to prepare them for it?

Miriam had fallen short. She'd given the raising of her daughters to a hired employee. Make no mistake, a loving and wonderful employee.

Nevertheless, Miriam had relinquished her most important responsibility, to nurture and raise her daughters to be able to take full advantage of the opportunities she'd worked so hard to gain for others.

Oh, dear God how could I have been so foolish? Have I let them down? How can I make it up to them? Is it too late? I don't even know them. God, I don't know what they like, what they want. I don't know their dreams or their goals. The loneliness they are doomed to experience is too much for my heart. I must let them go. I must find a way. They must experience life. Oh, dear God. Please give me another chance to make it right, please!

Miriam quietly sat at her desk and wept. It was the loneliest feeling she'd ever experienced. She could not shake the dark and empty vacuum of hopelessness she had for Fiametta and Adara. She could not escape the feeling of responsibility she alone bore and that she alone could rectify.

CHAPTER THIRTY-SEVEN
THE CONNORS
OCTOBER 1935

Mussolini's attack on Abyssinia that October brought the Italian cruise to an unscheduled end. For the safety of its crew and passengers, the *Conte di Savoia* returned to Genoa. There, the passengers disembarked. First-class patrons received compensation for their inconvenience. The remainder of the passengers simply had to accept the inconveniences of political unrest and be grateful they were, at the moment, safe. A greater concern for Harold was the potential of losing contact with Helen.

While walking the lido deck for the last time, he spotted her. "Ah, my dear—there you are!" Harold hollered over the heads of the people on the crowded deck. He could see Helen standing on her tiptoes, one hand holding her light pink cloche hat in the ocean breeze, the other clinging to her baggage amid the fury of passengers. She was frantically looking back and forth to determine where Harold's voice was coming from.

Harold caught Helen's eye. A burst of happiness flooded Helen's emotions. "Helen, stay where you are. I'll come to you!" Harold yelled above the roar of the ship's engines. He continued waving his morning paper over his head as he made his way through the crowd toward Helen.

"Harold, I was concerned I might not see you again. I mean, without saying goodbye."

Harold perceived a more meaningful intention. "Perhaps we should allay those concerns and plan rather say hello more often." Harold's statement was open-ended. He wished for Helen to make of it whatever she wanted. He observed her body language. Having been Harold's guest to numerous events onboard, Helen was much more secure with herself and her desire.

"Oh, dear, dear, dear, dear. Whatever shall we do, Harold?" Helen teased. "I was just beginning to consider the possibility I might like you. I'd hate to see the opportunity to verify it come to an end."

"Helen! Then you shall join me in Paris!"

They shared a friendly embrace. "Wonderful!" Helen giggled.

"Have you been to Paris before?" she asked.

"Why, no? No, I haven't."

"Oh, I am so happy! I shall have a thing or two to show you in Paris. I studied there in my junior year. Do you love the arts?"

"My dear, I am certain I will love whatever we do together," Harold responded.

For two months, they enjoyed their days sightseeing in Paris and its outskirts. Evenings were spent dining, dancing, and discovering. Their chance meeting on their Mediterranean cruise was the beginning of a lifetime together.

Leaving France, Helen and Harold boarded The *SS Normandie*, the newest of the luxury liners, at Le Havre for her maiden voyage to New York City.

On the morning of June third, the passenger ship arrived in New York Harbor. Helen's family arrived at the pier early that morning to be among the very first to see the ship's passengers disembark.

"There she is. I see her! Helen! Helen!" Mr. Conner shouted. Helen waved and smiled. Her entire family was on the pier to greet her. As she approached them, her youngest brother broke from the family ranks and ran to give Helen a hug.

"What did you bring back? What did you bring back?" He anxiously inquired. "Did you bring me something? Huh, Helen? Did you bring me something?"

"Well," a nervous Helen began. "I did bring *someone* back. Mama, Daddy, I would like you to meet Mr. Harold Haughton."

Helen stepped aside as Harold set his luggage down on the pier decking, politely tipped his hat to Mrs. Conner, and extended his hand to meet Mr. Conner.

Mr. Conner immediately assessed the situation and surmised Helen's friend to be more than a casual acquaintance. He'd always trusted Helen, and she'd never done anything to betray that trust. She was a young woman now and young women tend to find young men. If this was a gentleman Helen was interested in; it was best to put forth the most welcoming posture. If this Haughton fella was less than a gentleman in the eyes of the entire family, Mr. Conner had five strapping young sons at his side to dissuade Mr. Haughton's prolonged stay.

Harold was by no means the least bit reluctant with the introductions. "Mr. Connor, sir, Helen tells me you are in the fabricating business."

"Why, yes, yes I am. We manufacture primarily screws and bolts. We are just getting into custom sheet fabrication for the automobile industry."

"That's quite a coincidence. My family also is in the metal industry, Haughton Manufacturing. I doubt you've heard of us. We're not that well known yet but–"

Harold was immediately interrupted by a now quite animated Mr. Connor.

"But your father holds the largest contract the state of Indiana has ever awarded! He's become quite a legend in manufacturing circles.

Harold, it's a pleasure to meet you. Children, let's grab all of Helen's things and get home." Mr. Connor paused for a moment as Harold reached for his luggage. "Boys, gather Mr. Haughton's luggage, too," he said. "Harold, I am most interested in sitting down with you and learning more about your father's business. Yes, Benjamin Haughton is well respected in our industry, very well respected."

"Well thank you, sir. I know that he would be very humbled to hear you say that."

Helen had no idea. She looked over at Harold who simply gave her a wink and a nod as they continue walking to the automobile.

After supper, Mr. Conner invited Harold into the study for a port and continued conversation about the industry.

"So, Harold. Tell me a little bit about the history of Haughton Manufacturing."

Harold relaxed comfortably in the plush William and Mary leather chair. "In 1903, my father opened a tool and die shop in Indianapolis. He made a variety of products; the majority of products were for the city of Indianapolis and its smaller businesses. He was a custom manufacturer, so he made whatever the customer needed."

Mr. Connor sipped his twenty-seven-year-old 1908 Guedes vintage port. "What was his first product?"

Harold chuckled as he hesitantly told the story. He was careful not to ruin the impression his father had made upon Mr. Connor. Harold acknowledged Haughton Manufacturing's humble beginnings. "Interestingly enough," Harold paused for a sip of the smooth Tawny port. The sweet caramel flavor was warm and soothing. "He began stamping toe tags for funeral homes throughout Indiana. He still says his greatest accomplishment was convincing funeral homes the deceased needed an upgrade from the pulp-board toe-tags being used."

Amused by the genesis of such a reputable manufacturer, Mr. Connor pressed for more information. "Ha! Interesting, and then?"

Now more resolute, Harold continued, "Actually, with the outbreak of the European War, those became a profit center all their own. The tags were being ordered for everything that might otherwise be damaged under wartime conditions. My father is a simple man. He does not like to venture into things he does not fully understand."

"Ah, a very good trait, and what about you?" Mr. Conner queried.

"I enjoy learning about those things I do not understand. However, I too believe it is important to do what you do well. Do it with every fiber of your being to the best of your ability. If you have the opportunity to do something, be the best!"

"And what are you best at?"

Sensing Mr. Connor's question had a deeper intention, Harold responded, "Well, sir. I trust I am becoming fairly adept at presenting myself to the family of a young lady with whom I've become quite infatuated."

"Hmmm," Mr. Connor raised an eyebrow and pensively curled the tip of his handlebar mustache. The room was still. Neither man made a move nor said a word.

"And have you had much practice at it?" Mr. Connor asked as he held his port glass against the candlelight admiring its rich golden caramel colors.

Harold understood exactly what Mr. Connor wasn't asking.

"Mr. Connor. My father also taught me when you do something, do it right the first time."

There was a long pause. Harold was not at all uncomfortable with the silence. He was a determined individual, not given to hesitation when there was something worth fighting for. Mr. Conner could see this in Harold, and it was penetratingly magnetic.

"Harold, my boy. How about another port?" Mr. Connor's interrogation was complete. Harold had made the grade.

"Mr. Conner, I would enjoy that very much."

In the months that followed, the Conners and Haughtons became friends. Although both families were in the same industry, Haughton and Connor were respectful of one another's individual business endeavors.

On the evening of June 27, 1936, not quite one year after their first meeting, Helen Bernadette Connor became Mrs. Helen Haughton.

PART FOUR
NOT EXACTLY

CHAPTER THIRTY-EIGHT
JUNE 5, 2017

"So, your grandfather took over the business and left it to your dad and uncle," Asha stated matter-of-factly.

"Not exactly," Carrie replied. "Asha, nothing in the Haughton family was simple." She took a sip of her gin and tonic. "I think two is my limit today. I don't know how my dad and his team got anything done after their three martini lunches!" Carrie paused for just a moment, "Who am I kidding? They probably didn't!"

"So, you were saying your great-grandfather didn't leave the business to your grandfather?"

"Not exactly."

Carrie gazed around the room and became lost in her surroundings. "Asha, imagine my great-grandfather and grandfather sitting at this table and discussing business, isn't that crazy?"

CHAPTER THIRTY-NINE

TRANSFER OF POWER

JANUARY 4, 1937

B enjamin and Harold made their way to their favorite booth. St. Elmo was humming with business.

"Can I bring you gentlemen anything to drink?" the waitress asked.

Benjamin responded, "Coffee. We'll both have coffee, dear. No sugar, no cream. Black coffee, thank you."

Harold could sense that this was not the usual luncheon. There was something far more urgent in his father's voice. It was time for Harold to begin his journey. It was time to begin transitioning Haughton Manufacturing to the next generation.

"Son, there are any number of ways to get what you want in life. It is the wise man who first considers the well-being of others. By so doing he inspires a willing dedication from those he employs, to assist him in achieving his goals. Pay your employee more than your competition is willing to pay. You will have the dedicated service from the very best workers in the industry."

Harold listened intently to his father's words. It seemed all so simple. It was an adaptation of the "Golden Rule." Benjamin Haughton had expanded Haughton Manufacturing by living the principles he'd preached for years: faith, integrity, responsibility, commitment, servitude, generosity, humility, and most importantly—love.

"Father, I have been dedicated to those principles and committed to the care of our Sacred Thread. It was important to me that Helen's family understand our industry. I think it is remarkable the relationship you and Mr. Cannon have fostered."

Mr. Haughton nodded his head in agreement. "Son, it is remarkable that you have found such a beautiful wife. She strengthens our Sacred Thread." He leaned forward as he spoke. "Harold, we love Helen. The two of you are fortunate to have one another." These were sentiments Harold had not often heard. Benjamin continued, "That's not to say there wasn't a time I was concerned about your lack of humility."

Both men chuckled as Harold recalled a previous conversation he'd had with his father concerning the value of humility:

"If a man exhibits too much humility, the world will conclude he has too much to be humble about."

Benjamin continued, "I do believe you have met your match, son. She is strong and determined. She will keep you on the straight and narrow—with or without your cooperation!"

Harold chuckled. "Father, I knew from the moment I met Helen I wanted to spend my life with her. I don't know how I knew, but I knew. She is everything I could ever hope for in a wife. She makes me a better man."

"Son, always honor Helen. Make certain to honor her as your wife! Never take for granted the lofty position she holds within your marriage. Honor her for all she does, but most of all," Benjamin looked deep into his son's eyes and repeated himself. "Hear me now; honor her as your wife—and ultimately honor her as the mother of your children." Benjamin sat back in his chair before continuing. "Too often men fail to recognize the Godly authority a woman has over the home. When this happens, women seek appreciation outside the home. We are living in a new world." Once again, he paused to sip his coffee.

"Mind you, it is a good thing; a very good thing—women's rights. But a woman must not be forced to turn away from their authority in the home to stoop to a man-made authority elsewhere. Do you understand what I am saying, Harold?"

Harold was compelled to ask, "Dad, are you regretful? Do you regret your mother's influence outside the home?"

Benjamin glanced over Harold's shoulder and out the window. The streets were bustling with businessmen and women making their way to and from lunch. His attention then returned to the interior of St. Elmo as he considered his response to Harold's question. "No, Harold. I am not regretful for her influence outside the home. I am extremely proud of your mother's influence. She will be remembered for many years to come for all she has accomplished within the women's rights movement—even beyond Indianapolis. I love your mother, and she loves each of us: you, Fia, Addie, and me. I suppose, if I am regretful at all, I am regretful that I did not more openly share my needs. I played the part of the self-made, self-reliant man. In my mind, to display needs would have been to display weaknesses. Had I known better, your mother might have been more fulfilled through her influence within our home. I've needed her so much more than I ever expressed."

Harold was receiving a life lesson he would not soon forget.

"It is not a matter of restraining a woman from her God-given equality and opportunity within society. It is the failure of men to recognize the God-given honor due to her within her home and for her family. This failure will ultimately disrupt the very underpinning of the family unit. Harold, mark my words, women will always be successful in business. That will be a wonderful thing for commerce. Not all women will marry. Not all women will have children. If that is their choice, then God bless them in their endeavors. But a new day is coming, and I believe it is already here where women will hold positions of authority within the industry as well as raise successful families. I take my hat off to each one of them. I am humbled by their dedication."

Benjamin took a deep breath; the moment had arrived.

"Son, the time has come for me to begin relinquishing some of the decision-making responsibilities to your authority. You've proven yourself and I am proud of you. Haughton Manufacturing will be stronger because of your influence." There was a glint in Benjamin's eye. "Mind you, I firmly intend to be around for a long while. Ha! Probably longer than you would like!"

They both laughed. Benjamin continued; his face now beamed with pride. "This is a new world, my boy. We are entering a new Industrial Age, and it demands new ways of doing business. You'll be present at all meetings. You will participate in every decision-making process. I will offer my opinion and experience, but the ultimate decision-making will be yours."

"Father, I am grateful for your words. I will do everything in my power to make you proud. I will do everything in my power to make our workers proud. I will protect the Sacred Thread and the family name. Most importantly, I will, each and every day, be grateful to God for my wife, and I will honor her position within our family."

Benjamin gave his son a broad smile. He once again sat back in his chair, raised both hands from the table, and with resolve, pounded its surface. "Harold, I'd like a drink!"

He then turned his attention to their server. "Young lady, what the devil are you doing giving us coffee? My partner and I need a couple of drinks! Let's get a couple of John Harvey & Sons Bristol Creams."

Harold interrupted. "Miss? Miss, excuse me. Would you make one of those a Martini Cocktail No. 1? French Vermouth, two dashes of orange bitters and three olives, please?"

Benjamin's countenance changed. He raised an eyebrow, folded his arms, and in mocked seriousness shook his head, "Well, well, well. There you have it! Only a minute into our first major business decision and you've taken the helm!"

Harold gave his father a long overdue hug. "Thank you, Father. I love you."

"Thank you, son. I am certain my love for you is far greater than yours for me—knowing what it is you are taking off my shoulders!"

The drinks were delivered. Benjamin raised his glass. Harold followed his father's lead. Benjamin stood so that every St. Elmo patron would witness his toast, "To you, MR. HAUGHTON, and to the legacy you will carry into the future. I love you, son. St. Elmo, I give you Harold Haughton, owner of Haughton Manufacturing."

St. Elmo erupted in applause.

JUNE 5, 2017

"You know, Asha, there are some funny stories about my grandfather. When my grandma Helen was pregnant with my dad, my grandfather's business acumen didn't transfer over to his role as an expectant father."

CHAPTER FORTY-ONE
DR. SMITH
APRIL 8, 1938

"Helen, wake up; wake up! Your contractions are three minutes apart."

Helen turned her head to find her husband with one hand on her stomach and both eyes staring at his pocket watch.

She sighed. "Harold, don't you think I am aware of my contractions?" she asked, as her head returned to the impression it had left on her pillow.

"But they are only three minutes apart! I must call Dr. Smith," his tone was resolute, but he wasn't prepared for Helen's own resolve. Her head was motionless this time as she instructed her husband. "You'll do nothing of the sort! I am very comfortable. I will let you know when it is appropriate to call the doctor. Right now, it is appropriate for you to let me get some sleep!"

Chastened, Harold replied, "Yes, yes, you do that, dear. I'll watch for the contractions."

She had just closed her eyes when Harold awakened her again. "Helen, Helen! Wake up!" he urged. "They are two minutes apart— TWO MINUTES! I must call Dr. Smith."

"Harold I'm-" she groggily began, but Harold had already left his post and raced downstairs in the disheveled suit he'd been wearing under the covers. She could hear the clicking of each number on the phone as he hurriedly dialed the doctor's number. After three rings, the doctor answered.

"Hello?"

The downstairs was cold, but Harold could feel beads of sweat gathering on his forehead. "Dr. Smith! Oh, thank God! She is having contractions. I have been timing them. They have been precisely two minutes a part—two minutes!"

"Well, wonderful, wonderful." Doctor Smith calmly responded. "Excuse me. Who is this?"

"I'm sorry, doctor. It's Harold, Harold Haughton."

"Well now, Harold, how does she feel?"

"How does she-how? She feels like she is about to have a baby!"

"All right Harold, I want you to calm down. I'll be right over."

"Thank you, doctor."

Helen heard Harold racing back up the stairs, taking two steps at a time.

Slightly winded, he announced, "The doctor will be right over, dear." Harold was unable to contain his concern. "How are you feeling? Can I get you something? Would you like some tea? Can I rub your back? Should I-"

"Harold," Helen gently interrupted. "I'm worried about you. Please calm down." Helen did her best to allay Harold's consternation.

Unable to assist his wife, Harold paced, vocalizing his thoughts. "Yes, yes. Calm down, yes. I think I'll have some tea. Yes, that's what I'll do. I'll make some tea. Would you like some-"

"Harold!" Helen raised her voice just enough to prevent yet another recitation of helpful menu items. She softly, gently pleaded, "Harold, dear, I would just like to rest, please."

Harold composed himself. He took a deep breath, "Yes, yes dear," he offered as if the choice had been his all along. "You should do that!"

He kissed Helen on the forehead and returned to the kitchen to wait for Doctor Smith. Had she not been so tired, Helen might have seen the humor in her husband's responses.

Harold had fallen into a deep sleep at the kitchen table when Doctor Smith arrived. The knock at the door jarred him from his sleep. Still groggy, Harold stumbled on the throw separating the kitchen from the living room. Doctor Smith could hear the thud as Harold hit the living room floor. After a moment, the front door opened. Without saying a word of greeting the groggy and disheveled Harold Haughton grabbed Dr. Smith's arm and pulled him into the living room.

Dr. Smith took one look at Harold and asked, "Mr. Haughton, are you all right, sir?"

"Me? Oh, yes. I'm fine, fine, doctor. You know, I've got to maintain control to keep Helen comfortable. She's having a baby you know."

The irony was not lost on the doctor, and he softly smiled. "Harold," he said, with his best bedside manner, "I want you to sit here on the sofa and rest. I'm going to check on Helen. I'll be right back." As he ascended the stairs, he couldn't contain the chuckle that escaped him.

Harold continued mumbling, "Okay, doctor. Yes, that's what I'll do. I'll just sit here, right here on the sofa; until you get back, right here..."

Knocking softly on the bedroom door, Dr. Smith spoke through the door, "Mrs. Haughton? Helen? Are you awake?"

"Oh, doctor," Helen breathed. "Did he really call you? Oh, dear, dear, dear, dear! Do come in," she invited. "I am so sorry, Harold means well, but he is very nervous—and he is making me nervous! Is there anything you can give him to calm him down?"

"Well, as I understand it, Dr. Haughton believes you are about to have a baby. Can we first check and see how things are coming along?" he asked.

"What I'm about to have," she replied, "is a nervous breakdown if Dr. Haughton's bedside manner doesn't subside!" They both softly chuckled.

"Helen," Dr. Smith began, "Your baby is in position for delivery, but it could be hours before that time actually comes."

She thought about the implications. "Doctor," she began, "How strong a tranquilizer can Harold be given?" she asked.

He laughed and answered, "Well, from my brief visit with him downstairs, I would suggest you contact Dr. Beaker."

Helen asked, "Dr. Beaker? Isn't he the veterinarian?"

"Yes, that's him. He specializes in horses. What your husband appears to need would only be available through him!"

Helen's burst of laughter was a well-needed release of anxiety. Dr. Smith urged, "Helen, I want you to get some rest. We'll have a lot to do in the next day or so. These contractions are all precursors to the ones for which we are waiting." Then he smiled, "You will know when the time is right."

Still feeling a bit sheepish about taking his time, Helen thanked the doctor and said, "I'm sorry you had to make the trip over."

"Think nothing of it, my dear," he assured her. "That's what I am here to do."

He closed the bedroom door, and upon reaching the bottom of the stairs he heard Harold snoring. Thinking it best to let him sleep, the doctor quietly let himself out and made his way back home.

4:00 AM

Harold's sleep ended abruptly with Helen's call. "Harold? Harold? Are you all right? Harold?"

Harold bounded up the stairs and into the bedroom.

"Oh, my dear! I'm so sorry! So sorry, I must have drifted off." He glanced at the clock; it was four o'clock in the morning. "What can I get you? What do you need? Would you like some tea?"

"Please, Harold, no. I'm fine," she answered. "I just thought you should know the contractions appear to be getting stronger, and I-" With those words, Harold burst from the room. With lightning speed, he was back downstairs dialing Dr. Smith's number.

"Hello? Hello? Dr. Smith, hurry! Helen's contractions are very strong. We need you here right away!"

By 6:00 a.m. on the morning of April 9th, things were noticeably progressing. The intensity of pain was mounting, and as much as she tried to keep silent (for Harold's sake and for hers), each contraction brought on a deep involuntary moan.

Twenty minutes later, the doctor arrived to see Harold seated on the porch. The image of Harold Haughton shivering in a disheveled suit was laughable, and it took the doctor a full minute to gain his composure before exiting his car.

"Good morning, Harold," he greeted. His demeanor was cheerful and steady. "How are you this morning?"

Harold dispensed with any greeting of his own and politely chided, "Thank God, you are here! The contractions are strong now, doctor, very strong."

Smiling, Dr. Smith offered, "Well, let's just have a look and see how Helen is doing."

Harold followed the doctor upstairs. "Harold," he began, "Why don't you wait out here for a moment while I examine Helen?"

Harold's nerves were at a fever pitch. He paced the upstairs hall, wrung his hands, and mumbled to himself. He stood outside the closed bedroom door, "Yes Doctor, yes. That's what I'll do. I'll wait out here; right here. If you need anything, I'll be right here."

"Thank you, Harold," Doctor Smith responded as he began his examination.

Harold pressed his ear firmly against the bedroom door directing all his energy to listening. He could only hear the muffled sounds of Dr. Smith's and Helen's conversation. Harold heard footsteps coming towards him from the other side of the door. Dr. Smith finally stepped out of the room and into the hallway to give Harold an update. "Things are moving along beautifully, Harold," he said calmly. "Helen's contractions are very steady—two minutes apart. I'll return in a couple of hours to see how she is doing."

Harold was wide-eyed with disbelief. "A couple... hours? What!? Doctor, she is having a baby!"

"Harold, relax," Dr. Smith assured. "She hasn't dilated yet. We are hours away from delivery."

"Dilated?" It was more than Harold could bear, "Doctor Smith! I do believe you are looking in the wrong place!"

Amusing as it was, the doctor politely ignored Harold's comment. Making his way to the stairs, he heard Helen call for him. He and Harold both ran into the bedroom.

"Doctor, my water has broken. What should I do now?" Calm until then, Helen had assumed the demeanor of a woman experiencing childbirth for the first time. The doctor turned to Harold and asked, "Harold, will you please excuse us for a moment?"

Harold exited, but this time he left the door ajar so he could hear.

The best physicians have a way of speaking matter-of-factly while still conveying confidence, experience, and—when it comes to the birth of a baby—joy.

"Hmm, my dear," he observed, "It looks like we might be welcoming your little one sooner than we expected." He smiled while giving instructions. "Helen, I want you to take nice slow breaths between contractions. When the contractions return, I want you to take very short fast breaths. Will you do that for me?"

"Yes, Doctor," she answered. "But may I sit up a little? Lying on my back has become terribly uncomfortable." To his knowledge, it had been her only complaint.

"You find a position that is comfortable," he said. "Have you tried lying on your side?"

From outside the room, they heard Harold's response, "Yes, dear, try lying on your side."

Helen could only shake her head in embarrassment.

After years of tending to the needs of anxious fathers-to-be while their wives labored to deliver their children, Dr. Smith stepped out of the room and found Harold bent over at the waist, hands on his knees, and breathing through his own mental contractions.

"My dear friend, would you be so kind as to make me a nice cup of tea?" the doctor asked.

Happy to contribute something, Harold answered, "Certainly, certainly, doctor. Anything I can do to be of help!"

Closing the door securely, the doctor returned to Helen's side. "I think our patient will make it, Helen."

At eight o'clock that morning, Harold was at his post, pacing in the hallway on the opposite side of the door. Occasionally he heard, "Ok... push, push! Relax now. Take a moment. We're going to push again very soon." Moments later, "And, now, Helen—big push! Push!"

Coaching gave way to a sudden silence. And then, the burst of a newborn's cry. "Helen," the doctor announced. "You have given birth to a strong and handsome son." After a brief inspection, he reported, "It appears all the parts are intact. Let me clean him up just a bit, and you can hold him."

Harold's composure would not last much longer. His heart was racing. He'd become dizzy from hyperventilating. He'd unintentionally mimicked Dr. Smith's breathing instructions to Helen, duplicating each short series of breaths, holding and then pushing. His eyes hadn't left the doorknob since he first heard the baby cry. The knob turned, the door opened slowly, and the doctor positioned himself so that Harold had an unobstructed view of his wife and child. Helen's radiance was more beautiful to Harold than the day they first met. He just stood there, eyes transfixed on the beauty, the miracle of mother and child.

"Sweetheart," Helen's voice was full of love, "Would you like to come in and meet your son?"

"We have a boy?" Harold's voice was childlike.

Harold looked to the doctor for confirmation. The beam on the doctor's face was all Harold needed.

"A boy?"

"Yes, my dear," his lovely wife affirmed. "We have a son. And quite a handsome young man if I do say so myself!" She repeated her invitation, "Harold, come in and meet Harold, Jr." Helen said.

He'd had the energy to race up and down the stairs numerous times, to pace the hallway until the wood flooring revealed a path caused by scuff marks. But now, Harold found he had little command of his legs as he slowly, cautiously, moved toward Helen and his new son. He reached her bedside, and with one hand he caressed her forehead. With the back of his other hand, he gently smoothed the face of his son. He was overcome by more emotion than a lifetime could offer. He kissed his son's tiny forehead, turned to Helen, and said, "No, my dear. You're holding Benjamin. Benjamin William Haughton, the second."

"Harold?" Helen inquired. "Your first son should be named after you."

"My dear," the new father continued, "Long ago I made my father a promise to protect and maintain the Haughton name, the Haughton virtues, and our Sacred Thread. I wouldn't have any of this if it were not for him. I wish our son's name to be Benjamin."

Helen nodded her silent approval. She understood and respected his wishes. She returned her attention to Benjamin. Speaking to her new baby, she said, "Ben, I only hope that as you carry your grandfather's name, you will carry with it the loving heart of your father." Mother and father softly kissed Ben on the cheeks. Harold looked up at Helen and said, "Thank God for His unspeakable blessings. I love you, Helen. I love you." Focusing his attention on the little bundle he continued, "And I love you, my son."

Two years later, almost to the date, and with no less dramatic spectacle provided by the expectant father, Ben's little brother, Harold, Jr., came into the world. The Haughton family was now complete.

CHAPTER FORTY-TWO

WAR!

DECEMBER 8, 1941

Their young boys were three and five when Harold and Helen sat with their attention riveted to their RCA Victor. The United States had been attacked By the empire of Japan. President Roosevelt stood before Congress:

"NO MATTER HOW LONG IT MAY TAKE US TO OVERCOME THIS PREMEDITATED INVASION. THE AMERICAN PEOPLE, IN THEIR RIGHTEOUS MIGHT, WILL WIN THROUGH TO ABSOLUTE VICTORY! WITH CONFIDENCE IN OUR ARMED FORCES, WITH THE IN-BOUNDING DETERMINATION OF OUR PEOPLE, WE WILL GAIN THE INEVITABLE TRIUMPH, SO HELP US, GOD! I ASK THAT CONGRESS DECLARE THAT SINCE THE UNPROVOKED AND DASTARDLY ATTACK BY JAPAN ON SUNDAY, DECEMBER 7, 1941, A STATE OF WAR HAS EXISTED BETWEEN THE UNITED STATES AND THE JAPANESE EMPIRE!"

WAR!

Helen's heart sank. It was unthinkable. Wasn't the war twenty-seven years earlier, "The War That Will End War?"

"Harold? What does this mean? Harold, you won't go, will you?

Will they call you? You mustn't volunteer. Harold, tell me you won't leave us!"

Helen pleaded while Harold sat stunned by the news. It took only a moment for him to gather his thoughts and respond. "Helen, I will do whatever I am called to do. We are at war, and I cannot shirk my duty to serve my country. If called, I will..."

Just then, the telephone rang. Helen answered. "Yes, yes, it is. Yes, he is. Oh, I see. Just one moment, please."

Tears welled in Helen's eyes. "Harold it's for you. It's Governor Schricker's office."

Harold bolted from his chair and took the phone from Helen. They looked at each other. It was as if they were looking at each other for the last time.

"Hello? Yes, yes, it is. Yes, I will."

Helen gasped, "No!"

"Helen!" Harold covered the phone as he gently chided her. "The woman simply asked if I would hold for Governor Schricker!"

"Yes? Yes, hello, Governor. Yes, we were listening too. Sir, I want you to know that the Haughton family is one hundred percent behind our president, and we will serve in whatever capacity we are called."

Helen fell back into her chair. Her arms hung lifeless at her side; her head fell forward as she began to weep.

The conversation continued. All Helen was able to hear were the continual affirmative responses from Harold.

"Yes! Yes, absolutely, Governor Schricker. We will begin the process tomorrow! Thank you, governor. Thank you for this opportunity to serve!"

Harold hung up the phone still trying to comprehend the content of the conversation.

Helen looked up at him, "Why? Why? You didn't even try, Harold! You didn't even try! You said yes to everything without hesitation; you seemed honestly happy to leave us and die in some God-forsaken war!"

"Sweetheart, I am going nowhere. The governor has requested that we immediately dedicate a portion of our production line to the government and the war effort. I have been requested to modify Haughton Manufacturing into a packaging manufacturer for military containers of all sizes. Do you see what this means? I will have to remain state-side to oversee the operation. Helen, we will be doing our part from home!"

Helen leaped into Harold's arms. "Oh, thank God! Thank You, God!"

"Helen, I've got to call Dad. We've got a lot of work to do and a very short period of time to do it."

The next day Benjamin and Harold began redesigning Haughton Manufacturing, converting three-quarters of the stamping line into a line capable of slitting, deburring, forming, welding, expanding, crimping, decorating, packing, and sealing a variety of military containers.

The military was primarily interested in a method of packaging and sealing the new type C field ration. Benjamin frowned upon the endeavor. He'd previously been asked by the fishing industry to manufacture a conveyance for Oligochaetes. He politely turned the business away.

Benjamin did what he knew he could do well. His company was now one of the top three metal fabricators in the eastern United States. Haughton Manufacturing could, without a doubt, manufacture the containers, but it had no experience synchronizing the receiving of multiple finished goods, then packing and sealing them. This was not their area of expertise, and Benjamin foresaw nothing but challenges. The number of items the new type C field ration was intended to convey would be a coordinating nightmare.

"Harold, what you are venturing into is not a can of worms; it is a vat of snakes!"

Nevertheless, Harold pressed forward. The financial investment Haughton Manufacturing would receive from the government would create a state-of-the-art packaging line Harold could see continuing long after the war was over.

"Dad, we'll let the military coordinate the individual items and they will send them to us already organized. The bottom of each container will be universal, so we can continually manufacture them. We'll spot-weld a key on each one for opening the container in the field and store them in Work-In-Process. The only challenge I foresee might be a remote possibility of sealing the wrong embossed top on a ration. However, if we only run one style ration on the line at a time, we'll avoid sealing a 'Chopped Eggs and Ham' top on a 'Pork and Beans' ration. Dad, it's Haughton Manufacturing's next opportunity. It's my opportunity to contribute to what you began. It's the next generation!"

Benjamin took a moment to consider Harold's plan. It was plausible, even doable. He gave Harold a long stare. Harold stared just as intently at Benjamin. He was awaiting an encouraging glint; it finally came.

"Harold, if you don't get this right, we will all be eating rations!"

Benjamin threw his arm around Harold's shoulders.

"Son, You just might make something out of this little shop!"

Both men laughed. Harold returned to the machine shop to discuss the modifications and timeline with his mechanics. Benjamin returned to his office to visit with Rosie and read the paper.

Harold Haughton's vision became a reality. Haughton Manufacturing soon became the leading container manufacturer in the United States.

CHAPTER FORTY-THREE
THE BOYS' STRENGTHS
MARCH 1951

"Train up a child in the way he should go: and when he is old, he will not depart from it."

— PROVERBS 22:6

For fourteen years, Harold poured himself into the expansion of Haughton Manufacturing. Throughout the war, the packaging division continued to expand. Haughton Manufacturing increased the dimensions of its containers and became one of the leading cold-rolled and tin mill backplate lug and tight head pail manufacturers in the nation. Haughton's ability to intricately lithograph and size-coat expanded containers set them high above the capabilities of their competitors.

Young Ben was now thirteen, and Hal (as Harold, Jr. was known) was eleven. Harold was very cautious introducing Haughton Manufacturing to the boys. He wanted to encourage their interest and sense of pride without becoming overbearing. In their presence, he was careful to face each challenge as a friend, a friend that would better himself and the corporation.

Young Hal would lose himself in schoolwork. He was fascinated with numbers and loved assisting his father during inventory. Harold used this time to show young Hal how to measure the thickness of each of the varying gauges of steel with calipers. Hal could then measure an entire stack of cut stock, divide by the thickness per inch and determine how many sheets were in each stack. Harold would audit his son's numbers by picking a stack already counted and asking Hal to count the individual sheets. Hal's numbers were always accurate; it was like magic to the youngster.

Ben? Ben would lose himself in girls.

Ben was not a particularly good student. School bored him, and he had a distaste for anyone telling him what to do. He'd spent numerous occasions in the principal's office. He was never guilty of doing something wrong. He simply refused to go out of his way to do anything right. Ben's personality gave his father cause for great concern.

Harold saw a bit of himself in young Ben. Ben was pugnacious. It didn't matter the topic; Ben's opinion was the correct opinion. He wasn't interested in sports other than water skiing and snow skiing. The primary attraction in both was the young girls Ben would meet!

Since Ben liked the snow, Harold decided to take his young son to Sugarloaf Mountain in Maine to watch the first ski races on Winter's Day. The races were named after Sugarloaf Mountain Ski Club Member Amos Winter, who helped cut the first trail up Sugarloaf Mountain. Its cutbacks and turns wound down a 1,800 vertical foot drop.

Ben had never considered the planning and engineering required to cut a trail into the side of a mountain. He asked question after question about the need for such precision and the methods for cutting the trails. Ben was not satisfied with broad answers. He wanted to know the details: how the run was planned. What was the process of finalizing designs? Who was the engineer? How were tons of rock removed while not compromising the integrity of the mountainside? Harold listened to Ben intently. Perhaps there was a glimmer of hope. Perhaps what he was raising was his next master mechanic. When they returned home, he would introduce Ben to the machine shop and engineering department where the nuts and bolts of the company originate.

CHAPTER FORTY-FOUR
PERFECT
FEBRUARY 4, 1953

He wasn't particularly hungry and apologized profusely for not eating the breakfast Miriam had prepared. She thought it odd and asked Benjamin if he was feeling well.

"I feel peculiar," Benjamin responded. "I don't know how to explain it. I feel peculiar my dear. I'm tired, very tired." He then shook his head in disbelief and laughed, "Ha! I haven't done anything to feel this tired."

It concerned Miriam. "Perhaps you should see Dr. Westmoreland," she suggested.

Still thinking about how he was feeling, Benjamin, shook his head in agreement. "Perhaps. Perhaps I will do that. I will see if he has time for me. Thank you, my dear."

Benjamin grabbed his Crofut & Knapp and made his way out the washroom door. As Miriam removed his breakfast from the table, she watched him grab a hand full of oats for Ginger. Benjamin patted the mare on the forehead and made his way to the garage. Miriam continued cleaning. Without thinking about it, she was awaiting the sound of the Cadillac's engine. It didn't come. Not hearing it, she once again glanced out the window. To her surprise, Benjamin was once again patting Ginger's head and giving her a second portion of oats. She walked from the kitchen and through the washroom door to the porch.

"Dearest, is there anything wrong?" she asked.

Benjamin looked up at her and smiled. He gave her that Haughton glint and said, "Wrong? Wrong? My dear, everything is perfect, just perfect. I was giving Ginger some of old Fil's portion, I suppose. I don't know why. Just thinking of her, just, I guess I was just... thinking of her." His voice trailed off.

Benjamin returned to the washroom door and gave Miriam a kiss. "I love you," he said.

Miriam was taken by his return and paused before replying, "And I love you dear."

Precisely twenty-eight minutes later, Mr. Haughton pulled onto Haughton Manufacturing's property. The gentle hum of the machinery was music to his ears.

"Perfect! Just Perfect," he said to himself.

Harold strolled from the machine shop towards his father's car. Rosie could see the two of them conversing before Benjamin patted his son on the back and began his walk toward the office.

"Good morning Mr. Haughton," Rosie greeted.

"Good morning to you, Rosie. My dear, you have never looked more ravishing."

Rosie gave Mr. Haughton a puzzled look which, in turn, sparked that Haughton glint, "Well, perhaps you did once or twice... but at the moment, I simply can't remember, ha!"

"Well, thank you, Mr. Haughton. I placed a few checks for you to sign on your desk."

"Thank you, Rosie. I'll get right to them after I put up the flag."

Mr. Haughton gathered the flag, proceeded to the flagpole and proudly raised Haughton Manufacturing's American flag. He stepped back and admired the beautiful Stars and Stripes gently swaying in the light morning breeze. "Perfect!"

He returned to the office. "Rosie, would you please get Dr. Westmoreland on the phone for me?"

"Certainly, sir." Rosie paused for a moment. Intuitively she sensed something unusual in the moment. "Is everything all right, sir?"

"I'm tired, Rosie. It's an odd tired; a happy tired—if such a tired exists. Bothersome though. Miriam thought I should see Dr. Westmoreland."

"Right away, sir. Yes, you do look a little flushed. I'll contact Dr. Westmoreland for you right away."

"Thank you, my dear. I want to thank you very much for taking care of me." Rosie sensed his words of gratitude transcending the simple act of contacting Dr. Westmoreland.

Mr. Haughton retired to his office, closed the door, and sat at his desk. A few minutes later, Rosie paged him to let him know that Dr. Westmoreland was on the phone. There was no answer. Thinking he'd gone to the production area, Rosie called Harold's phone.

"Harold, is your father in the production area? Dr. Westmoreland is on the phone for him."

"No, Rosie. Father is not out here. Why would Dr. Westmoreland be calling father?"

Harold hadn't noticed anything unusual when his father arrived— their greeting was brief. Benjamin was parking the Cadillac when Harold strolled out to greet him. Exiting the Caddie, he moved to give his son an embrace, something Harold was unaccustomed to.

"Good morning, Father," Harold said. He returned his father's affection. He had just repaired one of the leather belts operating the spray booth portion of the assembly line, and he was covered in grease from head to toe. "Father, you're getting your suit soiled."

With a laugh, Benjamin offered, "Harold, my boy, it's a suit!"

Then, firmly grasping Harold's shoulders while moving him to arm's length away, he looked at him intently and said, "Mind the thing that matters, son." They held each other's gaze, and then, abruptly, Benjamin asked, "So, what are we working on this morning?"

Harold shared the same passion for the machinery as his father, and when he answered, his enthusiasm was clear. "Well, Father, the lead strapping broke for the coatings and spray booth areas. That put too much tension on the support strappings and, well, I removed the entire segment of the production line and re-strapped it."

Looking at the man his son had become, Benjamin smiled admiringly. Benjamin laughed. Harold knew it wasn't at his expense; instead, the laughter came from the shared delight father and son found in the work.

"Don't you just love the problems?" Benjamin had asked him. "Ah, my boy; they are wonderful! They've been my closest friend—kept me sharp—kept me working. Never dread them, Harold. They will keep you busy. They'll make you better... Granted, you don't want them to be friends for any length of time!" They once again joined in laughter. "Ah, but the challenge of facing them, solving them, and removing them is thrilling!"

"Harold," Rosie continued. "Your father was looking a bit flushed. I thought he was acting peculiar. Dr. Westmoreland is actually returning your father's call."

Harold's brow furrowed slightly as he looked down as if seeking an answer on his greasy coveralls. He shook his head, "That doesn't sound like Father. Did you check in his office?" he asked.

"I paged him," she answered, "but there was no response."

Harold didn't hesitate. He rushed through the back door into his father's office finding Benjamin slumped over his desk. He was breathing, but his breaths were dangerously shallow. "Rosie!" Harold shouted. "Call for an ambulance!"

As Rosie dialed, Harold spoke softly to his father. "Father, don't leave us. Don't leave us now!" Harold repeated his pleading as he gripped his father's body under the arms and around the chest, lifting him from his chair and lying him gently on the floor. "Please, Father, please stay with us," he begged, as he awaited the arrival of the ambulance. Once the ambulance was on the scene, the attendants immediately worked to stabilize Mr. Haughton. Once stabilized, they wheeled him to the ambulance.

The siren and flashing lights brought all production to a standstill. Word quickly circulated that Mr. Haughton had taken ill. Everyone rushed to the front office to ask how they might assist. Mr. Haughton was not just an employer. For many of Haughton Manufacturing's employees, he was the only father they'd known, the only friend they'd truly enjoyed. All were overcome with emotion and concern.

"Harold! Will Mr. Haughton be all right?" one of the employees called out. Like a firestorm, others began peppering Harold likewise until Harold held up his hands to quiet them.

Finding his composure, Harold addressed them all. "Please, please, everyone. We don't know how Father is right now. They are doing everything they can. Forgive me; I must go to the hospital. I know Father would appreciate you showing your support by your prayers and the completion of your duties. I ask you to restart the line. I will be back as soon as I have more information."

The men immediately returned to their stations. One by one they repeated, "For Mr. Haughton!"

Harold asked Rosie to call his mother, Fiametta, and Adara to tell them Mr. Haughton had been taken to Indianapolis General by ambulance. Harold would be following in his own vehicle.

Arriving at Indianapolis General, Harold found his father already in surgery. Three doctors were working to save Benjamin's life. Dr. Westmoreland stepped out of the operating room to give Harold an update on his father's condition. Harold jumped to his feet.

"How is he, doctor?" he asked.

"Harold," Dr. Westmoreland explained, "Your father has suffered a hemorrhagic stroke. It is deep within the lower back part of the brain. There—there continues to be significant bleeding."

Harold was dumbstruck. It seemed only moments before he and this unbreakable man had embraced. How could this be happening?

The doctor continued, "I'm terribly sorry, but I feel it is necessary to prepare you and your family for the worst."

"Yes," Harold replied, only faintly hearing the prognosis. "Yes, thank you, doctor. Is there any chance of survival?"

Dr. Westmoreland looked at him squarely, slowly shaking his head to convey his answer. "I'm afraid it will simply be a matter of time. I am very sorry."

At first, the words held no meaning—just words. Harold backed away momentarily from the doctor. He turned and sat unaware that he'd returned to where he'd previously been seated. His elbows rested on his knees to brace his trembling chin cupped in his hands. It was then that he weighed the doctor's words in silence—the finality of his painful words began to register.

"Yes," Harold said, staring down at shoes that had tracked his dusty footprints from the machine shop through the emergency doors and to the waiting room. Another moment of silence passed. Harold looked up and nodded, "Thank you, doctor. Thank you. Please, make him comfortable."

"Harold, we are making certain he is comfortable," Dr. Westmoreland assured him. "We will relocate him to a private room so you and your family can be with him."

As the unthinkable became reality, the foggy surreal—focused, Harold fought back his emotions and returned to his previous position —his eyes staring at the floor.

"Doctor," his voice quivering, "How long?"

"Harold," the doctor began, "We don't know. It could be days; it could be hours. Your father's in God's hands now."

Harold lifted his chin from his hands, and as if some greater inner strength had taken over said, "I understand." He stood and turned to Dr. Westmoreland. "Thank you, doctor, just make certain he is comfortable."

Fia, Addie, and Miriam arrived forty-five minutes later. They were directed to Mr. Haughton's private room. Harold was sitting on the left side of the bed holding his father's hand. Miriam quickly rushed to the head of the bed on the right side.

"Benjamin, Benjamin dearest, it's Miriam. Can you hear me?" Benjamin's eyes fluttered slightly at the sound of Miriam's voice. Miriam turned to the girls with utter excitement. "You see? Do you see? There is always hope! Benjamin, if you hear me open your eyes."

Benjamin's eyes continued to flutter.

"Call the nurse, call the nurse!" Miriam shouted.

Fia ran to the nurse's desk and told the nurse that it appeared as if her father could hear them! Perhaps he was trying to communicate! The nurse looked up from her monitors and gave Fiametta an angelic smile. She told Fiametta she would immediately contact the doctor to get his personal update on Mr. Haughton's condition.

"Thank you! Thank you ever so much!" Fia said. Fia ran back to her father's room. "The nurse said she would call Dr. Westmoreland right away. He will be here any moment." Fia reported.

"Do you hear that, dear? Dr. Westmoreland will be here in a moment. He'll have you good as new," Miriam said as she patted her husband's lifeless hand.

The four of them continued to chat amongst themselves until they were interrupted by a knock at the door. It was Dr. Westmoreland.

"Hello everyone."

Miriam immediately jumped to her feet. "Dr. Westmoreland," she paused to drop the formalities, "James, let's get Benjamin well so we can get out of this place and bring him home."

Dr. Westmoreland's face was stern. He did not acknowledge Miriam's request but asked everyone to follow him. They followed him across the hall to a large conference room.

"Please have a seat. I know this is a very difficult time for all of you. Miriam, I would be less than honest... It would be cruel of me to tell you Benjamin has any hope of recovery. He is fading as we speak. The portion of his brain that has been affected controls his voluntary muscle movements. He may still hear you; may still respond—for a while, but it is simply a matter of time before he passes. I am very sorry."

As if someone flipped a switch, a now very thoughtful Miriam Haughton lovingly reached over and patted Doctor Westmoreland's hand.

The room became deafeningly silent. Moments passed.

"James, I understand. Thank you for all you have done to make Benjamin comfortable. He's always enjoyed avoiding you!"

Everyone quietly chuckled. Miriam then said, "We are so very happy that you are here with us. Benjamin would no doubt recognize we are the ones who are in good hands. As always, he would be right. Thank you. I'd like to return to my husband's room if that is all you have to share."

"Absolutely, Miriam. I'm keeping Benjamin and each of you in my prayers."

Doctor Westmoreland left the room and walked down the hall. Fiametta, Adara, and Harold returned to the same positions they had previously occupied at Benjamin's bedside. Miriam joined them. As she looked at her husband, her memory took her back to a place only she and Benjamin would remember.

She was hanging laundry to dry in the morning sun. Miriam was an early riser, and she relished the routine of managing the household for the two of them. By the time Benjamin was out of bed and shaven, his breakfast of melon, sago, vegetable hash, broiled veal cutlets, and fried tomatoes had already been prepared. The aroma of fresh coffee greeted him long before he entered the kitchen. She watched him as he ate, listened as he told her of the challenges he would likely face at the tool & die shop, and warmed to him as he expressed his gratefulness to her for the perfect breakfast. She called his attention to a bit of unfinished breakfast that had come to rest in his mustache, and they laughed together as his repeated dabbing never quite found the mark. She lovingly took the napkin from him, moved her face close to his, cleaned the leftovers from under his nose, and kissed him gently on the lips. "I love you, Miriam," she heard him say, and she replied, "I know." After a second kiss, she added, "And I love you, Benjamin."

The weather was warm, and she stood in the doorway of the kitchen and watched as he opened old Fil's gate and led the mare to the carriage. Benjamin took great care with Fil as he placed the tack and carriage straps for his ride to the tool and die shop he'd inherited from his father. Task completed, he returned to the washroom, grabbed his Crofut & Knapp from the coat rack, and wished her a good day. Miriam offered another kiss and said, "I love you."

He held her close and said, "You are a very good woman." She watched Benjamin and old Fil clamor down the path, out to the road, and on to what would eventually become Haughton Manufacturing.

The next scene passing swiftly through her mind was different. Instead of leading old Fil to the carriage, she watched sadly as Benjamin simply greeted the mare with a fistful of oats, a few affectionate words, and a pat on the horse's forehead. Miriam remembered the spring in his step as he moved through the doorway, gathered his coat, and hurriedly kissed her. She interrupted his gait with the words, "I love you."

Without an embrace, he called out over his shoulder, "You are a very good woman!" He unlatched the garage doors and-

The shrieking scream of the ventilator's alarm shook Miriam from her reverie and beckoned her closer to her husband's side. Her memories were replaced with a flurry of disjointed thoughts. The brutality of change now haunted her. She disdained how ruthlessly the simplicity of horse and carriage was replaced by the cacophony and mephitic stench of automobiles. Had that been the moment she hopelessly recognized her world was changing? Was her fixation on women's rights evidence of her inner protestations over the societal paradigm shift manifested in Benjamin's admiration for mechanized progress? She didn't have a suitable answer. She only knew as she sat by this man whom she loved, she would trade every club meeting, march, and speech for his embrace.

Her next words came, not from an activist, but from the woman who'd watched his Cadillac transport him to the business he loved. "Dearest? Dearest? It is Miriam," She blinked back tears. "We are here with you. We are all here with you. Fiametta, Adara, and Harold."

Although his eyes were closed, Benjamin's lips moved as if to respond.

Miriam kissed him on the cheek. "I so love you, my dearest," she said, allowing her tears to flow.

In just a whisper he replied, "You are a very good woman." His eyes seemed to twitch—perhaps a last fading Haughton glint. Then, to everyone's surprise, they slowly opened. Everyone could see the tremendous effort it was taking—but he turned his head slightly towards Miriam and whispered, "I so love you, and always will."

Benjamin's eyes closed. Harold could feel his father's grip tighten. With every word, he tightened his grip more. Pulling his son close, Harold heard his father's last admonition, "Son!" Benjamin, in his final moments, whispered, "Mind the thread."

His grip loosened. Another moment passed. He inhaled deeply, opened his eyes for the last time, stared into eternity, and with a final glint breathed the word, "Perfect!"

Benjamin William Haughton was now a memory.

CHAPTER FORTY-FIVE

RICHARD'S RECOGNITION
MAY 27, 1953

Their meeting with Irvin Bateman, legal counsel for Haughton Manufacturing, was brief. Benjamin had never composed a last will and testament. Miriam now owned Haughton Manufacturing.

Harold would continue running his father's business. He'd trained for it for the past sixteen years, from sweeping the floors and cleaning the machines to becoming Haughton Manufacturing's Master Mechanic. He was intimately knowledgeable about the entire manufacturing process. While he mourned his father's passing, he was ready to fully assume all his father's responsibilities.

In Miriam's grief, she quietly wrestled with logic and principle. True, it was logical that Harold should run Haughton Manufacturing. Legally, she now owned the business until her passing or until she transferred the title to Harold. However, Miriam continued to be haunted by unfinished business.

Richard Edwards was now 72 years of age. With the passing of Benjamin, his partner and friend, Richard was ready to step aside and encourage Harold to make his own decisions, set his own course, and continue the Haughton legacy.

On May 27, 1953, Harold received Richard's letter:

My Dear Mr. Haughton,

Harold, it is wonderfully appropriate I address you as Mr. Haughton. Your father was a tremendous man of integrity. I am proud to have known him as my closest and dearest friend.

You, sir, are every bit as knowledgeable as he, perhaps even more so. The world is beginning to spin too fast for this old man; I am having difficulty keeping up. Harold, it is time for me to relinquish my small portion of time with Haughton Manufacturing into the hands of a thirty-six-year-old man whom I have grown to admire and respect.

I will always be a phone call away should you wish to discuss business or just have a chat. Please do not hesitate to reach out to me.

My very best to your mother and sisters.

With great confidence in you, I remain your friend,

Richard

Richard would continue to be a source of security for Harold. Richard and Benjamin shared the same life and business values. Should Harold ever have questions, Richard's advice would be as sound as if given to him by his father.

Richard's last bit of business was to make certain the exclusive contractual agreements from the state of Indiana continued. He made a personal request to visit Governor Henry F. Schricker. He and Governor Schricker had differing political viewpoints, but Richard's father had helped Governor Schricker early in the governor's career. He knew the door would be open to him.

Governor Schricker was more than happy to maintain business with Haughton Manufacturing. He knew of Benjamin and Miriam Haughton. He admired their social and financial commitments to the Hoosiers and was more than willing to participate in their history of good will to society. He also remembered Harold and his father's modification of Haughton Manufacturing for the war effort.

Harold pulled into Haughton Manufacturing's parking lot. Richard chuckled to himself, "Another Haughton, another Cadillac." Harold drove a 1948 Series '62 Convertible. His father compelled him to stay with Cadillac. It did not surprise the late Benjamin Haughton that his son would purchase a convertible. Harold would always take his father's advice and add a little bit of Harold Haughton to the finishing touches.

He sat for a moment looking at the corporation his grandfather and father worked so hard to establish. Momentarily overwhelmed with the enormity of the responsibility that was now his, he remembered the last words his father whispered to him, "Mind the Thread."

His mind suddenly flashed back to the last time his father drove onto these grounds, the very day he died. He vividly recalled being covered in grease from head to toe and his father giving him a hug. The conversation was seared into his memory,

"Father, you'll get your suit soiled."

"Harold, my boy, it's a suit! Mind the *thing* that matters."

Harold did not realize how much his last two conversations would mean to him. In Benjamin's heart, after all was said and done, after all the money had been made, after all the notoriety was received, after all the things had been acquired, the Sacred Thread was the single thing that mattered!

Tears momentarily blurred Harold's vision. His vision was transfixed on the beautiful building that was now his responsibility and his alone.

The flag had not yet been raised. It would be his first new responsibility.

CHAPTER FORTY-SIX

JUNE 5, 2017

"Oh my gosh, Carrie! So, the story about your grandfather never owning the company isn't true," Asha concluded.

"Not exactly." Carrie again replied. "Of course, when my great-grandfather died the responsibility fell upon my grandfather to run the business and to expand everything my great-grandfather had started. It's what my great-grandfather always intended."

"And your grandfather was already doing that," Asha commented. "Your great-grandfather made the announcement, right here!"

"Yes, that's true, but in reality, my great-grandmother Miriam legally owned the business. It was kept a secret until she died."

"Okay, but when she passed your grandfather owned it outright." Asha paused waiting for a response from Carrie—the expected response didn't come.

"Carrie? Right?"

CHAPTER FORTY-SEVEN

WONDERFUL!
AUGUST 22, 1953

After Benjamin's passing, Miriam's health rapidly declined. In her soul, she realized how much she'd sacrificed for suffrage. She'd poured herself entirely into every endeavor she undertook. There were no regrets; no, not really. She would never admit to herself or anyone else regretting her investment in such a noble cause. In Miriam's mind, she simply ran out of time. It was nothing she could have controlled, not time. Time moved too quickly for Miriam to enjoy the life she originally intended with Benjamin. At only sixty-eight years of age, her only desire was to once again be with her husband.

Fiametta did all she could to care for her mother at the same time care for her sister, Adara. Addie was now an adult with no physical challenges to speak of, but she'd never grown out of her affliction of "happiness and contentment." Addie was slower than the others. It was noticeable to everyone. The Haughtons would never acknowledge it. Addie was, and always would be, just as she was originally diagnosed, "Afflicted with happiness and contentment."

Fiametta drove Miriam and Addie each day to the newly constructed wing of the Women's Club. The new wing contained a beautiful indoor swimming pool, a recreation room, and a dining area. Addie was enrolled in numerous continuing education classes, swimming, and dance. These functions allowed her to socialize comfortably and participate in productive volunteer work for the club and for Marion County.

Even though Helen protested, Miriam's relentless persuasion resulted in her participation in the women's club functions increasing. She was, however, attempting to raise Ben and Hal. She enjoyed meeting new members who, like herself, became members through the "encouragement" of their mothers-in-law. Helen maintained a pleasant relationship with her mother-in-law, Miriam, and her sister-in-law, Fiametta. She visited with them several times each week. There was a very special place in her heart for Addie, and it was quite obvious Addie adored Helen. Although Addie was Helen's sister-in-law, Addie always referred to Helen as, "Mrs. Haughton."

Sharing time with Addie was one of the reasons Helen continued to participate in the women's club. Addie never voiced a complaint. She carried no malice towards a living soul. She perpetually smiled, and every day was, "Wonderful!" Her innocent, childlike attitude of continual anticipation was refreshing.

Helen pondered whether Addie might enjoy life more fully, living with her and Harold. Addie was perfectly capable of accomplishing specific tasks, she loved Ben and Hal, and her greatest pleasure was the thrill of making others happy.

That night at dinner, Helen approached the subject with Harold. "Harold, I really believe Addie would be happier here."

"Helen, we do not need Addie any happier!" Harold's response shot from his lips as if they'd been cautiously awaiting Helen's suggestion.

"Harold, behave yourself! You know what I am saying."

"I know what you are suggesting. You are suggesting I live with my sister—again! I have paid that debt. You simply do not understand the pressure it places upon me." Harold argued.

"If you feel responsible for Addie or Fiametta, you have no one to blame but yourself. They are adults. No one expects you to protect them. Those days are past." Helen responded.

Harold realized Helen's suggestion was probably a good one. Having Addie live with them would take pressure off Fiametta who was providing care for their mother and handling the books for Haughton Manufacturing. Addie could also help care for the boys and manage the home.

"Let me give it some thought. I suppose I am not totally against the idea-"

Before Harold could finish what he was saying, Helen exploded with joy, throwing both arms around his neck and repeating, "Thank you so much, Harold. Thank you, Thank you!" She gave Harold a kiss and said, "You have such a warm heart. I love you for taking care of your sister."

Exactly what he had just been told he would no longer be doing.

Addie was forty-one years of age when Helen approached Miriam and Fiametta about Addie living with them. Fiametta was grateful for the suggestion. It would be a welcomed reprieve. Miriam consented to allow Adara more time with Harold and Helen. She was too ill to fully comprehend Addie would be permanently living with her son and daughter-in-law.

On Sunday, August 22, 1953, immediately following church, Addie moved into her new home. She slowly climbed Harold and Helen's staircase, her face beaming with anticipation. Harold and Helen followed as she reached the top and walked down the hall towards her new bedroom.

Addie stopped before opening the door. She glanced back at her brother and sister-in-law as if to ask, "Is it all right?" They gave her a nod of encouragement. Her hand reached forward to take hold of the crystal doorknob. She hesitated momentarily as the light from the late morning sun peered through the hallway window, creating a prism of colors from the facets in the crystal. Her movements were slow and deliberate as she enjoyed the colors kaleidoscoping onto the hallway walls around her. Addie was savoring every moment. She glanced back once again to make certain Harold and Helen were equally excited.

Addie turned the knob, opened the door, and disappeared into the room.

Harold and Helen stood in the hallway. They listened. No sounds at all. It was disturbingly quiet. Helen grasped Harold's hand as they walked towards the open door. There stood Addie; her open palms were extended far above her head.

"Thank you, thank you, Jesus! It is just the way you promised!"

Sky-blue walls, white crown moldings, and a fluffy white comforter adorning her new queen-size bed welcomed Addie. The beautiful assortments of Gerbera daisies provided splashes of color throughout her room.

"Addie, do you like your room?" Helen asked.

Addie quickly turned; her hands were now clutched tightly under her chin. She rocked back and forth with a smile as broad as Helen or Harold had ever witnessed.

"Oh, Mrs. Haughton! It is wonderful!"

CHAPTER FORTY-EIGHT
MIRIAM'S PASSING
DECEMBER 21, 1955

In the very early morning, Miriam Haughton was granted her one remaining wish. She slipped quietly into the presence of God and the arms of her husband Benjamin. Her passing was a sad blessing. Fiametta called Harold with the news.

"Harold, it's mother. Harold, I couldn't wake her this morning." Fiametta paused, but instinctively Harold knew what was coming next. "She is with Father, Harold. I don't know what to feel. I'm sad; I'm happy. I feel an enormous weight has been taken from my shoulders and replaced with even greater guilt for having such feelings at all."

He'd been preparing himself for such a call. Still, there was a bit of remorse that he and his mother had never thoroughly enjoyed a close relationship. She would pass, never having read a story to him, taken a walk with him, or openly expressed an interest in his thoughts and feelings.

"Fiametta, I will be right over. Is she still there?"

"Yes Harold, I didn't know what to do, who to call. The house is so cold, Harold."

"Fia, don't worry yourself. I will make the calls and be there in a few minutes. Why don't you call Reverend Lacey and ask him to come over? Light a fire in the fireplace and make some tea for us. I will take care of everything."

"All right, Harold, thank you ever so much."

Harold called the sheriff's department and the coroner. Reverend Lacey would be able to provide comfort for Fiametta while he worked with the authorities.

The ride to Fiametta's home gave Harold time to reflect on his mother's passing. Although he tried, he could do nothing to conjure what he believed to be an appropriate emotion. He stood there alone and realized how much it reminded him of the emptiness he'd felt every day of his childhood. There were no fond memories, no sleepovers, and no childhood parties. There was suffrage, suffrage and speeches. Harold lamented how little he knew his mother and how little she seemed to desire to know him.

She must have been a wonderful soul when she married father, he thought. Harold would be resolved to love her for that.

Harold pulled into Fia's driveway, parked, and walked towards the front door. As he climbed the steps Fiametta met him on the porch. There were no words spoken as they hugged one another. Fiametta broke the silence, "She is still in the bedroom."

Harold gave his sister one last hug and opened the screen door, separating them from the inside of the house. He walked down the hallway to his mother's room. Miriam was lying in bed as if peacefully sleeping. He stood over her lifeless body, still desiring to feel something, something perhaps deeply hidden, that would assuage his guilt for feeling nothing at all. With actions far too mechanical in Harold's mind, he turned and left the room. He walked down the hallway and began a mental list of arrangements to be made. His mother was gone, and there were things he now had set into motion. Entering the dining room, he was met by the Reverend Lacey who was consoling Fiametta.

"I'm terribly sorry, son. Your mother was a strong woman

respected by the many people whose lives she touched. She will be greatly missed," Reverend Lacey said as he shook Harold's hand.

Harold could think of no appropriate response. He smiled and tipped his head in appreciation for the reverend's kind words.

Uniformed police arrived shortly thereafter, followed by the coroner. Having nothing else to do for the moment, Harold walked back into his mother's bedroom and once again looked upon her lifeless body. His feelings were, as they had been since he was ten years old, emotionally disconnected.

Fiametta entered the room and moved quietly up to Harold. She placed a hand on his shoulder, and though it startled him for an instant, he welcomed the interruption to his private struggle for feelings that wouldn't materialize. Still standing behind him, Fiametta rested her head on his shoulder. As if reading his thoughts, his sister remarked, "She really was a wonderful woman, Harold."

Harold closed his eyes and thought, *are you honoring Mother's memory, or trying to convince me?*

The two remained as they were, and Harold admitted, "Fia, I don't know what I feel right now. It troubles me. I'm standing here looking at this great woman who brought me into the world, and I have little sense of loss, little sense of sadness. Is that wrong, Fia? I feel sorrier for the women who respected her leadership and will now have to continue on without her."

Just then, Reverend Lacey entered the room. He walked over to Miriam and whispered, "God's rest and peace be with you, my dear sister." Fia and Reverend Lacey began to discuss service details, their voices faded as Harold's mind recalled a different conversation.

"But mother, he's so handsome, and he comes from a good family," Fia protested.

"Fia," Miriam began, "I understand he is very handsome, and your father and I have known the Idleman family for a long time-"

"Then, why-" Fia's interruption was cut short by her mother's powerful single-handed gesture.

"Silence! As I was saying, dear, we have known the Idlemans for a long time. But Fia dear, do you realize that Mrs. Idleman has never once darkened the doors of the women's club? And it is not because she hasn't received numerous personal invitations. I have invited her myself. Her husband simply will not allow it. Do you understand what that means? She does not possess the courage to think for herself on such matters. She willfully submits to her husband's wishes without any rebuttal. Do not think for a moment that young William Idleman would depart from his father's actions and his view of women."

"But, Mother!" Fia protested. "Billy is different. He loves me! He tells me I can have what I want and do as I wish!"

"Fia," Miriam said, her voice steady, "Please sit with me." The two sat on the sofa. Miriam took a deep breath and spoke, "Dear, your father tells me he loves me, and yet he spends his days fawning over machinery, inventory, and production. God, help the young lady who falls in love with your brother. His devotion to industry will far surpass that of your father. The woman he marries will see him on their wedding day and their honeymoon night. Soon he will become no more than the father of her children. Harold and William are cut from the same mold, Fia. Work will always be their first love. Neither of them will see the woman they marry as any more than an unpaid housekeeper. That, my dear Fia, is the life I am protecting you from. Unfortunately, I can do nothing to save your brother's future wife from a similar fate. Your father has already trained him in the *ways of men*, and as the Bible says, *'when he is old, he will not depart from it.'*" Miriam nearly spat out "ways of men,"—a phrase Harold equated with his mother from that moment until now.

Reverend Lacey spoke, interrupting Harold's memory. "Do you know what your mother's wishes were?"

Harold, recognizing it was evident to Fia and Reverend Lacey that his attention had been elsewhere, excused himself. "I'm sorry, Reverend; no, no, we are not aware of any special requests-"

Fiametta put her hand upon Harold's hand causing him to stop talking. "Yes, Reverend. Yes, we do know." Harold was taken aback. They had never spoken of Mother's wishes. Fiametta then turned to Harold and smiled. Giving his hand a loving squeeze, she continued, "You know Mother. She always had to be in control. Her wishes are in our safe along with her will."

Harold had never paid much attention to his mother's will. It sufficed that he would own and operate Haughton Manufacturing while most of her other earthly goods would go to Fia and Addie. He would make certain that Fia received the larger portion of their mother's liquid assets since she had so faithfully served their mother after their father's passing.

His sister retrieved the legal folder containing their mother's last will and testament from the safe and handed Harold an envelope addressed directly to him. The envelope bore their mother's handwriting. Another envelope was addressed to "The Minister of the Methodist Episcopal Church."

There were three copies of the will, one for each child. Fiametta hesitated giving Harold his copy. "Harold, Mother instructed me to have you open her letter before reading her will." Fiametta insisted.

"Why?" Harold asked.

"Harold, please open the letter," Fiametta abruptly turned and left the room.

February 8, 1953

My dear son,

I do not know what events will have taken place between the writing of this letter, written only four days since your father's passing, and this day which has inevitably come for me. I trust we have grown closer.

The fact that you are reading this letter indicates I have remained steadfast in my decision. It is with great confidence in you and your ability to do well for yourself, to care for your family, and to succeed in business that I, with a full understanding of my decision have left full ownership of Haughton Manufacturing to your sisters Fiametta and Adara. I do not mean for this to cause you pain. You will run it. You will make it greater, stronger. You have become a man in what, to my great sorrow, remains to be a man's world.

I have been plagued for years by the question, "What will become of your sisters?"

You, my son, have finished college, you've traveled around the world, you've found a wife, and have begun a family. You know your father's business. You know how diligent he was in training you to run it. You have run it well. Continue! Your family, and the families of generations to come, depend upon you. You must now set aside your personal disappointment and strive for that which really matters.

During my life, your sisters were in isolation. I prepared women across the country to be strong, courageous, and proud, but offered Fiametta and Adara only spectator's seats to applaud me in my efforts.

I must take this one opportunity I have to repay them for the years and the experiences my cause took from them.

You are your father's son. Continue to make him proud. Do not let this come between you and your sisters. This is my decision and mine alone.

I remain,
Mother

Harold folded the letter and carefully placed it back in its envelope. He took one long last look at Miriam Haughton and set the envelope and her will on the bed beside her.

"Rest well now, *madam*. Rest well."

CHAPTER FORTY-NINE
THE AUDIT
MARCH 11, 1963

H e'd entertained the thought of leaving Haughton Manufacturing. He was still young—let his sisters try to run a manufacturing firm with no business background and no manufacturing experience. He realized, however, Fia would simply sell the Haughton legacy, the legacy created by their grandfather, expanded by their father, a birthright intended to be continued through him.

He possessed the intellect and business acumen to develop his own stamping and packaging organization, but he could not bring himself to compete with whoever purchased the family business. To do so would be to go against every fiber of decency, every fiber of the Haughton Sacred Thread his father so diligently stood for and so faithfully passed along for his safekeeping. As much as he fought a sense of bitterness and betrayal, he was committed to carrying Haughton Manufacturing forward for future generations. Harold would humble himself and remain the general manager, working primarily for Fia and hoping that upon her death, she and Addie would pass the corporation on to Ben and Hal.

Under Harold's leadership, postwar business boomed. Haughton

Manufacturing was close to maximizing its production capabilities. The employees enjoyed the security of maximized production. Harold was concerned. Haughton Manufacturing's customer mix was too narrow. Seventy -three percent of the business was committed to government contracts; it was a liability.

No business owner wants to consider the possibility of losing a customer, but inevitably it happens. Harold knew losing a government contract would mean losing a large swath of business and revenue. He preferred the security of multiple smaller contracts with multiple businesses, businesses large enough to be profitable but small enough that Haughton Manufacturing would remain a primary supplier. Harold reasoned that the loss of a government contract would send repercussions throughout the industry, fodder for the competition and an even greater burden upon his sales force to replace the lost production and revenue.

While Harold ran Production and Sales, Fiametta handled the family's and the business's books. Sound accounting principles were important, but Harold reasoned if you don't manufacture a product, you won't have anything to count! Manufacturing and sales were the most important areas of the business. As long as he maintained control of these areas, as long as his sister kept at arm's length from production, Haughton Manufacturing would continue to expand and be profitable. That is, until Hendrich, Boggs & Co., Certified Public Accountants of Indianapolis, Indiana, conducted the audit.

Harold was sitting at his desk when he was served the package containing the audit results. He called Fiametta and invited her to dinner to discuss important details the audit revealed. She'd declined the invite citing she'd made a previous engagement with the women's club.

"Fia!" his voice tinged with panic, "You have no idea the gravity of the situation. The Federal Government is coming after us for corporate tax evasion. I received a telephone call from a friend of mine who works at the U.S. Courthouse. He says they are also auditing my personal finances; it does not look good! Fia?" Harold had never felt such helplessness in his life. "What have you done?"

"It's quite simple, dear brother. I've done nothing."

Her nonchalance sent Harold into a tailspin. He could foresee that he would be the one drawn into the center of the maelstrom.

"What do you mean *you've* done nothing? Are you saying there has been a mistake? Fia, are you saying you did file our corporate taxes, and you've done nothing wrong?" He could only venture hope that he had somehow misunderstood his sister. "Fia, you did our taxes, didn't you?"

"Harold," she began in a voice that was faintly reminiscent of his mother's. "We are Haughtons. How much have the Haughtons done for the state of Indiana? Tell me. How many of its citizens do we employ? How many ancillary businesses do we support with the purchase of raw materials and finished goods? Who else holds fifteen state contracts within our industry? I'm certain you have contacts at the state department. Besides, I'm not guilty of anything. You are the general manager of Haughton Manufacturing. I always told you to be more involved with the finances."

The twisting, whirling sensation ceased almost as quickly as it had begun. "So, you are telling me you willfully did not file?"

"The government has oodles of money," Fia flippantly remarked. "They seemed to have done just fine these past three years without taking ours. Now, you just run along and take care of this. They know you. I really must go, Harold. The ladies have been patiently waiting."

Her words were followed by a click and then a dial tone. He struggled to catch his breath. His father had instructed him on every aspect of production. He'd admonished Harold to love the problems inherent to the manufacturing process, but even Benjamin Haughton could not have predicted such a situation brought on by another Haughton. Had the meaning of the Sacred Thread never been communicated to his sister?

CHAPTER FIFTY
JUNE 5, 2017

"My grandfather didn't legally own the business. On paper, he worked for his sisters. He couldn't free himself of the responsibility my great-grandfather entrusted in him. He could not evade his promise to protect his sisters and mother."

Carrie paused. Asha could see she was struggling with her thoughts. "Carrie, I don't need to know anymore. Perhaps I already know too much. I'm sorry for making you upset."

Carrie did not acknowledge Asha's apology, but she continued. "Asha, what I am about to tell you is very personal. It is never spoken of within the family. I only know of it because Grandma Helen told me the story one time. She said she would never speak of it again, but I had to hear the truth."

CHAPTER FIFTY-ONE

FULL CIRCLE
MARCH 11, 1963

"Irv! Hello, Irv, I am sorry to call you at home. I wouldn't do it if I didn't feel it was–"

Irv interrupted, "Harold, you are a friend. You can call me anytime you want. I'm your attorney. The clock is running—by the way. You sound terrible!"

"Irv I'm afraid I've got a problem here. Fiametta did not file taxes for the past four years. Irv, I am personally being charged with federal tax evasion. I manufacture signs and license plates! I don't know anything about taxes."

"Wait a minute, Wait a minute, Harold. We must be very careful what we say here and how we say it. What I hear you saying is that your sister was not aware of the fact that she was depended upon to file the taxes."

"If that is what you heard, Irv, you heard me incorrectly. Fiametta willfully did not file our taxes."

"Then you have a problem. I hope you've kept up your relationships at the courthouse. You might be needing to call in a marker!"

"Irv, my relationships could not be any more solid. I simply want to clear this up the fastest way possible."

"Harold, let me get in touch with an associate of mine. His name is Lloyd Blankenship, and he's an expert in this field. Look, the Internal Revenue Service must prove that an underpayment was intentional. You don't need to panic. If there was a mistake, you'd have to pay the deficient amount and probably a fine or interest on the money. Let's take this one step at a time. You've got a good name with the government; you've had absolutely no problems in the past; I think things will be fine."

"Thanks, Irv, let me know what Lloyd says as soon as you talk with him."

Although Irv did his best to ease Harold's mind, Harold was sickened by the packet sitting on his desk.

"Irv, I don't know, I've got a bad feeling about this."

"Harold, what did you have for lunch? I think the bockwurst might be backing up on you!"

On April 23, 1963, Harold Haughton was flanked by Irv Bateman and Lloyd Blankenship as they entered the U.S. Courthouse. The three men walked through the enclosed interior courtyard. Their footsteps echoed throughout the building. Much of the original 1902 architecture remained. Mosaic tiled ceilings, white marble walls, and white and green marble columns, although beautiful, gave Harold a cold and hollow feeling in the pit of his stomach. They made their way up the stairs to the southeast corner of the second floor.

The courtroom, elaborately finished with gilded beams, paneled ceilings, and beautifully colored marble floors, created an atmosphere quite different from the architecture they'd just passed. Harold continued into the courtroom while Irv and Lloyd stood just inside the door. His mind was twisted in pain at the thought of his even needing to be there. He walked up to the bronze railings and ran his fingers across the iron gates. Gripping the cold metals caused Harold to shiver. This was a room where lives were changed —forever!

The men heard footsteps coming down the hall. The lightness of the step and the shortness of the stride told them that a female was about to enter.

"Good morning, gentlemen."

The attractive, albeit diminutive, red-haired woman greeted the men with a noticeably authoritative handshake.

"I'm Barbara Hawthorne, legal counsel representing the State of Indiana. It is a pleasure to meet you."

Not wanting to appear rude Harold released his grip from the iron gate separating courtroom spectators from the Bench. He turned and made his way to the back of the room where the three attorneys stood. As he drew closer his stride shortened, and his pace slowed.

She reached out her hand to shake his.

"Hello Harold, It's been a long time. You remember me, don't you? Barbara Louise McCleary? It is so good to see you once again.

The State versus Harold W. Haughton went to trial on September 13, 1963. The financial statements of Haughton Manufacturing from 1952 through 1955 indicated Haughton Manufacturing had inflated deductions and under-reported income. The evidence was irrefutable. During 1952, Haughton Manufacturing avoided paying taxes altogether. This was no oversight. This was tax evasion.

Fiametta was found guilty of gross negligence in the affairs of Haughton Manufacturing. She would never again be involved in the financial affairs of the business. She was required to pay all back taxes, interest on those payments, and $110,000 in penalties.

For Harold Warren Haughton, the State, represented by Barbara Hawthorne, pursued maximum sentencing. The Judge stated that Harold Warren Haughton's blatant disregard for federal law while enjoying long-standing benefits from exclusive contracts with government entities was reprehensible. In addition, State Counsel was able to show that Harold, on numerous occasions, offered special luncheons, dinners, and entertainment to representatives of the government. In the eyes of the Court, these were damning evidence of his attempts to bribe government representatives for personal gain.

Harold Warren Haughton was sentenced to six years in the Terre Haute Federal Correctional Institution. He would serve three years before being released.

Haughton Manufacturing lost every state and federal contract it had enjoyed for over forty years.

Harold was a broken man. His enthusiastic gait had become a slow shuffle. In his mind, he would forever remember his father's warning, "My boy, the good book says, *'When pride comes, then comes disgrace, but with the humble is wisdom.'*" Emotionally, he would forever wear the shackles he had been fitted with at Terre Haute.

The future and what would remain of the Sacred Thread were in jeopardy.

Ben was 25 years old when he and Hal took over what little remained of their family's once-thriving business. They retained the manufacturing facility. The corporate office was sold to cover legal costs and fines. The two brothers were left with a building and a few customers. Those few made up only 25 percent of their former customer base. They did, however, retain almost all their employees.

One by one the men and women shared their commitment to Haughton Manufacturing with the brothers. "We're not going anywhere Ben; nowhere Hal. Your father has treated us like family. We are dedicated to him, to you, and to the revival of Haughton Manufacturing."

Harold was a shell of the man he had been—but Ben and Hal were grateful they still had their father. Beaten and bruised with deep-seated feelings of guilt and embarrassment, Harold could still muster a spark of enthusiasm when watching his boys rebuild the business.

The state had taken away every one of his memorable achievements. In Harold's mind, for generations to come, the only memory of his involvement would be a dark blot in the family's history.

Harold turned to God for peace. He was burdened with the painful understanding of his father's concerns. Perhaps he could instill his father's admonitions in the hearts of Ben and Hal.

The three men sat in Harold's office. "Boys, I want to read to you a few things from the greatest business book ever written. It's called the Bible."

Ben stood up and immediately made his way to the exit.

"That's it for me—"

Harold stood from his chair, "Sit down, Ben!" Harold demanded. "You've made your feelings about the good book very clear, but your bone-headed disregard does not change the truth of it. So, sit down and listen!"

Ben, still standing, his left hand on the doorknob ready to bolt from the room responded, "Dad, I do not hate the Bible—I do not believe in it! I do not hate someone or something I do not believe exists. There is no God who cares for me like I do. I do not depend upon anyone. I do not expect anything from anyone. I will make my way through my life. You want to see God? I am my god! I can touch me; I can depend on me. I face life and I face it on my terms. If you want to be part of my world, the world I create, you are welcome—*but it is my world!*"

Ben had thrown fuel on a simmering fire. Harold, in a voice reminiscent of the days when his step was brisk and his vision clear, demanded, "Young man, you will return to your seat this instant! As long as I am living and sitting in this chair," he paused and pointed a threatening finger in Ben's direction, "these grounds are my world! Your pride will one day be your undoing; pride goes before a fall!"

Ben begrudgingly returned to his seat next to Hal. Hal leaned over to Ben and whispered, "You get up like that again, and I will personally deck you! It's bad enough we've got to sit through Sunday school while the company is going to hell in a handbasket. Don't get him started on a lecture or we will be here all day!"

Harold continued, "Proverbs, ah, here it is, the Book of Proverbs. Proverbs 11:3, *'The integrity of the upright guides them, but the crookedness of the treacherous destroys them.'* Here's another one, Proverbs 27:2, *'Let another praise you, and not your own mouth; a stranger, and not your own lips.'* Another, Proverbs 28:1, *'The wicked flee when no one pursues, but the righteous are bold as a lion!'* One that haunts me and will till the day I die, Proverbs 22:1, *'A good name is to be chosen rather than great riches, and favor is better than silver or gold.'"*

Harold then pulled a yellowed and brittle piece of paper from its pages.

"Boys, you may not understand the theology in these verses; I don't understand it all, but the truth of them is irrefutable. Your grandfather spoke of them often. Here is what he wrote:

"'In every family, there exists a Sacred Thread. When properly woven and maintained, it binds the hearts of family members from generation to generation. It is a thread comprised of faith, integrity, responsibility, commitment, servitude, generosity, humility, and, most importantly, love. It is a fragile thread. It often requires mending. Should any one of the components become compromised, the entire thread is weakened. Left unattended, this fragile thread breaks, thus subjecting all that was previously accomplished to be lost in the annals of time.'

"Boys, for Haughton Manufacturing to continue for generations to come, *you must* recognize our Sacred Thread, protect it, nurture it, and pass it on to your children making certain they understand its importance and the importance of passing it on, stronger than before, to their children. I will add one further instruction to my father's words of wisdom, one more passage from the book of Proverbs. Proverbs 31:10 through verse 31:

'WHO CAN FIND A VIRTUOUS WOMAN? FOR HER PRICE IS FAR ABOVE RUBIES...'"

Hal's eyes rolled. He leaned over to Ben and whispered, "That's twenty-one verses! Is he going to read all of them? How many more verses are there in that Book?" Ben had to chuckle. The shoe was now on the other foot!

After just a little over one minute, Harold was concluding the passage.

"'... AND LET HER OWN WORKS PRAISE HER IN THE GATES.'

"Boys, this speaks of a virtuous woman. A woman stays in the home, caring for it and for the family. If you never listen to anything else I say, remember this—*business is no business for a woman!* You keep her happy, and you keep her in the home!"

Ben and Hal looked at each other. They were counting the seconds. As young boys, they'd determined when their father did not speak for seven seconds his lecture was over. Their heads slightly bobbed as they counted, five one-thousand, six one-thousand, seven one-thousand!

"Okay Dad, thanks for the inspiration. Ya want anything from Mcdonald's?"

Harold closed his Bible and placed it back in his desk.

"Boys, this morning your mother fixed me a perfectly good bologna and cheese sandwich. I'm going to sit here and enjoy it."

CHAPTER FIFTY-TWO

GRANDPA HAUGHTON'S PASSING

OCTOBER 21, 1988

Harold Haughton was now seventy-two years of age. Arthritis had so crippled his body he could barely hoist the Haughton Manufacturing American flag.

His days were quiet. He would sign a few checks, read his morning papers, sip his coffee, and visit with the pretty girls working in the office. He would then return to his office, lock his door, and take a nap on the worn leather couch. Later he would shuffle through the production area, making certain to greet each employee and carefully inspect the quality of the products being made. The employees always took the time to acknowledge his presence. Harold, Mr. Haughton, was a legend.

Harold took pride in what his sons were creating. The container division was doing especially well. They'd expanded into the world of plastic containers. Railcar quantities of Allied Chemical and Union Carbide 101 HDPE were continually being pumped from railcars on the adjacent spurs into loading bins. A continuous draw of resin would then be pumped directly into eight Cincinnati Milacron 500-ton injection molding machines. The stamping and forming divisions were now heavily into construction products. Roofing materials, roof-to-wall connections, gutters, and electrical panel boxes now shared a large portion of the Haughton Manufacturing product mix. Haughton Manufacturing had been revived.

Harold thought back to the days when the old belt-driven systems powered the line. A sudden melancholy fell upon him like a cloak.

As he made his way back to the office, he experienced a sensation he'd never felt before. It was as if he could not catch his breath. A sudden unprovoked fear swept over him. He staggered before collapsing against a stack of pallets. Mike Vagaro rushed to his side before he fell to the floor.

"Mr. Haughton, are you all right? Sir, are you all right?"

"I don't know. I don't know what's come over me. I-I feel quite fatigued. I..." Harold attempted to take a deep breath. "Mike, I'm not getting any air! I'm breathing, but I'm not getting any, any-" His feet went out from under him. He was gasping for breath, holding the left side of his face. "Oh, dear God. The pain! It is in my jaw. I'm leaving you! I feel it... I'm leaving you!"

Mike attempted to shout for help, but the pulverizing sound of equipment drowned his cries. He left Mr. Haughton on the floor and raced to the central production office to summon emergency help.

Having called for an ambulance Mike then raced back to Mr. Haughton who was now unconscious. The production line stopped. Word spread throughout the plant that Mr. Haughton was in a serious condition. Several of the office personnel stood in the street to guide the paramedics to Mr. Haughton's side.

Mr. Haughton's face had turned an ashen gray. Ben and Hal rushed through the group of medical personnel to their father's side.

"Excuse me, gentlemen. You are going to have to step back."

"He's our father."

"Gentlemen, the medical team is doing everything it can right now. You must step back and let them do their jobs."

A police officer arrived at about the same time as the paramedics. He asked Ben and Hal if he could speak with them for a moment.

"What is the gentleman's name?"

"Haughton. Harold Haughton," Ben replied.

"Age?"

Ben could not remember. He looked to Hal for assistance. Hal was the numbers guy. Hal was paying close attention to the activity surrounding his father. Ben tapped his shoulder.

"Hal, the officer wants to know Dad's age."

"What? Oh, oh, I'm sorry, He is seventy-two, officer; born March 4th, 1916."

The police officer asked if he had any health problems. Ben angrily replied, "I suppose you would call this a health problem!"

Hal backhanded Ben on the shoulder. There was no reason to get nasty with the police officer. "Ben, you go to the hospital with Dad. I'll drive over and get Mom. This doesn't look good. It doesn't look good at all. Drive carefully."

Hal and Helen arrived at the hospital. A security guard took them just outside the emergency room where Harold was undergoing a battery of tests. Ben emerged from the room. Helen was sitting with Addie when Fiametta arrived.

Ben pulled his brother aside. "Hal, it doesn't look good. Dad has suffered a heart attack. There is quite a bit of blockage and muscle damage. The doctors said to prepare Mom for the worst."

The two boys walked over to where their mother was sitting. *How do you do that?* Hal thought to himself. *How do you tell a woman, your mother, that the man she has loved for over fifty-two years was about to die?*

Helen was nervously rocking. Addie was holding her hand and Fiametta was lovingly rubbing her back. Hal spoke, "Mom, the doctors are not giving us much hope. Dad has suffered a massive heart attack. His arteries are blocked, and the valves are calcified. There is quite a bit of muscle loss. I'm afraid we are going to lose him."

If ever Ben and Hal doubted the strength of their mother, they were about to be corrected. "Boys, if God calls your father home, it is better than if he remains here suffering. You cannot lose someone when you know where they are." Helen had turned the table and was reassuring them.

The doctor walked out of the room and over to the assembled Haughton family. "Folks, I am terribly sorry, we were unable to revive him."

Helen bowed her head.

"Thank you, God. Thank you for not letting him suffer. I am at peace knowing he is with You, and we will one day be together again." Ben walked a few yards away and stood next to the drinking fountain. He found no peace in useless words to a non-existent God.

In his will, Mr. Haughton requested that upon his death the family hold a private memorial service. There would be no need for unnecessary expenses. No need for speeches prolonging the event. Harold would have the last word. In a letter to the family, he wrote:

My dear family,

I've thoroughly enjoyed the life I was given. I have been most blessed by God with the very woman spoken of in Proverbs 31. Helen, I await you. Don't get me wrong, you don't have to hurry, but I await our reunion. Boys, mind the thing that is important. Mind the Sacred Thread. It is my prayer that you both recognize it, protect it, mend it when it requires mending—do so with your own blood, sweat, and tears if necessary—but mind the Thread and pass it along to your children, strengthened! Be humble in your success. All good things come from God. Be grateful.

You'll have to forgive me for not attending.

I remain,
Your loving husband and father.

CHAPTER FIFTY-THREE

JUNE 5, 2017

"When Fia and Adora died, they left the business to my dad and my uncle Hal."

"What about you and Lonnie? Was your relationship with Ben and Pauline always bad?" Asha asked.

"Probably," Carrie thought for a moment. "But we weren't aware of it. She was always nasty to Dad—we were her audience." Carrie paused. "Asha, you have to understand, originally there were fun times." Once again Carrie paused and then began to laugh. "There were funny times!"

CHAPTER FIFTY-FOUR
THE FOURTH OF JULY
JULY 4, 1989

The entire Haughton family celebrated the Fourth of July at their Lake Tippecanoe cottage. Lonnie and Carrie pulled onto Kalorama Road. Lonnie thought back to the previous year and his first Fourth of July celebration as a family member.

Lonnie had only heard about the cottage. The thought of staying with the entire Haughton family made Lonnie a bit nervous. Carrie encouraged him. He and the girls were now part of the family. Everything would be fine.

Ben and Pauline arrived at the cottage three days before Lonnie and Carrie. Lonnie had envisioned the Haughton's Lake home to be a cute little bungalow. He had no idea how expansive and beautiful it really was.

The driveway was a manicured lawn. It was as if driving on the fairways of the Tippecanoe Country Club. It led to the rear side of the cottage. Although stunning in its own right, it was deceiving. It hid the expansive compound of Haughton Manor. Lonnie took inventory of everything he was seeing. There were two garage doors situated in a river-rock facade with a window situated to the right of the doors. The window muntins created the appearance of small individual lights. Its window box welcomed guests with a beautiful array of native flowers.

This was Ben and Pauline's second home. They owned three. Their home in Clearwater Pointe was warm, charming, and comfortable. It was everything you could ask for—other than their two other homes. The Tippecanoe Lake house provided a spacious resort for Ben, his family, extended family, and friends. HBBH was the Haughton's Bahama Beach House. This oasis was a beautiful Spanish-style, single-level 2,200-square-foot home. Its sturdy construction and inlet location proved to be safe year after year during the fiercest of Bahama storms. It had two bedrooms and two baths. Its back porch was thirty-five feet from the Haughton's private beach, providing 1,200 feet of warm sand and ultimate privacy.

There were striking similarities between each of the homes, although they were aesthetically different. Ben told Lonnie, "I'm not too smart, so I like to keep everything simple. Every home has the same appliances. From the vacuum cleaner to the range, everything is exactly the same. That way, I don't have to learn about a lot of different things!"

As Lonnie and Carrie walked around the side of the cottage, Lonnie realized how massive this 'little cottage' really was. He was walking into a resort. The entire first-floor exterior was river rock. The second floor was shaking. There were three decks leading to the beach and a private pier. The first deck, which was actually the second floor, was just off the kitchen. It was covered by a large forest green retractable awning protecting the outdoor barbecue and dining area.

The master suites opened to a deck where a large hot tub and fire pit were situated. The third and lowest deck was a large overflow area used for dining or relaxing. The entire property perimeter and retaining walls were river rock. It was breathtaking.

The remainder of the property was beautifully terraced and manicured with shrubs and bushes.

The interior of Haughton Manor was, from floor-to-ceiling, knotty pine. A large river rock double-sided fireplace took up one full side of the family room wall and divided the family room from the game room. The accent to the knotty pine in each room was river rock. The lakeside view was magnificent from every floor. Simply framed floor-to-ceiling windows displayed the beauty of sunsets on Lake Tippecanoe.

The house had two master suites located on the lower floor under the main entrance. Upstairs there were six bedrooms, all knotty pine, all accented with river rock. There was also a grand room the Haughtons used when entertaining friends. Haughton Manor comfortably housed the entire family.

There were so many wonderful memories at Haughton Manor. Many of the memories were of previous Fourth of July celebrations, not the least of which was the explosion, rocking Haughton Manor one early July 4th morning.

It was a huge explosion, shaking windows and toppling glasses remaining on the large coffee table. Everyone from every corner of the cottage ran into the family room fearful of what they would find. There was no carnage, no fire. The room was intact, except for the layer of ashes that covered a nine-foot area in front of the fireplace and behind the fireplace into the game room. In the middle of the sprawling ash was soot-covered Grandma Helen, who, to start the festivities, had just thrown an M-80 firecracker into the fireplace. "Oh, dear, dear, dear, dear, dear! Honest to Pete!" she exclaimed—surprised at the power of the blast. "Now, *that's* how you start a Happy 4th of July celebration!"

As they pulled into the driveway on this their second July 4th celebration together, Lonnie thought about his own history-making memory.

Each July 4th, the HOA in Tippecanoe Village would anchor a pyrotechnic barge in the middle of the lake to showcase their wonderful fireworks display. Radio WRSW would simulcast oldies and patriotic songs throughout the display, culminating with Ray Charles singing, "America the Beautiful!" After the fireworks, the family would return to the cottage for fresh blueberry pie and homemade ice cream.

On his maiden voyage, still attempting to become part of the Haughton family (by no means an easy task), Lonnie and Ben seemed to be getting along quite well. Carrie, Kathy, and Pauline were sitting at the stern. Ben found the perfect spot to anchor.

Lake Tippecanoe is a beautiful, glacially created lake. It is 123 feet deep and is a premier spot for boating, fishing, and skiing. That night, there was hardly a ripple in the water. Ben directed Lonnie to open the starboard storage bin and tossed the anchor overboard.

"Put on those gloves, Lonnie, and just loosely hold the rope as the anchor goes down. That way, you'll catch any snags in the line before they go overboard. I want to make certain the anchor is on the bottom so we are not drifting during the show." Ben said.

Lonnie crawled under the windshield and to the bow. There were two storage bins at the bow. Ben said to open the starboard side bin. Lonnie looked back at Carrie. Carrie casually pointed to the right side. Lonnie, with seemingly no hesitation, carefully opened the starboard bin and put on the gloves stored with the anchor. He then carefully removed the anchor from its positioning atop the coiled rope. The boat was a beautiful 1976, 26-foot Sea Ray, and Lonnie wanted to be careful to not ding any portion of the vessel with the anchor. Lonnie was struggling to make a good impression, and this was no time for accidents.

He held the anchor over the starboard side of the boat and carefully lowered it into the water. The rope gently flowed through Lonnie's gloves. Everything was perfect. Lonnie's heart swelled with pride. He was working with Ben on his first family outing.

Pride suddenly turned to sickening panic as the end of the rope slipped through Lonnie's fingers.

"Lonnie? Is the anchor down?" Ben asked.

"Well, yes, It's down, Ben."

"Is it on the bottom?"

"Oh, oh, I assure you it is on the bottom!" Lonnie regretfully responded.

Ben looked over the windshield towards Lonnie. "Where's the rope? Didn't you cleat it?"

"Didn't I what?" Lonnie asked.

"Didn't you cleat it?" Ben asked again.

"Ben, I never thought I would be throwing an anchor out that wasn't fastened to something. I am terribly sorry."

The girls attempted to hide their laughter. Ben did not appear to be amused. Lonnie felt as if he had just been gut-punched.

Moments passed.

"Oh, well, that's the way it goes." Pauline attempted to console Lonnie.

Everyone was motionless, the girls at the stern, Ben at the helm, and Lonnie feeling very exposed and unforgivably guilty at the bow.

Ben could contain himself no longer. He suddenly exploded a guffaw that released the tension for everyone, but Lonnie. "Oh, my gosh. That's the funniest thing I've ever seen!" He continued to laugh uncontrollably.

Lonnie stood there, trying to keep his balance in the gently rocking boat. The infectious laughter finally caught hold of his emotions, and he joined in the merriment. It was at his expense—but it was a memory that would never be forgotten.

"Happy 4th of July everyone!" Ben shouted between snorts and cackles.

It was a good time; a good memory. It was family.

CHAPTER FIFTY-FIVE

FAMILY DINNER AT ST. ELMO

MAY 17, 1991

As Carrie and Lonnie walked up the slate path to the Haughton's front door, they could not help but admire the manicured landscaping. Lonnie casually commented, "Their landscaper must be spending a lot of time on this. It is absolutely beautiful."

The landscaper is spending a lot of time on something, Carrie thought to herself as she rang the doorbell.

"Oh, it better not be those pesky Dustins again," Pauline shouted—speaking in a forced volume to make certain Carrie and Lonnie heard. It was a good sign. Pauline was in a playful mood. The front door opened, and Pauline gave Lonnie a warm hug as he and Carrie entered.

"How have you kids been?" Pauline asked. Pauline's Jersey accent and the gracious welcome could throw an unsuspecting visitor off balance. Gentle and caring one moment, Pauline could transform into a viscous striking viper the next. Lonnie and Carrie were always cautiously prepared for whichever Pauline would answer the door.

"Ben, it's the kids; get down here!" Pauline shouted. "Your dad drives me crazy. Sometimes, I think he has selective hearing. Ben, get down here!" Pauline continued. "All he ever thinks of is himself, Ben!" Pauline's shout became more forceful as her jaws tightened.

"I'm coming, I'm coming." Ben finally responded as he made his way down the stairwell "Hey, hey, hey, hi Carrie, hi Lon!" Ben greeted them as if surprised by the visit he'd initiated.

Pauline broke in, "What were you doing up there?"

"Well, Paul, you asked me to change the bedding for the dog, and I couldn't find a fresh pillowcase for her pillow," explained Ben.

"Oh, for goodness' sake. You're so stupid. You know darn well where I keep the pillowcases," argued Pauline.

Ben had a little chuckle in his voice, his shoulders began to bounce as he looked at Lonnie and Carrie but responding to Paul said, "Well, I know where you keep my pillowcases—but they're not as nice as the dog's!"

Everyone but Pauline laughed.

"You just wait Haughton! I divorce you and you'll be in the streets, while the dog is living a life of luxury—and on your dollar!"

Lonnie recognized those piercing eyes and protruding vein just above her left eye. Pauline was not about to let the conversation end.

It was always this way when the four of them were together. Pauline would unmercifully berate Ben about whatever came to mind, and he would sheepishly take it on the chin. Pauline wanted a fight. Without a proper sparring partner, she'd escalate the attack until Lonnie came to the rescue with a witty line that would, for the moment, normalize relations. Lonnie was already preparing himself to make a defusing impromptu comment.

"Well..." Ben seemed to linger on the word as if singing it, "I don't think the dog has it too bad right now."

Rage filled Pauline's eyes. "You're an idiot!" she fumed.

Lonnie thought to himself, *We've made it from the porch to the entry-way. I wonder how the rest of the evening is going to go.*

As if the curtain had come up on an entirely new act, Pauline's countenance was suddenly altered. She took Carrie's hand and gushed about Carrie's blouse. "It's lovely sweetheart. It's simple—but it complements you well."

"Thank you," replied Carrie. "I got it at Ross for twelve dollars."

"Well, it looks every bit as if it were twenty-five," Pauline responded while softly stroking the mink collar around her black leather Loro Piana.

Carrie politely smiled.

Ben said, "Hey, why don't we have a little drink before heading to dinner?"

"Ben, we'll have something when we get to the restaurant," Pauline snapped.

"Well, I just thought-" Ben began but was immediately interrupted.

"You didn't think, that's the problem. You never think. Everyone has to do what you want to do. It's Ben's way or the highway. Just stop it! You never think about the other person!" she continued.

"Paul, I was just inviting everyone to have a drink," Ben sheepishly responded.

Pauline glared at Ben. This pause was Lonnie's cue to step in. Lonnie jokingly interrupted, "I suggest we get going so I can order two drinks to make up for the one I'm losing right now!"

Although Pauline's jaws remained tight and her eyes piercing lasers, the vein above her left eye had subsided. Lonnie knew his comment was enough to defuse the situation—for the moment.

The ride to the restaurant in Ben's Cadillac was as pleasant as riding with a loose and angry hornet could be. Carrie spoke up first, "Dad, did you see the landed price we got on stainless strapping?"

Ben replied, "Ya know, Hal said he saw the invoice come through and thought it was a mistake. We need more mistakes like that!" They both laughed.

"Oh, you two, is that all we're going to talk about all night? Work?

Get a life you two. There's much more to life than your stupid business," Pauline sarcastically stated.

Ben began to chuckle, "There wouldn't be more to life if it wasn't for our stupid business."

Everyone but Pauline laughed.

Pauline turned her head as if to look out her passenger side window, "You're an idiot."

The two couples arrived at St. Elmo.

"Geez, Ben. Is this the only restaurant in all of Indianapolis?" Pauline began to chide.

"I don't know," Ben's voice lilted quietly mocking Pauline's comment. "It seems to be doing pretty well."

"You're a stick-in-the-mud, Haughton! And I'm tired of the same waiter every time; what's his name?" Pauline asked.

"You mean Bennet?" Ben responded.

"Yeah, Bennet. We always seem to get Bennet. Can't someone else wait on us?"

Ben's forehead wrinkled as a puzzled look came to his face. "I don't know, Paul. He's always been very nice to us; very accommodating."

"He's too darned nice; he hovers; he's annoying." Pauline thought for a moment and then continued, "I think he puts on his act because you tip so well!" Pauline said mockingly. "That's all they want. They all want your money!"

"Well, Paul if you want somebody else to wait our table, I'll ask for someone else," Ben reluctantly replied.

"You can't do that!" Pauline shouted in disgust. "Honestly, Haughton, don't you have any brains?"

Of course, Ben loved St. Elmo. He could remember his father taking him there and the stories his father would share of Ben's grandfather taking him. St. Elmo was peaceful. When Ben brought his family, it was like a reunion. Everyone from the chef to the busboys knew and enjoyed Ben. Their gracious hospitality had always seemed sincere; in fact, Ben always felt Bennet was particularly focused upon Pauline's comfort.

Ben paid for valet Parking and asked the valet to park his Cadillac in a safe place. The extra ten dollars was insurance his car would be safe. The Valet always knew following dinner there would be more tens for the presentation of an unharmed car.

Lonnie opened the door of St. Elmo for Carrie. Before the others could enter Carrie was warmly greeted by Bennet, "Mrs. Dustin, you are a beautiful sight to behold."

Carrie blushed, but she enjoyed every bit of the extra attention the family was always given. She could hear Pauline's moan of disbelief following close behind her.

"Carrie, it is wonderful to see you! And I see you brought your lovely younger sister," referring to Pauline. Pauline's criticism of Bennet vanished in an instant. Critical as she could be, Pauline never grew weary of such greetings—even from Bennet. As long as ample attention was given to her, it would be a nice evening.

"Mr. Haughton, we have a beautiful table prepared just for you," Bennet announced as he proceeded to gesture for the family to follow.

It was a special table. A very special table. It had been the Haughton's table for as long as Ben could remember.

Since Pauline was being charmed, she presented herself with grace and appreciation. Lonnie looked at Carrie. They both held the back of their necks. It was a private signal between Carrie and Lonnie, when Pauline would instantly change her public demeanor—whiplash!

"Look at the shirt Lonnie is wearing. He always looks so nice when we go out. Why can't you take the time to wear something nicer? Geez, Ben, you always wear the same old shirts. You're stuffy and old. Lonnie, where did you get that shirt?"

"Actually, you bought it for me, Paul," Lonnie hesitantly replied.

Pauline smiled with knowing pride...

"You bought mine too," Ben interjected.

"Oh sure, twenty-five years ago," Pauline snapped.

"Well," Ben shrugged. "Thanks for buying good quality. Lonnie, you'll be able to wear that shirt a long time, too." Ben's shoulders began to shake as he chuckled. Lonnie and Carrie joined him with the light laughter.

"Oh sure, Haughton." Pauline mockingly attempted to point her arthritic finger at Ben. Its deformity sent it off the mark and towards an older gentleman sitting behind Ben and to his left. For a moment the gentleman thought Pauline was pointing at him. His eyes then locked on to Lonnie's eyes. Both men quickly looked away a bit embarrassed, nevertheless chuckling to themselves.

Ben continued to laugh quietly. His shoulders continued to bounce. He seemed unfazed by Pauline's ridicule. "Look at him, just look at him, laughing at his own jokes." Pauline was stoking her own fire while at the same time causing Ben's shoulders to bounce even more noticeably.

"How do you think I feel when you wear such old clothes? You never care about your appearance. Look at the hair in your ears. You're like an old senile man. You don't even groom yourself." Pauline continued her attack on Ben.

"Lonnie always grooms himself nicely. He cares how he dresses in public for Carrie. Geez, Haughton. The world doesn't just revolve around you. You've got to think about others. How do you think it makes me feel when you look like this?"

"I don't know, Paul." Replied Ben. "Ya think they'll still take my money for the dinner?"

Ben continued his lighthearted chuckling. His shoulders were ever-so-lightly subsiding as his belly gently tapped against the table.

Pauline had stoked her fire to the point of exploding. It was time for Lonnie to work his magic.

"Well, the truth is, Carrie picks out my clothes and lays them out for me on the bed, I simply slither into them."

It wasn't a notable statement, but it was enough of an interruption to once again avoid a total detonation of Pauline's fury.

"Yeah, well, how do you expect anyone to respect you as a successful businessman if you don't look the part?"

In an instant, Carrie's and Lonnie's hearts sank. Dinner had taken on a foreboding, dark, and eerie gloom.

PART FIVE
TURN OF EVENTS

CHAPTER FIFTY-SIX
JUNE 5, 2017

"Oh my gosh, Asha! Look at the time. We've got to get back to the office."

Carrie shuffled through her purse for her credit card.

"I should pay for this one, Carrie," Asha said. "You provided the entertainment!"

As the two women walked to Carrie's car, Asha asked, "When did Pauline turn her hatred towards you and Lonnie?"

CHAPTER FIFTY-SEVEN

CHRISTMAS 1991
DECEMBER 21, 1991

I t was nineteen degrees when Lonnie and Carrie left their home in Hunter's Crossing for the Haughton's Christmas celebration. They would have celebrated together on Christmas Eve, but the weather outlook was questionable for the 24th, and the roads were already becoming icy on the 20 miles of roadway between Hunter's Crossing and Clearwater Pointe.

This was Carrie's and Lonnie's second year of marriage, and their second Christmas dinner with the Haughtons. Lonnie remained in awe of the homes in Clearwater Pointe; they were massive. Every home was custom-built, reflecting the individuality of its occupants.

The Haughton's home was situated above a stunningly beautiful garden. A slate path wound through the garden and up to a magnificent double-door entryway. Four white columns and white board-and-batten shutters accented the clinkers surrounding the first floor. It was considered an average home in the neighborhood. To Lonnie, it was the vision of success. The most beautiful home he'd ever seen.

They pulled into Ben's and Pauline's driveway. Carrie could feel the needles of cold air biting at her cheeks. She loved the seasons. There was something about winter that signaled completion. It soon would be time for the earth to replenish itself with green blankets of sod and canopies of leaves.

Lonnie opened the back of their Pathfinder where most of the surprises were transported. Carrie carried the cranberry salad she'd been protecting in her lap along with a very special package.

They made their way up the slate path, the surrounding gardens were covered with two inches of snow. Reaching the double doors they took a deep breath. "Well, this is it!" Lonnie said.

Carrie gave Lonnie a warm smile. There was a glint in her eyes, signaling something very special was about to happen.

Lonnie touched the doorbell and was momentarily startled by the triumphant sounds of Mannheim Steamroller encompassing them. Ben opened the double doors wearing a red stocking cap, holding a double leather strap of solid brass sleigh bells, and vigorously proclaiming, "Ho, ho, ho. Merry Christmas, Merry Christmas! Ha, ha, ha, hi kids, come on in, come on in. Let me take your coats."

Ben paused for a moment and with a glint in his eyes said, "On second thought, you know where the closet is—LET ME TAKE THE GIFTS!"

The three of them laughed and hugged.

Pauline delayed her entrance giving ample time for pleasantries to be exchanged and the focus to turn to her.

"Hi kids!" She said as she made her way down the stairs.

Ben stepped to the left, Lonnie to the right. This left an open path directly to Carrie. The Christmas lights in the doorway highlighted Carrie with colors. Carrie stood there beaming. She didn't say a word. She just stood there.

Pauline's countenance immediately transformed. "You're pregnant!"

There was a conflicted mixture of joy and a hint of jealousy in Pauline's pronouncement. "Come on, you two. I can tell. You're pregnant, aren't you?" It now sounded more like an accusation than a question.

Carrie turned her attention to Ben, "Merry Christmas, you two. You are going to be grandparents!"

"What? WHAT? Really? REALLY?" It took Ben a moment to realize what was being said. Once he grasped Carrie's news, he could not contain his excitement. "Oh my, oh my! Can I get you a drin—" The words stuck in Ben's throat. "Can I get you a chair? Are you okay? How do you feel? When is the baby due?"

Ben's rapid-fire questions were so cute they were comical. "Oh, my gosh! This is wonderful. Man-o-man, this is some news. Wow! I can't get over it. We're going to be grandparents, Paul!"

Neither Carrie nor Pauline moved. Like two prizefighters in opposing corners of the ring, Carrie stood in the doorway, and Pauline stood directly across from her in the foyer.

"Isn't it wonderful, Paul? Oh my! That's super, just super!"

Pauline had not changed her expression or posture since Carrie made the announcement. "I knew it as soon as I saw you." Pauline turned and made her way back up the stairs.

Ben invited everyone into the family room where the fire was blazing, the miniature Dicken's Village was alive with all the festivities of Victorian England, the punch bowl filled with eggnog awaited its presentation, and the beautifully decorated Dutch Pine Christmas tree filled the family room corner opposite the fireplace.

Ben began pouring eggnog. "Oh, no, no, no, no eggnog for my grandchild!" Ben proudly apologized to Carrie.

"Ben, you and I will just have to make up for the two of them!" Lonnie joked.

"Dad, where's Paul?" Carrie asked.

Lonnie recognized the tone in Carrie's voice. She was not so much asking a question as she was drawing attention to the fact that Pauline was still conspicuously missing.

"She probably had to wrap a few more things upstairs. Paul, Paul come on down and let's get this celebration started. Paul?"

Ben paused. "I'll be right back."

Ben left the room and made his way upstairs. Carrie took Lonnie's hand. "I don't know what it is, but something is not right, Lonnie."

"Ha! Nonsense! What could be righter? I've got my wife, she's got our baby, and I'm drinking my father-in-law's expensive spiked eggnog!"

Lonnie attributed Carrie's comment to the heightened sensitivities of a pregnant woman. That is, until they found themselves in the family room alone for the next ten minutes.

Pauline was the first to enter. "Okay you two, let's get this dinner started." Her tone was expressionless. It was as if she was really saying, "Okay you two, let's get this dinner over with."

Pauline walked directly over to the stove. She removed stuffing, mashed potatoes, creamed peas, and candied yams and placed them on the island in the middle of the kitchen. Ben took the foil off the turkey.

"Okay, it's time to start carving I guess," Ben said.

"What better time would there be?" Pauline mocked. "You are such an idiot sometimes."

"Paul, I was just-" Ben was immediately interrupted by Pauline's continued chiding.

"Just what? Talking to the bird? Honestly, do I have to tell you everything? Yes, it's time to carve the turkey—so carve it already!"

Pauline was now shrieking. Her Jersey accent now accentuated by an irritating nasal quality. Lonnie grabbed Carrie's hand a little tighter and whispered, "Remind me to never doubt your intuition."

The four sat around the dining room table; three of them had a good time. It was fulfilling to see the pride in Ben's eyes; his first grandchild.

He pelted Carrie with question upon question. Ben could not get enough information. Every answer Carrie gave him initiated yet another volley of questions about her answer.

Pauline finally spoke, "Geez, Ben, you've had two daughters. You'd think you'd never been around a pregnant woman before, let her eat."

Lonnie wondered if Paul was supporting Carrie, or if this was simply an endeavor to change the topic of discussion.

Following dinner, everyone shared in the cleanup. Lonnie gave Pauline a kiss on the cheek and thanked her for all the preparation, the beautiful presentation, the decorations, and the hospitality. Pauline turned, smiled, and said, "You are very welcome. Thank you for helping Dad carve the turkey and for the cleanup. At least one man knows what to say and do."

Pauline turned to Carrie and said matter-of-factly, "I know you two have a long ride back and the roads are icy. Congratulations on your news. It is very exciting." She was bringing the evening to a close. Lonnie and Carrie felt it was just as well. Someone might have accidentally mentioned the baby again.

They'd been on the road for ten minutes, ten minutes of absolute silence. Lonnie and Carrie were privately assessing why they felt so empty after finishing a Christmas dinner. Lonnie spoke first, "Okay, babe, this evening was just plain weird! Did I say or do something wrong?"

"No, Lonnie, it's just Pauline. She's jealous, she's always been jealous!" Carrie continued to watch the light snowfall as they drove.

"Jealous of what? Your cranberry salad?"

Carrie turned to Lonnie, "Lonnie, Pauline is jealous because I'm pregnant."

He shook his head, "No, that's simply not possible. No one is that hateful—not even Paul."

"Lonnie, I'm telling you, life is not going to be easy for us once our child is born. We have to protect him or her. I don't mean Paul would do physical harm, but she has an uncontrollable mean streak. She will not hesitate to be a negative influence."

"What do you mean by negative influence?"

"I don't know, I've just got a very uneasy feeling. You saw how she left the room for over ten minutes. Didn't you feel the temperature of the room drop when she returned? I mean, really! She was as cold as ice the rest of the night. I wish we'd never gone over there."

"Okay, I get that. But what did you mean by negative influence?"

"Pauline would not do anything obvious. She always leaves a back-door excuse for her actions causing the person questioning her to look foolish; she's a master of control. She would do little things. Let's say we have a son. Let's say in kindergarten he paints a picture and says it's his family. Pauline is the type to say, 'Are you sure? It doesn't look like our family to me.' She'd just do something to diminish the moment—unless she was the central figure. I just have a bad feeling."

"Carrie, you're pregnant; and you had too much Christmas dinner. You're just upset because we all enjoyed the eggnog and wine while you drank water!"

Carrie knew he was trying to lighten the discussion, and she gave him a loving slap on the shoulder.

"Okay, Lon, you just watch. She will do whatever it takes to put us in the background so that she owns center stage!"

Lonnie thought for a moment and laughed, "Well, she certainly isn't going to get pregnant—and you don't just buzz into Gucci or Neiman Marcus and pick up a baby from the sales rack."

CHAPTER FIFTY-EIGHT

BEN'S BIG PROBLEM

JANUARY 14, 1992

Lonnie arrived at PALCO early. Today would be a stressful day. As the General Manager of PALCO Manufacturing, a leading custom plastic injection molder in Indianapolis, it was Lonnie's responsibility to immediately implement the previous year's Q3 and Q4 objectives. Of primary importance is hiring an individual whose expertise includes ISO and QS implementation. PALCO's move into the medical field demanded an entirely new business model. It would be a multi-million-dollar investment, but the anticipated ROI would be three years.

It was 6:45 AM when the phone rang. "Who the devil would be calling at this time expecting someone to answer? Hi, thanks for calling PALCO Manufacturing, I'll be happy to help you!"

"Hey, Lonnie, It's Ben."

Lonnie looked at his watch once again. Perhaps it was later than he'd thought. 6:46 AM. "Ben? Is there something wrong? Is Paul okay? Are you okay?"

"No, no, no, Nothing wrong. Uh, I just wanted to know if you could have lunch with me today?"

"Well, Ben, I'm kind of swamped today. Could I take a raincheck on that?"

"It's pretty important that I talk with you today, Lon. I've got a problem—a big problem."

Family first, give until it feels good, life is short—enjoy living it! These were principles Lonnie believed in. It was now time to put them into practice. "Ben, there is nothing too important that will keep me away from having you pay for lunch!" Both men chuckled. "Would you like to meet at St. Elmo?" Lonnie asked.

"No, no, let's go somewhere different. I don't know, you have a place out your way where we can catch a bite?"

Early in Lonnie's career, Ben taught him that words have meaning. Listen carefully for messages that were not intended. In this case, Lonnie heard Ben say, 'somewhere different' rather than, 'someplace different.' Ben was not focused on a place to eat as long as it was somewhere other than a place where they wouldn't be recognized.

"Sure, sure, Ben, let's try the Weber Grill; say 12:30?"

"Okay, okay, that's the new one in northern Illinois, right?"

"That's it!"

"Okay, thanks, Lonnie. Thanks a lot. I've got a big problem here. Thank you."

Lonnie immediately called Carrie. *What the devil could this be about?*

"What did you forget?" Carrie asked.

"Nothing, I didn't forget anything," Lonnie replied.

"Lonnie, I am getting ready for work and I don't have a lot of time. What is it?"

"Well, if you don't have time, fine. Have a nice day, and I'll tell you about my meeting with your dad tonight."

Lonnie hung up the phone—he was irritated. Carrie wasn't the only one working for a living. He felt minimized—his call just wasn't important enough for her to be interrupted.

Moments later, his phone rang. It was Carrie. He considered letting the call go to voice mail.

Why should I always be the one who is available at the drop of a hat?

It was a selfish thought. The fact was he was available, and Carrie was calling back. The phone rang a third time. Lonnie answered. "Hello?"

"I'm sorry I couldn't take your call. I was running late. I put a load of laundry in so I wouldn't be doing it tonight. We'll have your stuffed bell peppers and a nice evening together. You caught me just getting in the tub. What was that about meeting with Dad?"

Lonnie felt like a heel. Of course, she was doing something selfless so they could be together later.

"Stuffed bell peppers? What's the occasion?" Lonnie asked.

"There's no occasion. I just wanted to make them for you. Why are you meeting with Dad?

"I really don't know. He sounded rattled; kept telling me he had a big problem and wanted to meet for lunch. I figured we'd go to St. Elmo, but it was obvious he didn't want to eat somewhere we'd be recognized or interrupted. It was just weird."

"Do you think he might want you to come back to Haughton?"

Before Lonnie could even begin to process a response, Carrie answered her own question, *"That* would be the last thing he would want to talk about. What on earth could it be? Do you think he and Paul are having problems again?"

"Yeah, that's my guess, but why in the world would he be calling me about it? I have absolutely no clue as to what this is all about. I'm not so sure I want to know!" Lonnie concluded.

"Well, have a nice lunch. Don't eat too much. I want you to save room for the stuffed bell peppers," Carrie instructed.

"Ha, I promise. I'll only have a pack of saltines and a glass of water..."

"That will be the day! Call me after your lunch. You've piqued my curiosity."

"Okay babe, I love you."

"I love you too, bye."

Lonnie had never been to the Weber Grill. He thought it would be an opportunity to see how the company that manufactured his grill prepared their meals.

It was 12:15 and bitter cold when Lonnie parked. Ben had already arrived. Lonnie made his way past the floor-to-ceiling windows and could see Ben waiting inside. He could also see that there were not a lot of quiet spots for a private meeting. One thing was for certain, at thirty-three degrees, they wouldn't be requesting patio seating.

Lonnie stepped into the revolving door and greeted Ben. The mixed aromas of sauces and grills and the warmth emanating from the central brick fireplace were just the welcoming chilled patrons desired.

"This place is going to be fantastic," Lonnie thought.

"Hey, hey, hey, Lonnie." Ben removed his hand from his overcoat and reached out for Lonnie's.

"Hey, Ben. Great place, huh?"

"Yeah, yeah. Maybe we can get a few tips on how to grill."

It was a charming comment, but Lonnie could tell Ben was otherwise preoccupied. His face seemed to sag in gloom. Whatever the purpose of the luncheon, Lonnie had never seen Ben look so worn.

"Let's get a drink, Lon. Let's get a couple of them. How's your time? Ya got time to talk?"

"I've got whatever time you need, Ben."

They were escorted to a booth just to the right of the fireplace. "Your server will be right with you. Could I bring you some water?" The hostess asked.

"Ya know what we need is some booze. Can I get a double Harveys?" Ben asked.

"I'll have Natalia come right over."

With that, the hostess walked over to the Smokey Joe's Bar. Lonnie could see that she was making an extra effort to get Ben's drink.

The two men sat quietly. Lonnie attempted to exchange small talk.

"What a tremendous marketing idea this is. Did you see the kettles they are using as part of their decor?"

Ben gave no response. He was focusing on the young woman who was approaching their table. Natalia greeted the two men. "Good afternoon, gentlemen. Welcome to the Weber Grill. Here is your double Harveys, sir. Is this your first time with us?"

Ben responded, "Yea, we've never been here before. It's nice, real nice. Thank you for bringing my drink."

"Certainly, sir." Natalia turned to Lonnie, "Is there something I could bring you, sir?"

The expression on Ben's face coupled with the awkwardness of the entire experience erased any thought of saltines and water.

"I'd like a gin martini, please, three olives."

"Absolutely, sir. May I offer a suggestion on our specials today?"

Lonnie responded, "Sure-"

But before Natalia could begin to speak, Ben interrupted, "We, we've got some serious business to discuss. We'll order in a little bit."

This was way out of character for Ben. Lonnie had never seen him this upset. Lonnie wondered whether he should have ordered three martinis—and one olive.

"Lonnie, I've got a problem, a big problem."

"Ben, what the heck is it? Is someone dying? Is it the business? What?"

"Lonnie, I've got to buy a baby."

There was a pause; a long pause. Lonnie gave way to a nervous chuckle. "Ha, for a moment I thought you said, 'I've got to buy a baby....'" Ben's jaws tightened. Lonnie would see the anger in his eyes. "Ben, what the heck are you talking about?"

"Lonnie, Pauline is really mad; really, really mad. I've never seen her this worked up about anything. Carrie is pregnant and Pauline wants a baby."

Lonnie shook his head to clear his mind and grasp what his father-in-law was saying.

"Wait a minute, wait a minute—wait a minute! Pauline, is *that jealous* of Carrie? What the heck does she want? She has everything in the world. You give her five thousand dollars a month of play money. She has three beautiful homes. She hasn't worked for God knows how long—and because Carrie is pregnant, she has to have a baby? Really? That's crazy! Do you hear what you are saying? Really?"

"Lonnie, buying a baby is less expensive than getting a divorce. This is my third marriage and I'm not getting any younger."

"Frankly Ben, that's all the more reason not to... not to... oh, my gosh, I can't believe we are even having this conversation, not to buy a baby!"

Ben ignored Lonnie's comment. "Look, I need to know when your baby is due."

"What? Our baby is due at the end of July or the beginning of August, Why?" Lonnie questioned.

"Pauline said that our baby has to be born before yours, and he has to be a boy."

"Wha–" Lonnie interrupted his own question.

It suddenly became very clear; MONEY! Pauline was shrewd—of this, there was no doubt. Pauline was thinking about the future. Pauline was thinking about inheritance. She was as shrewd as she was evil.

"Ben, have you thought this through? You are in your fifties! You have two beautiful daughters and a grandchild on the way. Do you really want to raise a child at this point in your life?"

Ben hated to be questioned, especially when he was wrong. He slammed both open palms on the table hard enough that patrons throughout the restaurant turned to see what was going on.

"I'm buying Pauline a baby!"

Ben's aggression was no longer a threat to Lonnie. Lonnie took a gulp of his Martini, "Okay, okay; calm down. So why the heck are you meeting with me about this?"

"Because You need to tell Carrie!"

CHAPTER FIFTY-NINE

JUNE 5, 2017

Carrie continued with the story as they pulled into the Haughton Manufacturing parking lot.

"Absolute evil, Asha; absolute evil." Carrie was saying as she exited the car.

"It's all about the money, Asha. After thirty-eight years of marriage, divorce would have cost my dad more than staying married. Pauline had other interests to keep her mind off the misery of being married to my dad." Carrie paused, considering whether she should continue. "We all knew Pauline had no real love for my dad—my dad probably knew too. He would drop little hints like, 'Well, it's Wednesday; landscaping day' and then he would chuckle and give that Haughton glint."

Pauline awoke early every Wednesday morning—after all, Kevin would be taking care of the landscaping. Pauline was very self-conscious about her looks—particularly on Wednesdays.

It was ten o'clock. With makeup applied, Pauline wafted down the stairwell in her St. John leisure apparel to pour herself a cup of coffee. Before leaving for work, Ben always prepared coffee for her. He would set the timer for eight o'clock, thinking eight was the usual time she made her grand entrance. Unbeknownst to Ben, it was different on Wednesdays. This left Pauline's freshly brewed coffee sitting untouched for two hours.

I hate that man, thought Pauline as she poured out the container and angrily remade a fresh brew.

Kevin was a six-foot, chiseled man, fifteen years Pauline's junior. His arrival took Pauline back to a day when such a young man would enjoy her company without monetary encumbrances. Time had removed any such possibility. For now, Pauline would enjoy Kevin's company each Wednesday. After all, Ben was paying for Kevin's expertise, and Pauline was enjoying the touch of this young man's unique abilities.

CHAPTER SIXTY
PAULINE PLACES HER ORDER
APRIL 16, 1992

Carrie's delivery window was between July 24th and August 4th. It meant that Ben's and Pauline's baby had to be born prior to the middle of July. Ben had the money to make things happen. Money was his key to solving everything. In Ben's world, everyone had a price, and if the problem was big enough to have an impact on Ben, he would simply pay to make the problem go away. Pauline was the only exception to this rule... she didn't go away. Her five thousand dollar a month allowance and the lifestyle Ben provided was motivation to stay.

Ben employed the services of three adoption agencies and two attorneys to find a young girl willing to put her child up for adoption. The criterion continued, the child had to be a baby boy, and he had to be born before July 24th.

On Thursday, April 19, Pauline received the call she had been waiting for. The adoption agency had found a young teenage girl who was willing to release her soon-to-be-born child to Ben and Pauline. The child, a boy, was due June 28th.

Pauline immediately went through her litany of questions. "The mother and father are both healthy right?"

"Yes, Mrs. Haughton, she was a cheerleader, and he was the high school baseball star."

"The father isn't too big, is he? I don't want him to grow to be too tall. I'll look odd if my son is too much taller than I am."

"Mrs. Haughton, there are certain characteristics we are not at liberty to discuss without the birth parents' approval."

"Well then, get their approval. Whatever it costs. He is white, isn't he? I mean, are they both? I mean, I love children of ethnicity—regardless—just not my child."

"Mrs. Haughton, both birth parents are Caucasian."

"Good, Ben would never stand for anything else."

There was no response.

"Well, okay then. We'll make plans to travel in the later part of June. You do understand that if the child is born any later you run the risk of losing the deal, right?" Pauline charged.

The woman on the phone took a deep breath.

"Mrs. Haughton, with all due respect. You do understand you are adopting a baby and not purchasing an automobile."

"Oh, of course, of course," Pauline chuckled. "You just make certain it is born in June or the earlier part of July."

"He will be born *when he* is ready to enter the world," the nurse said firmly.

"Oh, we are so excited!"

The phone call ended. Pauline immediately got out her list of phone numbers and for the next four hours called everyone she knew with the news; she was going to be a mommy!

Carrie was at work when she received the call.

"Hi honey, it's Paul."

Odd, thought Carrie. *The only time she calls me 'honey' is when I'm about to be blindsided by something.*

"Hi Paul, I've only got a couple of minutes, Dad needs some numbers for a Union Meeting this afternoon."

"Tell your dad to cancel the meeting. We are going to have a baby!

Isn't it wonderful? It will be a baby boy and he will be born before yours! I'm so excited. Transfer me over to your dad's phone."

"Certainly Paul, Love you."

With that, Carrie transferred the call. Her heart sank. She couldn't quite understand why this was affecting her so much. After all, it didn't diminish the value of her pregnancy or the love she and Lonnie already shared for their child. She felt guilty, guilty of falling prey to Pauline's evil manipulation.

"Don't let anyone take up space in your mind if they are not willing to pay the rent!"

It was one of Lonnie's favorite sayings. Carrie repeated it to herself several times as she continued working on the meeting minutes. It was an important meeting. There were several grievances to be discussed and preliminary discussions on Haughton's forecast profits and an employee increase schedule. It wasn't so much the employees wanted more money. Haughton Fabrication was still the highest-paying shop in Indianapolis. The employees wanted certain guarantees that were difficult, if not impossible, to make while the economy was struggling following the recession.

Carrie's phone rang. As she reached for the phone, she could see it was Ben.

"Yeah, hi, Dad."

"Hey, uh, listen Carrie. Contact Bob Percelli and let him, tell him we are going to have to reschedule the meeting."

"Dad, this is an important meeting. Are you sure you want to cancel a union meeting at the last minute like this?"

"Yea, yea, yea we gotta cancel. We gotta cancel. So, anyway, tell him I will call him later to reschedule, thanks."

Ben was finished with the conversation, and he abruptly ended the call. This left Carrie in the precarious position of responding to what would no doubt be an angry union leader's interrogation.

"United Steelworkers Union 1999, how may I direct your call?"

"Hello, Mr. Percelli, please."

"May I ask who is calling?"

"Carrie Dustin, Haughton Fabrication."

"One moment, please."

"Good morning, Ms. Dustin. I'll be seeing you in a couple of hours. How can I help you?"

"Good morning, Mr. Percelli. We've had something come up and we need to reschedule our meeting."

"Reschedule? Why in heaven's name are we rescheduling? We've got very important items on the agenda. They require immediate action."

"Mr. Percelli, I know this is highly unusual. Our relationship has been solid for years. I think you'll agree that there has never been an incident where Haughton Fabrication and the United Steelworkers' Union did not collaborate, hand-in-glove, in the best interests of our employees."

"Certainly, but a great deal of effort goes into preparation for these meetings, Ms. Dustin. Our relationship has been a good one. However, what we have done in the past has no impact on what needs to be done today. Your employees don't need to focus on memories. Their question is 'What will you be doing for me in the future?'"

"Sir, if I understand the agenda correctly, Haughton Fabrication can address the grievances independently. These are internal issues that require absolutely no monetary negotiations. A change in schedules for the individuals in question will appropriately address their grievances. Frankly, sir, these are more agenda fillers than they are actual grievances."

"Ha! Well, you are probably right about that. May I ask the reason for the cancellation?"

"Certainly, sir, Mr. Haughton is going to have a baby."

"What the..."

"What I mean to say, sir, is that he and his wife are adopting a baby and they just found an individual who is willing to give her baby to them."

"Wait a minute; wait a minute. Ben, is going to adopt a baby? We're talking about Ben Haughton—right?"

"Yes, sir."

"Tell him to delay our meeting for as long as he wants. That man needs counseling! I've got two grandkids who visit a couple of times a month. I love them but it only takes a couple of hours before they need to go home. How the-what the-is he all right?"

"Mr. Percelli, I am certain he is just fine." Carrie chuckled. "I'll relay your concerns to him."

"Yes, do! And tell him to see a counselor or something. Oh, dear Lord, is he nuts? Look, I'm sorry, I'm sorry. It's none of my business. But that's the craziest thing I've ever heard. Heck, after this news, I need to get a drink! Ms. Dustin, although I am not happy about canceling the meeting, It will have no bearing on future negotiations. Will you send me the forecasts in advance?"

"Certainly, sir."

"Can we get together next Thursday; let's say, one o'clock?" Percelli asked.

"I will make certain of it, Mr. Percelli."

"All right, all right, Just between you and me, the man has no idea how this is going to change his life. I mean completely! How the... well, never mind. I'll be looking for those financials, and I'll see you next Thursday afternoon."

"Yes, sir. You'll have those forecasts within the hour. Thank you for understanding."

"Understanding? I don't understand a thing you've said—absolutely crazy!"

"Goodbye, sir." Once again Carrie could not suppress a chuckle at Percelli's response.

"Goodbye."

As far as Carrie could tell the telephone conversation went well. She advised the shop steward and the employees of the cancellation.

"Crazy!" Carrie mused.

CHAPTER SIXTY-ONE
TEDDY'S ARRIVAL
JULY 3, 1992

July 3, 1992, at 9:27 AM, Theodore William Haughton, "Teddy" was born. He was a small baby weighing 6 pounds, 5 ounces, 24 inches in length. Ben and Pauline anxiously sat outside the delivery room awaiting their first opportunity to see their son.

At 9:40 AM, the pediatric nurse pushed through the delivery room doors holding a carefully wrapped bundle in her arms.

Pauline abruptly stepped forward and reached for Teddy.

"He's mine, give him to me."

Catching the nurse off guard, Pauline stepped directly in front of Ben and took Teddy out of her hands. Pauline now had Teddy. Ben stepped forward to have his first glimpse of his son. Pauline immediately turned her back to Ben and the nurse. Taking several steps away from them she carefully removed the blanket from Teddy's face and proudly enjoyed the first glimpse.

"Miss? Excuse me, Miss? That child will need to go into the nursery for observation. I just wanted to introduce him to you and your husband."

"Yes, yes, well, you've done that. When will he be ready to travel?" Pauline asked.

As Pauline was finishing her question the delivery room doctor, who had been observing the events through the delivery room door, walked directly up to Pauline and, with absolute God-like authority, reached for Teddy. Pauline sensed that she was no match for him. She reluctantly relinquished Teddy to his arms. He returned Teddy to the nurse and smiled at Pauline and Ben.

"Congratulations to the two of you. You have a very healthy boy here. The nurse will take him to the nursery where we will be placing him under observation for a couple of hours."

"Is there anything wrong, doctor?" Ben asked.

Pauline interrupted, "Yes, yes. Anything? We don't want there to be anything wrong. We paid a lot of money for a healthy baby boy."

The doctor sensed a true concern in Ben's question. He made known his feelings for Pauline by ignoring her and turning his attention directly to Ben.

"Sir, this is a very normal procedure. We will observe him for an hour. We check all his vital signs, take a blood sample, and check his blood sugar levels. We will go over every area of his body to make certain nothing was disrupted during the birthing process. We will bundle him up and keep him warm. I assure you; he is in good hands!"

"Thank you, thank you, doctor," Ben responded.

As the nurse turned to take Teddy to the nursery, Ben interrupted.

"Uh, excuse me? Can I see him? Ca-can I see him before you take him to the nursery?"

"Oh, my goodness! I am terribly sorry, sir. Here, why don't you hold your son." Pulling the blanket from Teddy's face once again the nurse softly said, "Young man, this is your new daddy."

The nurse smiled and gently offered Teddy to Ben's trembling arms. He hesitantly, awkwardly, reached out for his son.

"Oh, that's not the way you take a baby!" Pauline began to chide.

The nurse gracefully turned her back, this time blocking Pauline, and extended Teddy to Ben.

"That's perfect, sir. You will be a wonderful daddy; I am sure of it, congratulations!"

"Oh, wow! Wow! He's so small. Thank you for letting me hold him. Thank you, thank you very much." Ben's humble gratitude touched the nurse and doctor.

Pauline was counting the seconds. "Give him back to the nurse. He has to go to the nursery to be checked. You'd think you never held a baby before."

Pauline's words went totally unnoticed as was her presence in the room. Ignored, her rage boiled.

"Ben! Give him back to the nurse now! I want to get some breakfast."

"Oh, oh, okay Paul, I'm sorry. I never held the girls when they were born."

As he handed Teddy back to the nurse. "This was a real first for me, thank you."

They walked to the elevator Pauline mumbled under her breath, "You're such an idiot sometimes."

The elevator doors opened, and they entered. Seeing their mirrored reflections in the stainless-steel interior walls of the elevator, Ben chuckled to himself.

"I suppose I am..."

Three weeks later a similar scene took place.

CHAPTER SIXTY-TWO
MELINDA'S ARRIVAL
JULY 26, 1992

11:22 PM

"Give me one more push."

Carrie reared her back. From depths within her she'd never experienced, came a low powerful moan.

"That's it, that's it!" the doctor encouraged.

There was a hush. For a moment, time seems to stand still. Lonnie sat next to Carrie. With every contraction, he rubbed her hand more aggressively.

"Lonnie, you're rubbing my skin off!" Carrie shouted as she endeavored one last push.

The silence was broken by the first cries of a newborn infant.

"Carrie, Lonnie, what is your little daughter's name?"

Lonnie's tears flowed. He hugged Carrie. His emotions were too profound to express in words or gestures. He'd watched her body change as this new life was growing within her. He'd witnessed her selflessness as she cared for herself and their baby while continuing to maintain her chosen lifestyle as a loving wife. He'd now emotionally experienced his wife's hard work and pain during childbirth. He felt guilt, joy, fear, love but most of all—awesome wonder.

"We have a daughter!"

Lonnie looked into Carrie's eyes. They'd rehearsed this moment many times but neither could remember their planned response. Carrie simply smiled and nodded.

Carrie placed her hand upon Lonnie's and with total composure responded, "Doctor, her name is Melinda. Melinda Bria Dustin."

"Well, Melinda Bria Dustin, allow me to introduce your mommy and daddy to you."

Lonnie remained transfixed by the beauty of his wife. He lovingly stroked her hair as Melinda was placed upon Carrie's chest. Carrie took Melinda in her arms, Lonnie gently kissed Melinda's forehead.

"We need to get Melinda to the nursery. Lonnie, would you do the honors of carrying your daughter to the nursery?" the nurse asked.

"You mean I can? Me? Oh, absolutely; absolutely, yes! Her sisters are in the waiting room with Carrie's sister. Can I show her to them on the way to the nursery?"

"The whole family is here?" The nurse asked. "Why yes, by all means!"

The doors of the delivery room opened. Megan and Melody immediately jumped from the waiting room chairs to their feet. Lonnie walked over to them.

"Girls, I would like to introduce your little sister to you." Megan and Melody shrieked with delight! They hugged each other bouncing up and down and screaming with excitement. "Would you like to see her? Her name is Melinda."

"Yes, Daddy, yes please!"

Lonnie removed the blanket from Melinda's face. Her little nose crinkled slightly at the bright waiting room lights.

Melody, with unabated honesty spoke, "She's the most beautiful baby ever! I mean, except for Megan and me."

Everyone laughed.

Kathy was beaming. She couldn't have been more excited had she given birth to Melinda herself. "Lonnie, she is the most beautiful baby I have ever seen."

"I think she looks like her mom, Kathy. What do you think?" Lonnie asked.

"I don't know, I see a little bit of both of you in her," Kathy responded.

"Who do you think she looks like girls?" Lonnie asked Megan and Melody.

After a moment of careful consideration, Melody innocently responded,

"I don't know, I think she looks a whole lot like old Mr. Jensen down the street!"

Once again there was laughter.

"I've got to take your sister to the nursery now, I'll be right back."

Lonnie turned and made his way down the hall to the nursery. The girls threw their arms around Kathy's neck.

"Isn't this the most wonderful day in the world, Kathy?" The girls asked.

"The most!" Kathy responded.

CHAPTER SIXTY-THREE
JUNE 5, 2017

"Melinda and I stayed in the hospital the next full day for observation. I took the opportunity to make a few telephone calls to family and close friends. First on the list would be my dad."

CHAPTER SIXTY-FOUR
SOMETIMES I HATE THAT WOMAN!
JULY 27, 1992

"Hi Sweetheart, your dad is in the garage. Did you have your baby?"

"Yes, Paul, I'd like to talk to Dad, please. I want to give him the news."

"Well, what is it?"

"Paul, we have a baby girl."

"And her name?"

"Her name is Melinda Bria Dustin." Carrie reluctantly shared. "Paul, I'd like to give Dad the news myself if you don't mind."

"Ben, Ben, Carrie is on the phone! They had a little girl. Her name is Melinda Bria Dustin."

Vintage Pauline...

"I'll get him for you, sweetheart."

Carrie was seething.

"Hey, hey, hey! So, you have a little girl!"

Carrie could hear Pauline in the background firing questions. "Ask her how much she weighs. What was her length? Does she have hair? Is there anything wrong with her? Ben, give me the phone!"

Pauline would not wait for Ben to follow through with her orders. She commandeered the phone and the conversation.

"How did delivery go? Was it a natural childbirth? Is she feeding well? Are you breastfeeding? Does she cry much? You know, Teddy doesn't cry much. He is a very good baby."

"Paul, Paul, *STOP!* Please put Dad back on the phone."

"Ben! Ben, she wants to talk to you. Okay, sweetheart, here's your father. I hope they don't find anything wrong with the baby. Those things happen sometimes ya know."

Ben took the phone, "Hey, Carrie, how are you feeling? I bet you're tired."

"Actually, I am feeling great! I just can't wait to get home and begin our new lives together," Carrie responded.

"Yea, yea, well, it sure changes things. I know things have gotten pretty exciting around here these past couple of weeks. Pauline never puts Teddy down." Ben chuckled. "It's going to be fun having Teddy and, and—what did you say her name was?"

Carrie could hear Pauline shout out, "Melinda!"

"Right, Melinda, It will be fun to have the kids together!"

"It will be, Dad. I've got to run. There are a few other people I'd like to call before they find out some other way..."

"Okay, okay, well, we'll see you soon!"

"I love you, Dad."

"I love you, too."

At that moment, Lonnie walked into Carrie's hospital room.

"Sometimes, I hate that woman, Lonnie!"

"Gooooooood morning!" Lonnie sang out mocking the fact that Carrie had obviously started the morning on a negative note. As if he didn't know who Carrie was referring to, he asked, "What woman, Carrie?"

"Pauline!"

"Ha! I assure you, there's a very long line of people far more specific, far more committed, far more absolute, in their feelings—they hate her all of the time!" They both snickered. "What did 'sweet & sour' do this time?"

"I wanted to be the one to tell Dad about Melinda. But no, she had to play her dumb game and blurt everything to him before I could even say 'hello.' She knew what she was doing. I hate it when she does that."

"Carrie, it's Pauline, remember? Pauline's goal in life is to make everyone as miserable as she is. She's the saddest, meanest person I've ever had the misfortune of knowing. I thought buying a baby might soften her a little bit. Ha! Silly me!"

"They've been waking me up every three hours to feed Melinda."

"Really? I thought they would at least let you get some rest. Can't you use a pump or something so the nurses can feed her?"

"No, I've got to stimulate the productivity before going home."

Lonnie pulled up a chair alongside Carrie's bed.

"You'll be going home tomorrow though, right?"

"Yes, the doctor will probably release me after his morning's rounds."

Lonnie continued, "Kathy and the girls have the house looking spotless! I think they've wiped down every square inch with alcohol. I'm afraid to touch anything. When I do, Megan attacks me with an alcohol wipe!" Lonnie laughed. "We're all very excited to get the two of you home!"

CHAPTER SIXTY-FIVE
JUNE 5, 2017

Entering the building, Asha whispered, "So, it happened just the way Pauline wanted. She had a son, and he was born before Melinda."

Carrie was also careful to keep her voice low as they walked up the stairs. "That's what I mean, why does God let evil win?"

At the top of the stairs, Carrie and Asha separated, Asha continuing to her office, Carrie taking a seat at her desk. Asha began her payroll summary as Carrie reviewed inventory levels.

Minutes later, Carrie was interrupted. "Carrie?" Asha was once again standing in Carrie's doorway.

"Honestly, Asha! You are going to have to make more noise getting up from your chair. You scared me!"

Asha laughed as she continued. "It all happened when the two kids were born, didn't it?" Asha tilted her head just slightly. She squinted inquisitively as she asked, "Why? Why would such a wonderful life event be the beginning of such a horrible relationship?"

"I don't know, Asha, but that woman did everything she could to make us miserable. Lonnie had planned a quiet evening for all of us the day we came home. He and Kathy did the cooking. Megan and Melody served as my personal attendants, retrieving whatever baby items Melinda needed, disposing of diapers and making us both comfortable. It was to be the perfect homecoming."

CHAPTER SIXTY-SIX

HOMECOMING
JULY 28, 1992

The *"Welcome Home, Melinda!"* sign Megan and Melody painted was strategically placed over the front door.

Lonnie slowly approached the last turn which would lead them down a short block straight to their driveway. The pink, "It's A GIRL!" sign Lonnie, and the girls staked in the front lawn would be visible for Carrie to see as soon as they made that final turn. The girls were bouncing with excitement. "Watch, Carrie, keep watching!" Megan instructed. "Look straight ahead, Carrie—don't even blink!" Melody giggled with anticipation.

Lonnie made the final turn. Melody's giggles were replaced by a disappointed sigh. The sign they were so anxious for Carrie to see was blocked by the Cadillac parked directly in front of their house. As the Dustins pulled into the driveway, they couldn't help but notice Pauline puppeteering little Teddy's hand to wave hello.

Pauline yelled out the window, "Hurry up and get out of the car kids. Teddy wants to see his little niece!"

Lonnie thought to himself, *and so it begins.*

Carrie and Melinda were in the back seat with Melody. Megan was sitting up front with Lonnie as Pauline walked up to the window.

"What are you doing here?" Megan asked Pauline. "Sweetheart, we're here to celebrate Melinda's arrival," Pauline responded. Megan pleaded with Lonnie, "Daddy, does she have to stay?"

The question was both embarrassing and enjoyable. There was no way Lonnie could scold Megan for being impolite. He was thinking the very same thing.

"Megan, we'll take a little time with Pauline, Teddy, and Grandpa Haughton. Then we'll have all the time in the world to ourselves."

Pauline shouted back to Ben who was still seated in the Cadillac with Teddy. "Dad, we need to order a couple of pizzas."

"No, Paul, we'll have lunch together some other time," Lonnie stated. "It is important to me that the girls have time to bond with Melinda and equally important that Carrie and Melinda have time to rest."

Pauline barked back at Lonnie, "Oh, rest! I hope you're not going to be overprotective parents with Melinda. You know, that can do a lot of damage to a child. You're already overbearing, Lonnie, far too protective. Ya gotta lighten up a little bit. Let Melinda enjoy life!"

Lonnie mockingly responded to Pauline, "Paul, listen to me. Melinda is only two days old. I'll admit, I will not let her date, I will not let her drive. She will be given a curfew. She must be in her crib by 7:00 PM. If that's being too overbearing you might be correct, her future may be in jeopardy!"

Pauline laughed and flipped the back of her hand at Lonnie. "Lonnie, you are so silly sometimes."

Lonnie remained steadfast. "That may be true, but for right now I'm going to be the bad guy and ask that we spend one hour together, and then I'll have to ask you to leave so Carrie and Melinda can get some rest."

Pauline was aggravated, but she did not want Lonnie to know he'd gotten under her skin.

"Oh, nevermind, we were just dropping by for a second to welcome Melinda home and introduce her to Uncle Teddy. You kids have a nice afternoon." Pauline turned and marched back to the car as Ben, unaware of the conversation, was still naively walking towards the group.

"Aren't we staying for a visit?" Ben asked. Pauline walked past him towards the Cadillac. In disgust Pauline shouted back to him, "Get in the car, Ben. We'll make an appointment next time!"

Ben continued walking towards Lonnie and Carrie. There was an all-knowing glint in Ben's eye. He chuckled as he said, "It looks like things are going to get pretty exciting around here."

"Ben, hurry up; we're leaving!" Pauline shouted.

Ben glanced back at Pauline and then returned his attention to Lonnie and Carrie. "Yes, we're going to have some pretty exciting times. I'll see you guys later. I love you."

Carrie gave her dad a hug. Kathy had been waiting in the house for Lonnie's, Carrie's, and the kid's arrival. It surprised her to see her dad's Cadillac. Stepping out onto the porch she thought she would be welcoming the entire family. Instead, she found herself saying goodbye without having yet said hello. The girls gave Ben a hug. Lonnie and Ben shook hands. "Can I see that little cutie one more time before I go?" Ben asked. "Why don't you hold Melinda, Dad, and give her first welcome home kiss?" Carrie asked.

"Oh, that would be super, super!"

Ben carefully took his granddaughter in his arms. Carrie moved the blanket from Melinda's face so that he could see her. Her eyes were wide open and fixated upon his face. "Grandpa loves you, do you know Grandpa loves you?"

Melinda seemed to give a slight smile as Ben became more comfortable and began to rock her back and forth.

"Ben, we've got to go. Give her back to her mother!" Pauline shouted from the car.

Ben smiled once again. "I guess Paul wants to get going. Yeah, things are going to get pretty exciting..."

CHAPTER SIXTY-SEVEN
RAISING THE CHILDREN
JUNE 5, 2017

"There were so many missed opportunities: so many instances where an unselfish act could have positively impacted Teddy—but no. No, Pauline had her own motives. The opportunities? Disregarded, they would not have served her purposes.

"There was no sense of responsibility instilled in this little boy. Teddy was never allowed to complete anything. By signing him up for soccer, baseball, karate, or skiing, Pauline was simply purchasing bragging rights. Each activity would last until the weather was nice in the Keys or Pauline wanted to go to the lake. She would excuse their abandoning the team by saying Teddy was bored with inferior coaches or was unable to identify with the other children because of his advanced level of development."

Asha slipped into the chair directly across from Carrie.

"Teddy had no friends to speak of other than perhaps Preston Edmund. Pauline didn't care for the precocious little Preston and only tolerated his mother and father. They'd first met the Edmunds at Lake Tippecanoe when the boys played in their first 4th of July Lake Tippecanoe Junior POA Golf Tournament. Preston's father was a prominent attorney; his mother, every bit as braggadocios as Pauline, was a real estate mogul in the Tippecanoe Lake area. They continued to see each other on holidays and for a few weeks during the summer months —just long enough to not hate each other.

"Pauline boastfully preached sermons of permissiveness in her private religion of jealousy to the demise of any hopes Teddy could grow to be a socially normal individual."

Carrie began to mimic Pauline's flick-of-the-wrist motion as she continued,

"'Teddy gets bored so easily with regular children.' She would say. 'He's extremely advanced for a boy his age, ya know.' She would then gently stroke his hair and continue, 'Teddy would rather be with adults. Adults enjoy him.' He developed his sinister sneer reclining against his mother and proudly accepted her accolades.

"She regularly condemned Lonnie and me for being too controlling, too strict." Just thinking about Pauline's accusations rekindled a long-forgotten anger.

CHAPTER SIXTY-EIGHT

LONNIE UNLOADS
AUGUST 12, 2000

"Parents force kids their age to be involved with activities they don't even want to do. It's all for the parent's entertainment. I see it; I see it in you and Lonnie! You do the same thing with Melinda, her dance, her piano, and her theatre." Pauline paused to kiss Teddy on the forehead. "Let her live, Carrie! She's gotta experience life! You can't control a child like that, ya know? They will one day rebel. You just watch."

Although Teddy would never be allowed to fully participate in competitive activities, Pauline never avoided competition with Melinda. Melinda's activities rewarded her with numerous friends. She needed movement and thrived on physical activity.

Carrie made all of Melinda's dance costumes. It was a labor of love. Of course, Melinda always wanted to wear them for her Grandpa Haughton. Ben was the perfect grandfather—when he was allowed to be. On one occasion, Melinda sprang from her bedroom wearing her fully sequined costume for "Great Balls of Fire!" It was an eye-popping red sequined, full bodysuit with black and white sequined piano keys running down the entire length of her left leg. Grandpa Haughton offered her all his attention and applauded her as she posed.

"Oh, wow! That's beautiful, Melinda. Do a little bit of your dance for Grandpa, will ya?"

Melinda would giggle and perform her entire recital piece. Her eyes were always fixed upon his expressions. It meant everything to her to make her Grandpa Haughton proud.

Pauline? There was no mistaking. She made it very evident with her expressions—this was a painful ordeal. Another costume, another time-step, shuffle-ball-change. Her comment? "Well, that's a lot of money and time going down the drain. She's never gonna be a Rockette, ya know." When Melinda was awarded numerous trophies at her dance competitions, Pauline coldly brushed them off, "What good are they going to do you? They'll just collect dust."

Lonnie fumed. Carrie begged Lonnie to hold his tongue. Pauline was Pauline; she just had to be ignored. In Lonnie's mind, that was easy for another adult to do, but for a child, this was verbal abuse. Lonnie did his best to comply with Carrie's wishes, but when Pauline verbally abused his family, it was game, set, match.

Pushed to his limit, Lonnie was capable of being brutally honest. Pauline's comment about the Rockettes was more than Lonnie could take. She'd set herself up for a tongue lashing.

"Hey Paul—take a few moments." Lonnie's voice escalated to a higher pitch as his throat tightened and his rage continued to mount. "Take longer if necessary. See if you can think of something nice to say." He continued to challenge Pauline. "Go ahead, Paul, I've got time; I live here. I've got all the time in the world. See if in your vocabulary, in your thoughts, somewhere in that black heart of yours there is a single word of kindness!"

There was no dismissing the fury in Lonnie's eyes. Carrie cringed. Not willing to spar with Lonnie for fear of being further exposed as the bully she actually was, Pauline defused the encounter using it as a tool against Ben. "Ya see, Ben. Lonnie knows how to fight. You never fight. You just sit there."

"Lonnie isn't in the ring twenty-four hours a day," Ben mumbled under his breath.

It was like any other evening. When it was over, Pauline, Ben, and Teddy went home in a tiff while Lonnie and Carrie poured themselves a glass of wine and wondered why they continued to put up with it.

By her late teens Melinda had received acceptance letters from five prestigious universities. Emerson College in Boston and Harvard in Massachusetts were at the top of her list. Teddy, not having finished his sophomore year of high school, was encouraged to get his GED, and go to junior college.

Ben tried motivating Teddy with money. In Ben's world, money was the answer to any challenge. If there was a disgruntled employee, give him or her money. Getting Teddy out of the Navy after he, unbeknownst to Ben and Pauline, met with a recruiter and joined? Money. Teddy's traffic violations? The small possessions charge? It simply took the right amount of money to the appropriate individual or foundation, and Teddy's challenges disappeared.

It was time to encourage Teddy to move out on his own. Teddy didn't appear to have any intention of moving. "Ted, I'll tell ya what. You graduate from Ivy Tech, and I'll buy you a new car. They teach all that high-tech stuff you enjoy and are so good at."

Teddy thought about his dad's offer. He thought about it for another two years. Finally, Teddy decided to enroll—or so he said. Ben came to work more excited than Carrie had seen him in years. "He enrolled in Ivy Tech! Carrie, Teddy enrolled in Ivy Tech!"

"That's wonderful, Dad. Have you seen Teddy's application for entrance to Ivy Tech?"

"Well, no, I haven't."

"Dad, you might want to keep up on Teddy's education at Ivy Tech. What courses has he signed up for? Did he get his GED? How many hours does he need to get his associate's degree?"

"Uh, I don't know all that stuff," a puzzled Ben responded.

Carrie was attempting to be as gentle as possible. "Dad, you've got to ask. If you are going to give the kid a car after he graduates, you need to know what he is doing in school right now."

"Carrie, Teddy is really sharp about a lot of stuff. I asked him some of the questions you are asking me, and he showed me on his computer how legally he doesn't have to answer any of my questions. He has a right to his privacy."

"Not in my house he wouldn't!" The words involuntarily blurted from Carrie's lips before she could consider the ramifications. "Dad, who is paying for his classes, his books? Who is paying for his transportation? Does he pay for anything?"

Ben's jaws tightened. Carrie was no longer questioning Teddy. In Ben's mind Carrie was questioning his parenting. The battle was on. "Of course, he pays for things!" Ben emphatically argued.

"Where does he get the money?" Carrie immediately fired back.

"I give it to him—where else would he get it?" Ben was now shouting.

Carrie shook her head in disbelief. Did she hear him correctly? Was he aware of what he'd just said? *He really expects me to accept that as the logical, final word.* She thought to herself. She knew, however, that in her dad's world, it made total sense.

"Okay, Dad. I get it. You do what you want. I told you before, I will do everything in my power to help Teddy succeed. I just need to keep my job. I don't need to have a problem with you over this."

"I don't want a problem with you either, but you just keep pressing. Teddy is smart. He is real smart. He's got nobody but me. He and his mom fight all the time. It's a good thing he sleeps during the day and does his video games at night, or they'd kill each other. I've got to make sure he learns the business and makes enough money to get out of the house!" Ben turned to walk out of Carrie's office. Reaching the door, he paused and turned back, "The problem is you just don't like each other. You can be difficult sometimes, Carrie."

Ben was now parroting Pauline, and Carrie would not endure it any longer. "If I hear that one more time, I am going to scream! You call it whatever you want. You may be the only one he has, but I'm the only one expected to pay the price for it! I pay the price with his threatening tone of voice, his continual vile cursing, and his constant glares! And still, I'm the one you are expecting to train him. He can't even go back into the shop without Haughton Fabrication employees threatening a strike! Your son is disliked by everyone who knows him!"

Carrie regained her composure. "Dad, have you ever considered the possibility that Teddy has no friends because he's not a likable person?"

Carrie was speaking from her heart. She was concerned for the family, for the business. Someone had to mind what was important. Right now, working things out with her dad was the most important thing facing Carrie.

Ben looked at Carrie for a moment—he was thinking. He tilted his head back slightly, his eyebrows raised, his jaw jutted forward ever so slightly. In a very calm voice he said, "All my friends like him."

Carrie realized her father didn't want to hear the truth. He didn't want to hear it—and he never would. She felt a weakening hopelessness creeping over her.

That night when Carrie came home, she didn't even have to say a word. Lonnie held her in his arms and whispered, "Honey, whatever you went through today, I'm sorry. I love you so much!"

Carry wept.

"Lonnie, this is killing me. What do I do? What *can* I do? I need the job. Everything we have for the future is tied up in that job. He scares me, Lonnie. They all scare me. None of them have any principles. My dad is now on their side—I'M DIFFICULT! Three against one. It isn't fair, Lonnie. I've done nothing but try to help my dad make a place for that kid. He lies to my dad. He lies to everyone, about everything! I can't compete with that. I'm really scared!"

Lonnie decided that the possibility of a close family relationship had already been sabotaged. Pauline's jealousy of Carrie was obvious to everyone. Her rancor, however, was so palpable now, and her requital so vial no one would challenge her. Pauline had no filter, and her tongue was like an obsidian blade. Teddy had become an extension of that hate—a dangerous extension Carrie faced daily.

Lonnie had no desire to drive a wedge through the heart of whatever was left of a family relationship, but this draconian woman and her adopted tool-of-hatred could not be allowed to continue to hurt Carrie.

CHAPTER SIXTY-NINE

PRECISION METAL FABRICATION
MAY 25, 2016

B en arrived at the Corporate Office at nine o'clock and immediately went to his office to check his calendar. He knew that the owner of Precision Metal Fabrication was scheduled to arrive in the morning, but he could not remember the time.

Precision was the top metal fabricator in the nation. They'd pursued Haughton Fabrication for years, but Ben was never willing to sell. Today would be like any other day. Jim Franklin, Owner and CEO of Precision, would arrive with one or two of his top executives. They would meet with Ben and Carrie for two hours, discuss the present value of Haughton Fabrication and what PMB would be willing to pay to acquire it. Rejection would be followed by a luncheon at St. Elmo.

The scenario had taken place so many times, Ben wondered why Jim continued the ritual. Jim would laugh and say he knew one day he'd call at the right time with the right price. Ben jokingly would reply that the only reason he wasn't selling was he wouldn't be able see him anymore; he'd miss him!

The appointment was scheduled for ten o'clock. Jim had made the appointment with Carrie, and Carrie made certain the meeting was on a day Teddy was in the field making sales calls.

She arrived at nine-thirty. There was really no preparation necessary. Ben had no interest in selling Haughton Fabrication. It was,
however, good for Ben's ego to go through the ritual, and Carrie took it
as an opportunity to ask questions about the marketplace. Carrie was
not shy in questioning what PMB was doing and Jim was not reluctant
to ask specifics about Haughton. He believed he was sharing what
otherwise would be considered proprietary information with a
company he would ultimately own. Over the years, he'd grown to
enjoy and trust Carrie. When the timing was right, and a sale was
made, he would keep her on the payroll to run the New Indianapolis
Precision Metal Fabrication operation.

Jim and his coworkers arrived at ten o'clock. They were greeted
warmly by Carrie who happened to be in the lobby at the time. Carrie
already knew Tina from their previous visits. Tim was someone she'd
never met. They exchanged cards and Carrie escorted them to Ben's
office and upstairs conference room.

Ben got up and walked around his desk to meet Jim at the door.
"Well, Jim, how ya doing, how ya doing?"

"Hi, Ben, I'm doing well. Have you been taking good care of my
machinery?"

Ben began to chuckle. "Well, I've been doing some very expensive
modifications these past few months. I guess I should just send you
the invoices?"

Both men laughed and shook hands.

"Ben, you remember our CFO, Tina Yen, don't you?"

"Sure, sure, hi, Tina, it's nice to see you again."

Jim then turned to Tim Hurley, Chief Counsel of Business Affairs,
"This is Tim Hurley. Tim is our Chief Counsel of Business Affairs. I
thought it might be appropriate to bring him along today. What do
you think?"

Ben thought a moment. There was a glint in his eye as he
responded.

"Absolutely... if he likes a great New York strip. St. Elmo has the best!"

Jim laughed and shook his head acquiescing the polite interaction to Ben.

The five of them made their way to the conference room. Carrie transferred all her calls and Ben's calls to Asha's phone. She always preferred a caller get a real person on the phone rather than have calls go into a voice mail server. Carrie gave Asha instruction to simply take a message and she or Ben would return the call after lunch.

"Ben, we've been at this game a long time. I know how much Haughton Fabrication means to you; it IS you. I respect that. Precision is experiencing tremendous growth in the construction industry. We are currently reviewing contracts that go far beyond our capacity to provide product. That's why we brought Tim on. He's a whiz-bang at corporate acquisitions and we are going to be making many. Precision is prepared to offer you twenty million dollars for Haughton Fabrication. That includes payment of any outstanding debt and any contracts you might have in the offing. We would like you to be a member of the board of directors and Carrie to run the operation."

Jim turned his attention to Carrie.

"Carrie, I've known you for some time now. Your competency, professionalism, and manufacturing knowledge precede you. We share many of the same supply sources. Your suppliers say you can be tough. They say you are tough," he paused and winked at Tina and Tim, "Tough but fair and honest. When I hear of people like you in our industry, it makes me proud, and I certainly would be proud if we were working together."

Carrie genuinely blushed. "Jim, I, I don't know what to say to that. Thank you very much. I'm just doing my job. I love what I do and know you love what you do. Thank you for those kind words."

Ben interjected.

"Yeah, well, Carrie isn't going anywhere too soon. I need someone to keep me inline!" Once again everyone chuckled. "Nah, she does a super job, a super job. Ya know, Jim, I've got a son involved with the business now, too."

Jim looked puzzled. "I didn't even know you had a son, Ben. What does he do for you?"

"Well, ya know, Bud Matthews died awhile back..."

Jim interjected, "Boy that's a name that has to go into the Manufacturing Hall of Fame. The entire industry respected him. He was a walking encyclopedia of manufacturing knowledge. I met him only a few times, but my gosh, what an intelligent man. He was extraordinarily impressive."

Ben continued, "Yeah, well, he died, and it was a big hit for my brother and me. Ya see, he worked for both of us, both Haughton Divisions. So, to answer your question, I put my son, Ted, in Bud's position. He's taken over Sales for Fabrication. He's real smart, I mean real smart. Bud was good, but Ted has the technology. He's up on all that stuff."

Jim asked, "Where did he go to school?"

Ben became noticeably uncomfortable at the question. "Yeah, well, he has been studying for eight years and aced everything put in front of him. He's itching to get out into the real world and make his impact."

Jim looked at Carrie. She gave absolutely no evidence of what was going through her mind.

In the adjacent office, Asha's telephone rang.

"Thank you for calling Haughton Fabrication, my name is Asha, how can I best serve you?"

"You can serve me best by taking me off this forward and get me Ben!"

Teddy was brash; not the least bit polite.

"I'm sorry, Ted, your dad is in a–."

"Excuse me?"

"I'm sorry, Ted, Ben is in a meeting right now. I would be happy to take a message."

"GET BEN!"

Asha was not anticipating the possibility that Teddy would be calling. Her mind raced to find the appropriate response. She could not interrupt the meeting, but even more so did not want to be the recipient of Teddy's wrath.

"I am terribly sorry, Ted, Ben asked that I not interrupt him under any conditions. He and–I mean he is in a closed-door session. I wish I could help, but I can't interrupt."

Teddy cursed. Asha feared the phone would melt as she held it in her hand. Such profanity. She only hoped her misstep of almost mentioning Carrie went unnoticed.

"Look, I'm going to tell you once more. I want you to consider who I am. Consider it carefully; GET ME BEN!"

Asha took a deep breath and blurted, "I am sorry, I cannot interrupt the meeting. Would you like to leave a message?"

Teddy cursed once again and slammed the phone down.

"Well, Ben, you're just going to have to get used to seeing me. I will not give up until we've secured a deal." Jim politely affirmed.

Ben replied, "Jim, I think we're going to have a lot of good lunches at St. Elmo!"

The informal meeting ended. The group made their way to the stairs to go to lunch.

"Excuse me, Carrie? Carrie? Can I speak with you a moment before you go?" Asha looked distraught. Carrie asked her dad if he would wait a moment before leaving.

"Asha what is it? You look terrible."

"TEDDY HAUGHTON! TEDDY HAUGHTON CALLED!"

Asha began to cry. Carrie moved her back into her office. "Asha, what did he do? What on earth did he say?"

Asha tried to compose herself. "Oh, Carrie. He was terrible. He just wouldn't stop cursing and yelling. He scares me. He is so mad at me right now for not interrupting the meeting. I don't know what he'll do."

Carrie reassured Asha, "He won't do anything to you. I'll let him know I told you to hold all calls. You don't worry about it. Thank you for your support. Go ahead and go to lunch. I'll put calls on voice mail."

Asha turned off her computer and locked her books in her drawer. Carrie and Asha walked down the stairs together. Asha walked to her car while Carrie made her way to her dad's car.

At four-forty Teddy stormed into the office and up the stairs. Asha had already left, only Carrie and Ben remained. Before reaching Ben's door the profanities began. As Teddy exploded into Ben's office he ordered, "I want to know about the meeting! Who set it up? Who were the participants? and why wasn't I included?"

Ben attempted to reason with Teddy. "It was a nothing meeting, Ted. A nothing meeting. I knew nothing would become of it, and so I didn't bother you about it. You need to be out in the field. You don't need to have your time wasted in meetings that we know are not going anywhere."

"You're not answering my question, old man. You are getting too old to make decisions for my life! Don't ever decide for me who I need to meet and who I don't. You have no idea what you are doing anymore. Now I'm going to ask you one more time. WHO SET UP THIS MEETING?"

Ben rocked back and forth in his office chair.

"Well, Carrie was contacted by–"

Ben didn't even get a chance to finish his answer. Teddy cursed, abruptly turned, and made his way directly to Carrie's office. Ben followed. He feared what this confrontation might lead to. The office was empty. Carrie had left through the rear fire escape. Teddy looked out the window. She was just pulling out of the parking lot. He slammed his fist into the wall. A picture fell to the floor, and the frame and glass broke. Teddy cursed again. He pushed past his father, who was now standing in the doorway and went into his office. He slammed the door.

Ben could hear Teddy talking with someone on the phone. He glanced at Carrie's phone. None of the office lines were lit.

He prepared himself for another verbal beating when he got home.

Ben remained at the office until five-thirty. He delayed going home by driving to the manufacturing facility. He'd take time to visit with personnel while forestalling the impending confrontation. The fabrication plant was home to Ben. This was his place of solitude. The pounding of presses, grinding of mills, and whirling of conveyor belts were exciting. At the plant, there would be no arguments. Ben was always respected. Within the walls of Haughton Fabrication, Ben had full control. This was the center of his world, and the lives of those fortunate enough to be a part of it were his closest and dearest friends.

At six-ten, Ben decided to leave the peacefulness of the empty Haughton Fabrication offices. He imagined a war zone when he got home.

Ben pulled into the driveway and parked the Caddie in his three-car garage. He walked to the door that separated the garage from a short hallway leading to the formal entryway. Teddy's new car was in the garage, as was Pauline's. Ben took a deep breath and prepared to be attacked.

There was soft jazz playing on the stereo. The fireplace was lit, and a Harvey's rested next to Ben's La-Z-Boy recliner. Teddy walked in from his bedroom.

"Hi, Dad, you worked late. I thought you'd be home before me."

Ben was visibly confused by Teddy's peaceful greeting.

"Uh, yeah, yeah. Well, I wanted to go over to the plant and look at the expansion of the line. Yeah, It's looking good, real good. Have you seen it yet?"

"Dad, to be honest, I've been working so hard to make something out of the information I'm given I haven't had time to visit the plant. I really should. We should go there together." Teddy calmly responded.

"That would be super, super. What information are you getting that is causing the problem?" Ben asked.

"Nah, let's leave work problems there. We're both home now. Let's just enjoy the evening, Dad." Teddy's tone was soothing, caring.

"Ted, if you've got a problem, I want to know about it." Ben continued.

As the two were visiting, Pauline entered the room.

"Hi, sweetie, how was your day at work?"

"Oh, it was super. A good day. We had Jim Franklin and his group in today from Precision Metal Fabrication." Ben laughed. "He's always trying to buy the business, but I'm not interested. I mean, what would I do? I've had too many friends sell their business and die. No, I won't want to do that."

"I'm glad you won't sell, Dad. I've got big dreams for the business. It's a good corporation, but it can be so much better with technology. You've got a great group of loyal employees, but we need to reach out to the younger generation, my generation. I can do it—I know I can! It's just, just, well…"

Pauline interrupted. "Ben, we all know that Carrie is controlling the money. You always used to say that you couldn't do anything unless Hal gave you the money to do it."

Ben replied. "And Hal was real good with the money so we could do it."

Pauline agreed but added, "Ben, Carrie was trained by you. Other than that, she's been an elementary school teacher. Hal graduated with a degree in economics. Carrie? I don't even know what her major was. Ted is smart. He sees things, Ben. He sees things you don't see. You are too close to the situation. Too emotionally involved with your daughter. Teddy has found some things-"

Teddy abruptly interrupted as if scripted hours before. "Mom, not now. Now isn't the time. Dad just got home."

Ben's curiosity was triggered. "What? What is it you've found?"

"Go ahead, Teddy, Dad wants to know, Teddy?" Pauline sat next to Teddy and lovingly put her arms around him. "Teddy, he's your father. You must tell him." Ben was now sitting on the edge of his chair as

Pauline continued. "I know you don't want to cause a problem, but you are not the one who has caused it. Tell him."

Teddy appeared genuinely conflicted. There was a reluctance in his voice. "Dad, there are some suspicious things going on in accounting. I haven't been able to get all the information, I can't put my finger on it yet, but I think there are serious discrepancies. I hope they are honest discrepancies."

"What are you saying, Ted? What have you found?"

Teddy began wringing his hands and shaking his head as if he was facing a daunting, threatening possibility—too terrible to even discuss. "Dad, it's Carrie's numbers. I'm trying to determine why I am working so hard, but we are still losing money. The money is going somewhere, and I don't know where. We've got some help, professional help, to audit what has been taking place. When he is finished with his investigation, we'll have more information to discuss."

Ben didn't want to doubt his daughter, *but this* was his *son!* If it took an investigation to get to the bottom of the discrepancies, the investigation would proceed with his blessing. Ben was sold on the fact that Teddy was not wanting to create a problem. It appeared clear to Ben that Teddy was uncomfortable even discussing the issue.

Teddy's calm, professional manner gave Ben a sudden rush of pride. Any possibility Carrie would be given the benefit of the doubt vanished with Teddy's show of professional concern and emotional control. Ben sat back in his recliner. The taste of a good drink, the comfort of a warm fire, and the pride he felt for Teddy set his mind at ease. Teddy and Pauline soon heard the sound of soft snoring.

Teddy had been coached well.

CHAPTER SEVENTY
JUNE 5, 2017

Asha recalled, "Teddy was so angry with me on the phone. I couldn't get out of the office soon enough!"

"I feel the same way every time he comes in!" Carrie lamented. "I've just got to keep my head down and do my job." Carrie paused for a moment. "Even then, with the way Teddy has my dad wrapped around his finger, I'm probably doomed!"

"Carrie, your dad has to see what is going on; he has to! He doesn't want a confrontation with Teddy and ignores what is so obvious to everyone else. Carrie, he has to see it!" Asha was pleading her case unable to consider the alternative.

Carrie quietly smiled. She couldn't believe what was happening, how could she expect Asha to understand?

PART SIX
THE PLAN TAKES SHAPE

CHAPTER SEVENTY-ONE
PRESTON EDMUND
JULY 4, 2016

Flights and tee times had been scheduled weeks in advance. Most of the players—amateurs, arrived as the sky, just beyond the hills marking the back nine, was changing from pink to gold. Some would not be asking for mulligans until two-thirty when the harsh twosome of sun and humidity would outplay even the lowest handicappers. It was the Fourth of July, and a baking round of golf seemed just as patriotic as sweating it out at Victory Field, watching Indianapolis Indians baseball, and chowing down an Arni's Pizzeria pepperoni and cheese pizza.

Lake Tippecanoe Country Club was Preston Edmund's home course. To hear him tell it, he played to a +1 handicap, a level of play that never counted his foot wedges or miraculously located errant tee-shots, which, for other players, were deemed lost in the creeks lining the perennial ryegrass and Poa Annua fairways.

Teddy Haughton's return to Lake Tippecanoe and the Haughton Lake House was meticulously planned. His flight arrived at Indianapolis International Airport the prior evening—plenty of time to drive to Lake Tippecanoe, open the Lake House, and enjoy a good night's sleep. It was imperative he arrive at the clubhouse by seven o'clock.

Teddy's preparation required clockwork precision. His dress and appearance, even his gait, had to convey affluence. By arriving at the clubhouse by seven a.m., Teddy would be on the practice range at precisely seven-fifteen. This gave him time to strut, scope, and undoubtedly (in his mind at least), psych the rest of the field. Teddy would pace the putting green and driving range glaring at any golfer whose eyes he could catch—intimidating the weakest of the competition.

So, then why, he asked himself, of all days would his limousine driver choose this day to be late?

Teddy's blood boiled. Seven-ten—he was still waiting for his limousine. He called his mother. She was enjoying the last few moments of a deep slumber when the phone awakened her. She was still groggy when she answered the phone, but Teddy's cursing jarred her into action.

"Teddy, Teddy calm down! Sweetie, when the limo arrives, remain calm until you get to the Clubhouse. Request your clubs from the driver. Once you have them, simply walk away." Teddy knew he could always get the best advice from his mother, "Simply walk away." If Teddy had to wait for a ride from an incompetent driver, the driver would have to wait until his next customer to be paid.

Teddy arrived at the Tippecanoe Country Club at seven-thirty-six. He followed his mother's advice. He retrieved his clubs from the driver, carried them to the clubhouse entrance where a tournament attendant would take them to his assigned cart, and he simply walked away. This left the angry limousine driver arguing with the club parking attendant who ordered him to move the limo from the unloading zone; other players were waiting to be dropped off.

Teddy made his way to the locker room. He preferred a locker at eye level. Given the late hour, the only lockers that remained available were those on the lower tier. He slammed the palm of his right hand against one of the locker doors simultaneously popping a blood vessel just below his index finger. The pad beneath his finger immediately began to swell. He cursed the swelling, he cursed the locker door, he cursed the limo driver, and, most immediate, he cursed the time it was taking to prepare himself for his appearance on the course. For the moment, his freshly pressed golf pants and shirt assuaged his anger; he may have been later than he'd planned, but he looked good! He locked the locker door and walked briskly to the golf shop. It was now seven-fifty-two—his opportunity to make a menacing first impression had long passed.

Drinks were covered by the tournament, but golf balls were not. He needed Titleist Pro V1/X's, and the pro shop was sold out. By this point he could barely contain his contempt for the ineptitude of tournament sponsors whose plans didn't include enough V1/X's for him. He purchased Nike RZN Tour balls which always underperformed for his level of play. As he reached the counter to pay for the two 3-packs, the waist of his shirt caught a small burr of metal on the stainless-steel siding protecting the wood veneer of the counter. Teddy felt the tug. He looked down to see a 3-inch thread linking his shirt to the countertop corner burr. In anger he yanked it away causing another couple of inches to be sacrificed before the thread yielded and broke. Now, to the casual observer, Teddy would enter the mix of amateurs—another wannabe golfer, in an old shirt, with a noticeable snag.

That was it! Someone had to pay for the wretched morning he was having. He verbally assaulted the worker behind the counter for the damage to his shirt and demanded the golf balls be given to him as compensation. His vile outburst brought the part-time high school sophomore to tears. There was no way to prepare for Teddy's vengeance. Even a seasoned veteran clerk would have been hard-pressed to remain calm. Through tears, the young lady apologized and complied with Teddy's demand. As he turned away his scowl was replaced with a gratified grin. It didn't matter who it was; nobody interfered with the way Teddy wanted things to be. Stand in his way— pay a price. Ultimately, Teddy Haughton always got what Teddy Haughton wanted.

As he drove his cart to the practice tee, he shook his head in disgust. He'd paid good money to play in this tournament. He should have been treated with respect by the limo driver and the cashier in the pro shop. With what he'd paid to participate, he should be enjoying himself, not dealing with incompetence. He had enough of that at Haughton Fabrication. His sister and father were running the business; in Teddy's and Pauline's opinion, they were running it into the ground.

He pulled his Callaway XR 16 driver from the bag and teed up a practice ball. After taking several practice swings, Teddy stepped up to the ball. He adjusted the shoulders of his shirt to give himself ample room to make his perfect swing. He tugged at his pant leg making certain the break of its cuff was just above the tongue of his shoe. Placing his weight on his left leg, he tilted his head slightly, pre-cocked his wrist, and pulled the club back. Even the lowest handicapper would have to admit, his swing was a thing of enviable beauty. The ball sliced diagonally across the range, in full view of the other golfers. Teddy cursed. He stared at the swelling on his hand and repeated his litany of curses against the limo driver (long gone by this time), the pro shop cashier, the noticeable thread-pull on his shirt, the range ball, and his new Callaway XR 16 driver. He was seething. He teed another ball. He heard his mother's voice, urging him to calm down and remember he was better than anyone else. His next drive was—as in his mind his mother told him it would be—perfect.

At 8:20 a.m., Preston Edmund finished his eggs Benedict, tipped the server handsomely, and made his way from the Clubhouse restaurant to the driving range. Teddy was returning his seven-iron to the golf bag when he noticed Preston walking toward him. A smile lit upon Teddy's face. It was good to see Preston. Their relationship was the closest thing to friendship Teddy had ever known.

Teddy's plan was taking shape. Preston Edmund would supply the legal support Teddy required.

"Ted, my man! It's great to see you! What happened to your shirt?"

CHAPTER SEVENTY-TWO

A RAIN CHECK
FEBRUARY 6, 2017

At ten-ten a.m., Carrie noticed the red light blinking on the phone. A direct call had been placed to Ben's desk. She heard him hurriedly push his chair away from the desk and abruptly close the door to his office. This had become a daily ritual when Teddy was on the road making sales calls. Carrie could hear only half the conversation. Even then it hurt her to hear her father, her hero, cower to the person on the other end.

"I know, I know. No, you don't have to do that. No, I'll get it taken care of. I'm not trying to stand in your way. I need time to make decisions. Well, I am still the one making decisions, and I'll make them when I am ready to. I don't know, I don't know. Geez, Ted, back off a little. We'll get these things taken care of, but they are not the most important things we have to focus on. Ted, I've been doing this a long time. These guys... you can't play around with them. I've handled these things before and... Okay, okay. No, calm down a little. Ted, calm down! No. I'll work it out!"

There was a long pause.

"Okay, okay, look, I don't know... maybe you should just take care of it, maybe that's the best thing. No, go ahead and do what you think is right. Hello? Teddy? Ted?"

The red light on Carrie's phone went out. The conversation had ended. It ended just as every private red-light conversation ended, Ben Haughton giving in to Teddy's badgering, his threats, his foul language rants, and his relentless pounding. Carrie realized the constant attack was more than any man could sustain.

After a few moments, Carrie could hear footsteps approaching her office door.

"Uh, hey, it looks like Teddy will be out today. He's, uh, he's making some calls in Chicago." Ben took a deep breath, "He's got problems; yea, he's got a lot of problems. Business is tough out there. He's doing the best he can."

It was an unconvincing speech, but one Ben made after every altercation with Teddy. Ben believed it and in Ben's world that sufficed.

"He's smart, he's real smart. He gets on that computer and gets information so quickly. He's brilliant—it's kinda too bad, ya know? Really sharp people, like Teddy, they don't have many friends. There's really no one he can talk to. He's so smart."

It was as if Ben was daring someone to tell him the truth, the truth he already knew. Carrie realized that if she responded negatively towards Teddy, even if it was in Ben's defense, Ben would immediately turn the tables to protect Teddy. He'd invested every bit of himself into Teddy, and any criticism of Teddy was a direct attack against him.

Carrie stood in the way of Pauline's and Teddy's objective to secure all of Haughton Manufacturing and all the family fortune. Pauline had groomed Teddy well. Theirs was an unholy alliance seeking not only to bring Carrie down but to ruin her. She was at an insurmountable disadvantage. She would not contradict her father for fear of emotional and financial retaliation. She was terrified of Teddy because of potential physical retaliation.

"Hey, why don't we enjoy some lunch together? We haven't done that for a long time; just you and me."

Ben was right. It had been quite a while since the two of them enjoyed a lunch together. For a moment her enthusiasm almost got the best of her reasoning.

Carrie realized they would not be alone. Teddy would be the unseen third party. Teddy's problems would be the total focus of Ben's conversation. How difficult business is would be his reasoning. Carrie was not about to allow her father the opportunity to convince himself at her expense.

To be sure, the death of Bud Matthews left a void in the front office. Bud had been the salesman for both divisions of Haughton Manufacturing, the packaging division, and the automotive division. He was an irritating cuss—but he was intelligent. He could charm his way into the offices of any corporate executive. Why? Because Bud was totally committed to his product. He was convinced he had the very best product, and every potential client needed the product he had. Bud, having been with Haughton Manufacturing for thirty-eight years, knew both sides of the business and was an irreplaceable contributor to each. He understood business from Haughton Manufacturing's perspective but was also very much aware of the perspectives each of his competitors held. They respected Bud; many not only respected him, but they also genuinely liked him. He could make deals that left both Ben and Hal shaking their heads in amazement. He'd simply smile at them and say, "Never go to bed with the competition, but it doesn't hurt to date them once in a while."

Bud was gone, and in Ben's world, Teddy Haughton was the perfect replacement.

This was not the first time Ben attempted to find a place for Teddy within Haughton Fabrication. In each case, Teddy would arrogantly walk into the office and declare that he oversaw the future of Haughton Fabrication. The production team, the engineering team, and the shipping team threatened to walk if he was ever allowed to return to work in their areas. Shop Steward, Glenn Barkley, and the Steel Worker's Union Representative, Tony Vitale, met privately with

Ben. They managed to persuade him to drop any thought of mingling Teddy with the workforce.

Ben's brother, Hal, could foresee the untenable situation his boys would be in if forced to work with Teddy. This was the real reason for the separation of the two divisions into indigenous and autonomous corporations. It would give his three boys unobstructed opportunity to build Haughton Packaging.

Ben felt he had no other option but to bring Teddy to the corporate offices. There, Teddy could be kept under control and have no influence upon other employees—at least that was the way it was to have happened in Ben's world.

"Go to lunch, Dad?" Carrie stalled to consider her options. "I promised you some great numbers, and I'd like to take lunch to pull a few more things together for you. How about a raincheck?" Carrie responded.

"Oh, sure, sure." Obviously, Ben needed a listening ear; it would not be Carrie's. "Well, I don't know. I guess I'll just go and get something quick. I know you're busy. Okay; okay then. I'll, uh, I'll see you a little later."

There was a sadness in Ben's voice. Carrie could do nothing to ease his pain. He'd allowed this to happen, and while Ben was suffering, Pauline and Teddy were planning their next move.

CHAPTER SEVENTY-THREE
CHICAGO
FEBRUARY 8, 2017

The flight from Indianapolis to Chicago took just over an hour. Teddy had booked a room at the Hilton Chicago. He took the CTA from Chicago O'Hare directly to the Hilton. Today he would relax. The only thing scheduled was dinner with Preston Edmund, Esq.

Teddy's room was located on the twenty-first floor. The room might have been perfect for any other traveler. Teddy was the exception. The king bed was covered by a plush comforter. Teddy concluded that such a covering would no doubt harbor bacterium and pathogens, remnants from previous visitors. A shower curtain separated the tub from the sink area. It was spotlessly clean, but to Teddy the entire bathroom was a petri-dish contaminated by mold and fungi.

Teddy exited the room and returned to the front desk. Kelly Carpenter greeted him at the desk.

"My name is Ted Haughton. I am scheduled to stay with you people for five nights. The room you have given me is unacceptable! It's filthy!"

"Oh, my goodness! I am very sorry, sir. I will send housekeeping there immediately for you."

Teddy replied, "No, you won't! You will get me a suite with a Lake view. It will have a glass door surrounding a shower. I do not want draperies! I will return in two hours. I want housekeeping to make certain the room is perfect. Have I made myself clear?"

Kelly was completely overcome. All she wanted to do was help Teddy. His aggression prompted her to apologize for her inability to rectify the situation. She apologized once again and told Teddy she would get her supervisor. Moments later, a sharply dressed gentleman stepped from the back offices.

"Hello, Mr. Haughton, my name is Curtis Bering. How can I help you?"

Teddy was becoming more impatient. "You can help me by addressing my requirements for an adequate room. Ms. Carpenter was incapable of complying with my request!"

"Mr. Haughton, I assure you, Ms. Carpenter is one of our most highly regarded hosts. I will see what I can do to find a suite that meets your approval."

"And I want you to consider the inconvenience you people have caused me before charging me an exorbitant price for your mistake!"

"Sir, I will see to it that your new room is prepared to your liking."

Teddy exited The Hilton Chicago onto Michigan Avenue. The verbal confrontation he'd enjoyed with the front desk personnel meant nothing to him. It was all a game of manipulation and control. Teddy was pleased.

The warm Chicago sunshine greeted him. It was a beautiful Chicago afternoon.

He walked up Michigan Avenue, occasionally glancing at his own reflection in glass doors and windows. He crossed Balbo Avenue. Columbia College provided him with one block of solid glass, amplifying Teddy's self-indulgence and delight.

Two hours of strolling was enough exercise to prepare Teddy for his meeting with Preston. He returned to the Hilton, modified his visage to a scouring frown and approached the front desk. Kelly

Carpenter immediately retreated into the back office where, in perfect synchronization, Curtis Bering reappeared to greet Teddy.

"Mr. Haughton, I hope you had a nice walk."

Teddy ignored the comment. "I hope to finally have a satisfactory room!"

"Sir, we've made every effort to accommodate you. We have a beautiful one-bedroom suite with a lake view."

"I do not expect to be paying more for this!"

"Mr. Haughton, it is indeed an upgraded suite, but we are happy to extend it to you for your original contractual agreement."

Teddy took the key. "You should!"

Preston Edmund arrived early and requested Concierge to ring Teddy's room.

"Ted? It's Preston, I got here a little early so I'm down in the lobby. No need to rush."

"Preston! I hope you had a good flight, thanks for coming. I'll be right down."

"Let's get a drink when you get down here."

"That sounds great, I'm on my way."

This was the first time they'd been together since the Tippecanoe Country Club Tournament the previous July 4th. Teddy was interested in how, at such a young age, Preston had taken possession of his family's estate. Preston was interested in increasing his wealth by helping Teddy do the same. Their mutually self-absorbed arrogance was the groundwork for what would become a disreputable business partnership.

Teddy greeted Preston as if he were a long-lost brother. The two exchanged pleasantries and proceeded to the 720 South Bar for a drink.

"How's the golf game, Preston?"

Preston laughed. "Let's just say the course record is still intact! Yours?"

Teddy shook his head. "I've been under so much stress I haven't had time to think of golf."

Their server approached them.

"And what can I get you two gentlemen this evening?"

Teddy tilted his head back slightly, raised his eyebrow and gave the attractive young lady a "you know what I'd like" smirk. She responded by leaning over to him as if to share a deep personal invitation. Teddy's eyes widened with anticipation.

"To drink," the server politely responded.

Preston laughed.

"Strike one, my friend! Ha!"

Teddy recovered his fumbled flirtation by joining the laughter and requesting a glass of Chardonnay. Preston ordered a Drizly with three olives on the side.

"Ted, let's get an appetizer. How about the shrimp spring rolls?"

"Sure, and those pan seared scallops sound good. Let's get an order of those too."

Their server replied, "Let me get those appetizers going. I'll be right back with your drinks."

Teddy's attention was briefly interrupted as she walked past them and back to the bar.

"So, Ted, how do you expect the meetings to go? You prepared?"

Teddy leaned back and draped his arm over the plush leather chair.

"Preston, I was born for this meeting; but we can't stop here! Tell me about your dad's practice and how you've taken it over. How much control do you actually have? What about your inheritance? You mentioned he has several properties. What did you do to get control of them?"

"Here are your drinks, gentlemen. Your appetizers will be right up. Will you be staying for dinner?"

Teddy responded, "I wasn't planning on staying, but it's comfortable, and we're here. Why not?" Preston agreed.

"I'll give you some time to look at the menu. Let me get your appetizers, excuse me."

Preston returned his attention to Teddy's questions.

"Ted, you've fired quite a few questions at me. Let me break them all down into one simple question. Your question is, how did you take it all? right?

That was exactly what Teddy wanted to know, and how could he do the same thing?

"I'm sorry for the wait, gentlemen. I do believe you'll find your appetizers well worth it. Have you decided on what you would like as an entrée?"

Teddy took a moment to glance at her name tag. "Sarah, I'd like the veal loin medallions."

"And I'll have that pan seared salmon. Not too much of the butter sauce please."

"Great choices gentlemen! I'll get those right to the kitchen. How are those drinks?"

Preston looked at Teddy. Teddy was not giving any response.

"Sarah, why don't we get another Chardonnay and Drizly going?"

Sarah gave a pleasant chuckle. "Right away, gentlemen."

"Ted, let me tell you something. You've got to remain bold—heartless if that's what it takes. There will be plenty of opportunities to mend fences once you've taken everything and the others need you. And they will need you—they'll hate you—but they will need you, and you will always maintain control."

Teddy pondered Preston's words. Teddy quickly concluded that he was on the right track. Most people hated him already, and he didn't care.

"But I've got two sisters to deal with!"

Preston leaned forward, nose to nose with Teddy. Teddy had unintentionally stirred Preston's anger.

"Let me tell you something, pal. If you ever start a sentence with the word 'but' after I've given you sound advice, we are no longer working together. That's weak talk. I only work with ruthless warriors! Got it?"

Teddy did not budge. The two were still nose to nose.

"Don't you ever threaten me again if you want a piece of what I'm going to take!" Teddy retorted. "Yes, I got it!"

Both young men sat back in their chairs and began to laugh, satisfied they'd both pared that hole. Their second drink arrived. Preston proposed a toast, "To a long and mutually profitable relationship!"

After taking a generous sip, Preston continued, "Ted, here's how you handle your sisters. You don't have any! There is only one important person in your life; there is only one you are responsible to house, to feed, to entertain, and to enjoy—YOU! You don't owe anyone anything; no one! You have to know, deep in your inner being, that when you say something, it will be done. There are no options, and there are no interruptions. If you want it, it is yours—take it!"

The next morning, Teddy was awakened by housekeeping shoving the morning paper under his door.

CHICAGO BLEEDS, 4 DEAD, 45 WOUNDED IN FOURTH OF
JULY WEEKEND SHOOTINGS

"How can this place be so beautiful in the sunlight and deadly at night? This is just craziness!"

The phone rang. "Ted! You awake? We've got a long day ahead of us. How about meeting for breakfast at nine o'clock?"

"Yea, Preston, did you see the headlines? Are you sure we should plan an evening out on the Martini tomorrow night? These shootings are crazy!"

Preston laughed, "Welcome to Chicago!" Preston's casual laughter hid his underlying concern. This was a side of Teddy he had not anticipated. Was Teddy ruthless enough to do what it was going to require for him to take it all? "I'll be downstairs, Ted."

"I'm on my way!"

Although Preston was callous and narcissistic, he was also intelligent and nimble. For the past several months, Teddy had been sending Carrie's files to him. While they meant very little to Teddy, Preston realized Carrie was detailed and proficient. Her numbers were flawless. He carefully arranged her historical data graphing the company's P&L profile. The debt ratio was 20%. It was perfectly positioned for a buyout.

"Good morning, counselor," Teddy said as he extended his hand.

"Good morning to you, sir," Preston replied as the two shook hands. "Big day ahead, Ted; are you ready for it?"

Teddy flexed his pectoral muscles and threw his shoulders back. With an arrogant smile, Teddy said, "Don't you ever doubt me, pal. I didn't come this far to have second thoughts!"

Their meeting with Jim Franklin, Tim Hurley, and Tina Yen was scheduled for 3:00. Preston went through all the information and the charts. Teddy took careful time to study the charts and commit them to his photographic memory. This would allow him to speak with some semblance of understanding.

"Preston, I'm expecting you to do the majority of the talking. I know that Jim will be depending upon Tim to represent his requirements. You know what I want."

"Ted, I'm here for a purpose. You just let me do what I do well."

CHAPTER SEVENTY-FOUR

CONFERENCE ROOM CONFRONTATION

MAY 11, 2017

Carrie moved about the office with speed and accuracy. Seldom was there a wasted moment in her day. Today, she made final preparations for the afternoon's union meeting. The meeting would be at two o'clock. Carrie would begin briefing her dad at ten o'clock. This allowed her time to retrieve any information Ben thought to be advantageous for the discussion.

In the years they'd worked together, they'd established an efficient rhythm. Meetings with the shop steward and union representatives were always congenial and productive. Ben carried over many of the traits his great-grandfather Benjamin Haughton established. He paid his employees more than the competition, and he made certain they were all treated with respect.

At ten o'clock, Ben and Carrie met in the downstairs conference room. The room was shared by both Haughton Fabrication and Haughton Packaging. Carrie reserved the room for two hours.

She presented Ben with a powerful financial forecast that reflected the current downturn in industrial construction. Her data indicated that while business would remain stable, revenues would be lower than the previous two quarters. There had been some loss due to imports, but thus far the quality of those products left much to be desired.

As Carrie continued her discussion with Ben, Teddy burst through the conference room door.

"Ted, we're in a meeting right now," Ben politely explained.

"What, am I blind? You don't think I can see you are in a meeting?"

"Teddy, we're-" Carrie was harshly interrupted.

"Shut up. I've had enough of you. You're nothing to me and nothing to this company. If there is a meeting going on, then I am going to be in it and not some two-bit secretary no one respects."

There was no basis for Teddy's accusation. Carrie looked at her dad with eyes, begging him to protect her.

"Ya know, Ted, you're probably right about the meetings. That's my fault. I should have invited you. We're meeting with the Union this afternoon at two o'clock. Carrie is just giving me a financial update so that we have numbers to support our positions."

Carrie was shocked by her father's response. Once again, Teddy had gotten a free pass. She sat for several moments, attempting to regain her composure. Teddy remained in a position, blocking the door. Without saying a word, Carrie gathered her copies and returned them to her folder.

"Dad, if you and Teddy are going to have a meeting, I suggest you make copies for him."

Carrie got up from her seat and walked towards the door. Teddy would not move. They stood only two feet apart. Carrie would not make eye contact with him. She could hear his exaggerated breathing through clenched teeth.

"Ted, I think you better sit down so we can go over these numbers," Ben said.

"Are you crazy? Do you think I'd trust any numbers this idiot put together? I'll be at the meeting at two o'clock."

"Ted, I think you better sit down," Ben urged his son.

Teddy moved past Carrie to the conference table. He made certain his left shoulder came firmly into contact with hers. Carrie maintained her balance and stood her ground while hugging the folder tightly to her chest. Her back was to the conference table, and now to the two men. There was a threatening purpose in Teddy's shoulder contact. Carrie knew it was no accident. It was a warning.

"You make certain I have a chair at the head of the table. Got it?" Teddy demanded.

With Teddy now behind her, Carrie quickly made her way through the door.

"Did you hear me? Make certain there is a seat for me at the head of the table! Answer me!"

Carrie never looked back; she gave no response. The only sound was Carrie's footsteps quickly returning to the stairwell and the safety of her office. Once there, she locked her door.

Teddy erupted with vulgarities so disgusting the packaging division's receptionist got up from her desk and politely closed the conference room door.

Carrie placed her notes in her desk drawer and locked it and her computer. She then quickly made her way out the back door and down the fire exit steps. She was shaking uncontrollably. Her eyes filled with tears as she hurried to her car. Her shaking made it impossible to find her key. Suddenly there was a hand on her shoulder. Carrie screamed. Too petrified to turn, she looked up from searching in her purse for her keys at her reflection in the driver-side window. Standing behind her was Asha.

"Oh, my gosh, Asha, you have no idea what I have just gone through. I can't take it anymore. I can't take it!"

Asha put her arms around Carrie.

"I know what you went through. I know what you are going through; we all do. We've all heard. What is wrong with your father? What has happened to him?" Asha asked.

"Right now, I don't care, Asha. I've just got to get away from here. I cannot continually be abused like this." Carrie looked up to the clouds overhead. "Oh, dear God. I know I have to be in that meeting. Give me strength. Please keep me calm," Carrie pleaded.

Asha tried to lighten the moment, "Let me take you to lunch. I think you could use a nice gin and tonic. What the heck—if I buy my boss a gin and tonic, I can't get in trouble for having one myself!"

Carrie politely declined, "Thank you, Asha. You are a jewel. I think I'd rather just drive somewhere and eat my sandwich. I'll take a raincheck on that gin and tonic though."

"Carrie, you be careful. We worry about you. Don't ever be in this building alone with that maniac. He's dangerous, Carrie. We are all very concerned for you and for Ben," Asha warned.

Carrie was now calm enough to find her key and open her car door. As she drove out of the parking lot, she looked in the rearview mirror to give Asha a thankful wave. She couldn't help noticing, behind Asha, a dark figure peering out the conference room window.

CHAPTER SEVENTY-FIVE

UNION MEETING
MAY 11, 2017

C arrie made it a practice to distribute the agenda and notes a week prior to union meetings. She was always careful to prepare additional packets and have them available as participants arrived. After welcoming each union meeting participant at the door, she would hand them their packet and invite them to enjoy the light refreshments she'd prepared.

Union relations remained remarkably strong. Since Haughton Fabrication was already paying top dollar, the discussions usually focused upon future business opportunity forecasts.

There was good news on the horizon. The economy had been sluggish during the previous five years due to uncertain demands and difficulty obtaining credit. 2014, however, started with a burst of momentum. It was too soon to pull out the party hats, but a turnaround appeared to be in the making.

Carrie went over the agenda and asked if there were any questions or additions. There were none.

The members present included:

Bob Percelli - Senior Union Representative

Mike Dutro - Union Representative

Dorthy Falco - Union Representative

Rob Steiner - Shop Steward

Don Malone - Plant Manager

Tyler Dixon - Dayshift Foreman

Mohamad Ishmael - Night shift Foreman

Carrie Dustin - Controller

Ben Haughton - Owner, CEO

"Members, please open your packet. I would like to briefly discuss with you the financials for the last quarter of 2016 and the financials for the first two months of 2017. There is reason to be optimistic. However, let me remind you. Haughton Fabrication historically experiences a lag-time of about three months during economic increases and downturns before it is fully impacted. It is actually a very good thing, in both cases. It allows us to properly control our inventories and therefore decreases potential shutdowns that might otherwise occur. Don, could you speak to this, please?"

Don Malone, Haughton Fabrication's Plant Manager had been with the company for over twenty-seven years. He was hired by Harold Haughton Senior as were most of Haughton Fabrication's employees.

"Certainly, Carrie, as everyone seated at this table today knows, Haughton Fabrication does not experience any measurable employee turnover."

Union Representative, Mike Dutro interrupted, "Why the heck would there be? I've been trying to get a job here for seven years!"

Bob Percelli jokingly hit Mike over the head with his agenda. Everyone laughed. Don continued.

"All kidding aside, we do our best to stay ahead of the curve with regard to employee relations. The net result? Collaborative effort during the downtimes as well as a collaborative celebration during the upswings. Our economic indicators, residential growth, city improvement programs, and the automotive industry allow us the opportunity to prepare. And, by the way, the average number of years our sixty-six employees have been with Haughton Manufacturing is thirty-eight years. This team knows how to work together. We know how to do whatever it takes and how to do it right!"

Rob Steiner raised his hand.

"What Don is saying is very true. We've been through just about every economic situation you can think of—and we're all still here! Carrie, production has kind of plateaued for about half a year now. How do you and Ben see these indicators affecting production and the workforce in the near future?"

As Ben began to respond, Teddy abruptly walked into the meeting and made his way to the head of the table. He glared at Carrie and sat in the chair she'd reserved for him.

"Oh, hey everyone this is my son, Te–"

Before Ben could introduce Teddy to the union representatives, Teddy interrupted.

"Good afternoon, I am Ted Haughton, the future of Haughton Fabrication. I am a bit surprised this meeting has begun without me. I was told it would begin at two-thirty. I'll have to request Ms. Dustin to give me a quick update on what has already been discussed. In the future, Ms. Dustin, I'd appreciate it if you would give me the correct time for meetings I should attend."

The room became very tense. Carrie would not make eye contact with Teddy. She cleared her throat to politely respond to Teddy's request while her eyes remained fixed upon her notepad. Before she could say a word Bob Percelli spoke.

"Excuse me, who did you say you are?"

Teddy slowly and deliberately turned his head towards Mr. Percelli.

Without answering Mr. Percelli's question Teddy firmly asked, "And you are?"

Mr. Percelli reached out to shake Teddy's hand. He had his business card in the other hand. Teddy took the business card leaving Mr. Percelli awkwardly standing in front of everyone with an outstretched hand. Seeing he was talking with the senior union representative, Teddy spontaneously adjusted his posture and attitude. He graciously took Mr. Percelli's hand. Broadening his smile, he said, "Mr. Percelli, it is an honor to have a professional businessman in our meeting. I am Ted Haughton. I am currently exploring new revenue streams to get us out of the hole we've dug ourselves into as a result of our sloppy accounting practices and poor management. I'm next in line to succeed Ben in the ownership of Haughton Fabrication."

Teddy's first words to Bob presented so many loaded phrases, Bob didn't know where to begin.

"Ted, I can call you Ted, can't I?"

Teddy nodded affirmatively.

"Ted, I've been under the impression things are very much in control here at Haughton. You appear to have a different opinion. I'd like to hear about it."

Ben interrupted the conversation with a noticeably nervous chuckle. "Bob, Ted is kinda new at this stuff. He's very smart and very energetic-"

Teddy took back the floor. "Ben, Bob asked me a question, and I am very capable of answering it."

Teddy turned his attention directly to Mr. Percelli. "I'm sorry for that interruption, Bob. Haughton Fabrication could be so much more than it is. We've gotten old—stale." Teddy sat back in his chair and extended both hands over the table, palms up as if preparing to make a notable presentation. "With all due respect to the employees at this table, you are old. No one should ever stay in one company as long as most of our employees have."

Returning his attention to Mr. Percelli's question, Teddy continued, "As far as the future goes, how can I even guess? I have no confidence in the numbers I'm given. When I ask for financial statements, I never get them. We are totally at the mercy of loyal customers. As for the future? My generation, the younger generation, doesn't want to get our hands dirty. Why should we? Why work in this industry when technology is changing every second?"

Teddy paused to mentally applaud himself.

"That isn't the worst part. There is absolutely nothing special about what we do. Anyone can do it. And foreign competition is killing my opportunity to compete. Ms. Dustin orders foreign steel coils at horribly inflated prices. She then pays for their transportation to our facility. Our costs do not end there! Don still must prep the steel when it arrives so that we can manufacture parts. Our foreign competition, those same countries Carrie is purchasing our steel from, don't have all our costs. They are shipping finished goods directly to our customers. I see it; I see it every day!"

Teddy concluded, "No, no, sir. Without my intervention, without the influence of a younger mind, the future is not secure at Haughton Fabrication; not at all!"

No one moved. No one said a word. Teddy had sucked the energy out of the room. Everyone was embarrassed for Ben and Carrie. But Teddy was not finished.

"And you!" Teddy pointed an accusing finger at Carrie. "I don't know what you are doing to these numbers. I don't know where the money is going. But I'm going to find out!"

He then turned his attention back to Mr. Percelli.

"Bob, I believe you have a better understanding of where we are right now. I would like any further union communications to go directly through my desk. We've got to put some controls in place. In a time of crisis, I have to think of this company and its future. I'm paying these employees more than any other steel fabricator in Indiana—any of them!"

Sensing no resistance from Mr. Percelli, Teddy continued, "You people come in and make demands; you turn things upside down. I hope you can appreciate the fact that I'm trying to run a business at a great disadvantage." Teddy picked up the agenda packet and then scornfully dropped it back on the table. "There is no reason to be talking to you about anything on this agenda. Everything is question-able. This meeting is over. Bob, in the future, let's you, Ben, and me get together before we interrupt everyone's busy schedules."

Teddy stood up and shook Mr. Percelli's hand. Everyone left the room in total silence.

Ben arrived home at shortly after four o'clock. Pauline could sense he was not in the mood to take her verbal abuse.

"You're home awfully early, aren't you sweetie?" A saccharin Pauline observed.

"I had a bad day. I had a real bad day. It was one of the worst day's I've ever had. It was a bad day..." Ben continued to mutter to himself as he made his way to the wet bar.

Pauline briskly walked past him and to the bar. "Here, why don't you just sit down and relax. I'll pour your Harvey's for you."

Pauline knew very well how to manipulate Ben. Her gentle ways were always precursors to the venom she would spew later.

"Oh, thanks, Paul. Thank you, man, I had a real bad day."

"Do you want to talk about it?"

"I don't know, I don't know what happened. I was in a meeting with Carrie, and I guess..." Ben paused. He didn't want to incriminate himself for not inviting Teddy. Gathering his thoughts, he continued, "I guess she forgot to invite Ted. He was angry. He was really angry."

Ben pushed the handle of the recliner back and stared at the ceiling. Pauline brought Ben his drink. She turned the fireplace on and switched the music to soft jazz. It was the perfect setting to begin her attack.

"Ben, She hates Teddy, she absolutely hates him. I don't know if she is threatened by him or if she is just concerned about her inheritance, but she will do anything she can to keep him from the business!"

Ben was uncomfortable with Pauline's comments. "Ya know, Paul, Teddy can be pretty demanding sometimes-"

Pauline broke that train of thought. She wanted to take Ben down another track.

"She's difficult, Ben, everyone knows that. She is difficult and emotional. Your father always warned you to never let a woman run the business. You told me that. Look what happened to him. Look how his sister took advantage of him." He just sat there. "Ben, don't you dare let Carrie do the same thing to your only son!"

Ben's anger became visible. "No one is going to take advantage of Ted. You hear me? NO ONE! I'm the only friend he has. No one understands him. He is strong, he's smart. Carrie will never run the business-"

Pauline interrupted.

"Carrie will never work for him either. Ben, she will continue to undermine him. I've talked with Ted a lot. He doesn't trust her. He can't get financials from her. Ben, Teddy can't be trained if your controller is hiding things from him."

It was a carefully constructed web of deceit, and Ben allowed himself to be caught in it. Nothing Pauline said was founded. She and Teddy had discussed his takeover in detail. This was just the beginning.

His arrival was tempestuous. He threw open the front door so hard that it shook pictures hanging along the entryway.

"I hate her! I hate what she is doing to my father! I hate her!"

Teddy was home.

"Teddy, Teddy, what's wrong, baby?" Pauline temporarily withdrew her fangs and reached out lovingly for her son.

Teddy was in a rage. He was crying, his nose was running, his arms were flaying, he stormed into the family room and threw the notes from the meeting towards his seated father. They flew in all directions like confetti in a windstorm.

"You just sit there! You sit there in a comfortable chair, sipping your drink next to a warm fire while I am continually under attack. There is no way I can ever fix Haughton Fabrication if you continue to be blind to the lack of cooperation that woman gives me. She is crazy!"

Ben's blood continued to boil. He was angry. He was angry and his anger was directed toward Carrie!

Teddy continued, "What am I supposed to do? You want me on my own? You want me to find a place to live? You want me to better myself? How? How am I supposed to better myself and the company if I am forced to work with someone who is hiding something? I need a car. I need a home. I need to get out from under your thumb and be what I was always meant to be. I need to run Haughton Fabrication."

Ben's face became altered. The rage was replaced with a sick expression. "Well, Ted, I told you that I'd get a car for you when you graduated from-"

"Graduated? GRADUATED? Do you think your company has time for me to invest in myself? You're crazy too! By the time I graduate there won't be a Haughton Fabrication!"

"Okay, okay, tomorrow we'll go down and get you a car. You need that. Yeah, you need that to make your calls. We'll get you a car tomorrow."

"What about my housing? Do I have to stay here the rest of my life?"

Ben tried to reason with Ted. "We can find a nice apartment for you. Something closer to the plant."

"Apartment? What? Are you thinking of getting me into some cheap low-income housing?" Teddy turned his attention to Pauline. "Listen to that mom. Carrie lives in a nice community. I'll be living in the slums." He turned his attention to Ben, "Thanks, dad. Thanks a lot."

Pauline and Teddy kept this tag-team match going for another hour and a half. Ben could take no more.

"Okay, Teddy, what do you want? What will make you happy? What's the right thing to do?"

Pauline quickly answered. "He needs a house, Ben. He needs a new house."

"Mom's right! You're a businessman, you know that property is our best option. I need an investment. I need a new house. It's not about making me happy. It's about making smart business decisions. You see what I mean? You just can't do that anymore."

Without hesitation, Ben said, "All right, I'll buy you a house. I'll talk with Carrie tomorrow and get the name of her and Lonnie's agent."

Pauline looked at Teddy, and both smiled. What more could they ask? And Carrie was going to be forced to help.

Lonnie pulled into the driveway and opened the garage door. Carrie's car was already parked in the garage. It was unusual for Carrie to be home before him. He hoped she was feeling all right.

"Babe, I'm home. Are you all right?" There was no answer. "Babe?"

Lonnie walked down the short hallway and into the kitchen. It was empty. There were no signs of dinner preparations. Through the kitchen nook, he could see that there was no one in the back yard. Lonnie made his way upstairs towards the master bedroom. The doors were closed. He opened them slowly to avoid making any noises. Perhaps Carrie was not feeling well.

"Babe?" He whispered.

Carrie was in bed; asleep. Lonnie gently sat beside her. "Babe? Are you all right?"

Carrie opened her eyes and cried. She sat up in her bed, threw herself into Lonnie's arms and sobbed.

"Carrie, what happened? What's wrong?"

Through deep sobs, Carrie was able to exhale the word, "Everything!"

Lonnie set aside any notion of making whatever had taken place right. Carrie just needed to know he was there to support her.

Carrie sobbed until there were no more tears. Tearless cries were all that Carrie had left as she tried to explain what had happened earlier in the day.

"What is happening, Lonnie? What is happening to my life? Where am I going wrong? Where did God go? Where is He? Lonnie, I didn't do anything, and I was under attack all day. Where was God today? I had no protection. My dad just sat there like a useless idiot while his evil son tore me apart in front of an entire union meeting, and I did nothing wrong!"

Carrie looked up at the bedroom ceiling. "GOD, WHY ARE YOU DOING THIS TO ME?"

Lonnie attempted to console Carrie. "Carrie, God didn't do anything to you. He wants our best. We just happen to have evil people in our family. I am sorry you are hurt. Can you explain to me what happened?"

"No, No, I can't. I can't even explain it to myself. I prepared financial statements for Dad and Ted. I always give Ted the financials—he's just too ignorant to understand them. To cover his ignorance, he tells Dad that I am not giving him information. If I give him information and try to teach him how to make it useful, I'm told I am talking down to him. I can't win!"

Carrie continued, "I've told my dad. I know he wants Teddy to one day run the business. I told him I would do everything to help him. I don't want the business! I just want to have a job that allows us to live a comfortable life, that's all. It's like I am continually being set up. And today, TODAY, Teddy beat me up in front of all the union representatives, and my dad did nothing!"

"Wait a minute, wait a minute, wait a minute. What do you mean he beat you up in front of the union representatives?" Lonnie asked.

Carrie shook her head in disbelief. "He lied, he always lies. He told them he was late for the meeting because I didn't give him the right time. He said my numbers were all wrong. He said I hide financials from him; he basically said the business is falling apart because of me. He was the big cheese that would take care of everything. He was obnoxious, Lonnie. He's trying to get me fired and I don't trust my dad enough to think he couldn't do it!"

Lonnie tightened his hug. Their years of marriage taught him that this was no time to have answers. His role was to listen.

"Lonnie, I know I say it all the time but I don't know how much more of this I can take. This is my own family! This kid has lied to my dad about his schooling, lied to my dad about the workers in the shop, lied to my dad about me, lied to my dad about Bud. He just lies! He is a chronic liar. He is incapable of telling the truth!"

Carrie then mimicked Teddy walking into the meeting, chest out, glaring eyes—the big cheese.

"I know we're not supposed to hate, but Lonnie, it's hard. Can you imagine if I ever showed my anger, what would he do to me? In my dad's eyes, I'd prove every lie Teddy ever told him about me. I have to be so careful, so careful every moment. Oh, and get this, Pauline is on the phone with him every afternoon. That's just weird. He's a young man, and Mommy calls every day? It's like they are conspiring against me. Maybe I'm paranoid, but I can't help feeling something is going on."

Lonnie felt it was finally time to bring some logic into the conversation.

"Babe, you have enough tangible issues affecting your life without allowing conjecture to fill in any of the gaps. Hating Teddy won't help; he'd have won. I won't give him that luxury. But I cannot allow you to continue to be battered the same way the two of them are battering your dad."

As Lonnie talked, he could feel his own blood pressure rising. He got up from the bed and returned to the kitchen. He went directly to the drawer under the telephone and took out their personal phone and address book. Carrie slowly came down the stairs. Lonnie was unaware of her presence.

"Yeah, hello, Paul? It's Lonnie; I'd like to talk to Ben. Yea, I'm sorry he's not feeling well. I'll hold while you get him, anyway." There was a momentary pause. "Hello, Ben? It's Lonnie; I understand you and Carrie had a difficult day today. I'm sorry about that. It seems somewhat odd to me. Things went so well between you two and the business until recent years. Did you notice that, Ben? Ben, when I married your daughter, you had a little chat with me. We were at the lake. Do you remember the chat I am talking about, Ben? No? Well, Ben, let me remind you. We were having a drink on the porch, and you said, 'Lonnie, you're a good addition to the family, but I'm going to tell you something. You take care of my daughter. If you ever do anything to hurt her, that's it! It's all over.' Do you remember that, Ben?"

Ben quietly acknowledged the conversation.

"Ben, I think you gave me some good advice—I want to thank you for that. I'm going to return the favor to you. You take care of my wife! If you ever do anything to hurt her, that's it! It's all over. Do you understand what I am saying, Ben? Have I made myself clear?"

Ben stuttered momentarily. "I hear ya, I hear ya, Lonnie. We had kind of a bad day today. I hear ya. Thanks for the call."

Lonnie hung up the phone. He turned to return to the bedroom. Carrie was standing in the kitchen doorway. "Thank you, Lonnie. I love you."

CHAPTER SEVENTY-SIX

JUNE 5, 2017

"Asha, I don't expect you to fully understand half of what I've shared with you. I simply feel better knowing someone here is aware of what is happening," Carrie confessed.

"Carrie, everyone is aware! Everyone is aware and frustrated. There is nothing anyone can do about it if your dad isn't willing to do something." Asha replied.

Just then Carrie's telephone rang. "Thank you for calling Haughton Manufacturing, this is Carrie Dustin. I would be happy to help you." Carrie paused. "Oh, hi, Dad. Certainly. Yes, yes, I can come to the bank. What is our meeting about? Okay, is there anything I should bring with me? Okay, I'll be there in about twenty minutes." Carrie hung up the phone. Asha could see immediately that Carrie was shaken by the exchange.

"Carrie, what's going on?" Asha asked.

"I'm not sure, Asha. Dad wants me to meet him at Summit Enterprise immediately. He gave me no reason why we are meeting—it sounded to me he was avoiding giving me a reason."

At four o'clock, Carrie pulled into the Bank parking lot. Her legs became weak when she saw Teddy's car parked next to Ben's.

Carrie entered the bank and was greeted by Doug Honer, Summit Enterprise Bank Branch Manager. Doug escorted Carrie into a large office in the rear of the building. Seated in front of a large Victorian desk were Ben, Teddy, an empty chair next to Teddy, and another chair for Doug. Behind the desk was seated Bank President, Case Benedict.

Mr. Benedict stood as Carrie walked into the room. Doug pulled the chair next to Teddy out for Carrie to be seated. Carrie did not make eye contact with Ben or Teddy as she walked in and took her seat.

"Good evening, Ms. Dustin. I'm Case Benedict, President of Summit Enterprise Bank."

"Good evening, sir. May I ask what this meeting is about?"

Teddy turned and spoke directly into Carrie's right ear. Carrie never turned towards him but kept her eyes fixed ahead toward Mr. Benedict.

"We've found it! I knew there was something going on. We've found it!"

Carrie slowly and deliberately turned her head towards Teddy. She very firmly, but directly asked, "Found what?"

Teddy pulled out his cell phone. He quickly dialed a number. When it began to ring, he turned on the speaker. "Hello, this is Stephen Spence."

"Steve? Yeah, Steve? This is Ted Haughton." Teddy turned the volume up. "Steve, I'm sitting with Ben Haughton, Case Benedict, Bank President at Summit, Doug Honer, Branch Manager, and Carrie Dustin. Tell them about the account."

A befuddled voice on the other end of the call began to stammer.

"Ted, Ted, take me off the speaker! I told you not to make any moves! I told you we haven't found anything yet, except this one number. This is not the way to handle this, Ted."

Carrie interrupted.

"Excuse me, who are we talking to?"

Teddy was on the edge of his seat with excitement. "The account! We've had a private detective watching your every move. We found the account you've been hiding. It has your name and your social security number!"

A sudden peace swept over Carrie. It was visible to both Mr. Benedict and Doug as she sat back in her chair.

The voice on the other end of the call moaned, "Ah, no, Ted! No! This isn't right. You've got nothing!"

Teddy hung up the phone. He began to raise his voice. "That's right! I've found the hidden company account no one was supposed to know about. It's in your name, it has your signature, and it has your social security number. We are losing money. Everything points to you, and I want answers!"

Carrie turned her attention to Mr. Benedict. In a very calm, professional tone of voice said, "Sir, part of my responsibility as Haughton Fabrication's controller is to assess and modify processes so that time is utilized efficiently. In March 2014, Teddy began his employment with Haughton Fabrication. I was instructed to secure, for him, a company credit card. At that time, eight of our managers had company cards. Each of their cards was different. Each required separate payments at different times of the month. I contacted your branch and asked if we could consolidate the cards into one account at your bank while still allowing each employee to have their own individual cards. This would allow accounting to track their charges individually. Your people were very accommodating. I was grateful for their assistance. I simply had to come here and open a master account in my name to secure Teddy's card and consolidate the others. As you well know, it was necessary for me to give my social security number and signature to open the account and complete the transaction. Mr. Benedict, Mr. Honer, there is no hidden account. I am sorry my father and his son have taken your valuable time. If you don't mind, I will excuse myself."

Carrie got up from her chair. Mr. Benedict and Doug Honer stood. Teddy and Ben remained seated. Carrie shook Mr. Benedict's and Mr. Honer's hands and left the bank.

What Carrie had just experienced did not fully register with her until she pulled into Haughton Fabrication's corporate offices. Ben Haughton, her father, knowingly allowed his adopted son to pursue her with the full intention of ruining her name, ruining her ability to effectively work in the financial world, and therefore ruining her life. They had willingly violated Carrie in the presence of two financial professionals.

Carrie entered the corporate office. It was strangely quiet. No one looked up, no one said a word. Carrie went directly to her office. Asha met her in the hallway.

"Carrie, are you al–?"

"Not now, Asha!"

"Carrie, what happened? Teddy called when you left. He gave me some strange warning and then started laughing. What happened?"

"What did he say?" Carrie asked.

"He said I needed to be ready. Big changes were about to take place and I would be working for him. Is that true, Carrie? Tell me, is that true?"

Carrie realized Asha deserved an explanation. For the moment, she had to set aside her personal anger and assuage her most valued employee and friend. "Asha, you know the pressure I've been under because of Teddy."

Asha acknowledged affirmatively with a worried nod.

"It is worse than I thought. He and my dad hired a private detective to tail me—to investigate all of my transactions, all of my comings and goings. I have been under surveillance for a number of months."

"Oh, my gosh! No!"

"It gets worse. I just returned from Summit Enterprise Bank where my dad and Teddy accused me, in front of the bank president and branch manager, of opening a hidden account to siphon off company profits."

"Oh, Carrie!"

"I have never been so humiliated in my life! I'll tell you, God was with me. I felt a sudden calm where there should have been uncon-

trolled rage. I remembered immediately the day I consolidated everyone's credit cards. The Bank President was on his computer as I was
talking. It all unfolded in front of him as I was giving my
explanation."

"What did your dad say? What did Teddy say?"

"Nothing. Absolutely nothing. You just watch. It will be totally
ignored. In 'Ben's World' it never happened."

"Carrie, what are you going to do?"

Carrie was not willing to divulge any of her options. Although Asha
was a friend, she was also an employee. Carrie felt she'd probably told
Asha too much already.

"Asha, I'm going to keep my head down and work. There will be no
chats in the hall, no small talk. I am going to work, and then I am going
to go home."

Carrie gave Asha a hug. It was a confident hug. She gathered her
things and left the building. She hoped a confident hug would be
awaiting her at home.

Pauline was setting the table when Ben walked in.

"Hi, sweetie. How did your day go?"

"It was a bad day, Paul. It was a really bad day. This just isn't fun
anymore. I can fix machinery, but I can't fix these kinds of problems."

Teddy stormed in. "There she goes again, Dad! You saw what she
did, didn't you? You saw it—you were there! She set us up! She tried to
make fools out of us! She knew exactly what the account was but never
told anyone. I keep telling you; she hides information. She is more than
difficult; she is deceptive! You can't trust her, Dad. No wonder your
father told you a woman has no business in business!"

Pauline, knowing full well about the private detective and the
meeting asked, "What happened, Teddy? What on earth did she do
now?"

"Ah, Mom, what doesn't she do? She knows Dad is getting older.
She has his office and total control of Haughton Fabrication in her
sights!"

Pauline nodded towards Ben who had his back turned while pouring a Harvey's. Teddy took her cue.

"I'll tell you, Dad. It's obvious to me that she should never have sole influence over any of your holdings! She is irrational and secretive. I'd hate to think of what will become of your personal assets when you die."

Teddy's comment came out of the blue and caught Ben's attention. "What are you talking about?"

"You know what I'm talking about. You always have her take care of your investments. She handles your taxes. What do you do? No, wait. I'll answer that, I know what you do—You sign them! That's all you do. You blindly sign anything she puts in front of you. Just like your father did with his sister! If she is willing to take advantage of you at work who knows what she is doing with your personal finances? There's too much at stake here, Dad. You need someone who has your best interest in mind. I should be the sole executor of your will."

"Ya know Ben, Teddy is right. You've got to think about me, too. Who will I have looking out for my best interest when you die? Carrie? Ha! I don't think so."

Their comments bruised his pride. He took a sip of his Harvey's, slammed the glass down on the coffee table and said, "I'll tell you what we're going to do. We're going to see Jake Batemen tomorrow and make some adjustments to my will. That's what we're going to do!"

Pauline smiled. Teddy glanced her way and did the same. Not another word was spoken of the day's events.

As Carrie drove to Hunter's Crossing, she was sickened with reality. The evil she'd experienced that day clung to her like a contaminating spirit. She felt filthy bearing the residue of hatred she'd experienced. She knew beyond any doubt, Teddy would continue to wreak havoc without fear of repercussions.

As Carrie pulled into the driveway, Lonnie was getting the mail. He waved but there was no response. He could see through her windshield an expression he had not seen before.

"What did he do now?" Lonnie moaned.

"Not now!" Carrie firmly responded.

Carrie walked past Lonnie and into the house. Lonnie paused for a moment to let Carrie settle down. As he entered the hallway, there were articles of clothing leading to the master bath. Carrie was in the shower.

Lonnie knew something terrible had to have happened. "God? I hope you are listening. I have no idea what has happened, but please give me the right words to say to her."

Lonnie went downstairs and set the kitchen table. Thirty minutes went by. The shower was still running. After forty-five minutes, he heard the water stop. He waited for Carrie to come downstairs; she did not.

Lonnie went upstairs and opened the master bedroom door. Carrie was in bed. A myriad of thoughts ran through Lonnie's mind. What was the right thing to do? Lonnie decided to follow his heart and sat on the side of the bed.

"Babe, I have no idea what you have been through, but you are safe at home now, and I love you."

Carrie sat up in bed, threw her arms around Lonnie. He asked no questions, he said no more. He held her. After a few minutes, Carrie gently pulled back.

"Lonnie, they are after me. They not only want me gone, but they also want to ruin me—ruin us! I must leave Haughton Fabrication. I don't know what I'm going to do. I don't know where I'm going to go. I've been there too long, too long as a controller in a family-owned business. I don't know if I can compete in the financial world. I don't know if anyone will hire someone my age when there are so many younger CPAs out there looking for jobs. Lonnie, I am really scared."

Lonnie carefully considered all that Carrie said. Not knowing what had happened and not wanting to ask, he replied, "Babe, whatever we need to do, we will do it. You are not alone in this. And this isn't the first time you've felt this way. God has always pulled us through."

He realized he sounded preachy. He looked directly into Carrie's eyes and said, "Can I feel a little scared with you, so we can depend upon God together?"

Carrie found the strength to smile. "That would be just fine with me."

The next morning, Lonnie got up and jumped in the shower. Carrie remained in bed. When Lonnie stepped out of the shower, he noticed Carrie was still in bed.

"Babe, you've got to get up and get ready."

Carrie rolled over and said, "I'm not going in today. I need some quiet time to sort things out. Let's talk later when you get home."

The thought of talking about Haughton Fabrication, Teddy, Ben, or Pauline when he returned from his day's work was depressing. "Okay, if you need anything, just give me a call."

"I need a job. *That's* what I need!"

"Babe, if that's what you need, it's out there looking for you. You just have to find each other. God's got a bird's-eye view of the whole thing. It will happen."

"Thank's, Lonnie. I'll cook something special for dinner."

He kissed her goodbye and left for PALCO.

Carrie decided to call Kathy. She anticipated Kathy to be busy and she would leave a message—Kathy answered the phone.

"Hi Carrie, what's up?"

"Hi, Kathy. Have a minute?"

"Sure. You caught me on my break."

"Listen, I want to bring you up to date on a few things. Have you talked to Dad lately?" Carrie asked.

"I had lunch with him last Friday, why?" Kathy responded.

Carrie told Kathy the chaos Teddy was creating. When she told Kathy about being tailed by a private detective, Kathy gasped. "No way! No, he didn't! Dad didn't know, did he?"

"Dad knew, Kathy. He just sat there and let Teddy violate me. It isn't enough that Teddy lies about me, and Dad believes him-"

Kathy interrupted.

"Come on now, Carrie. Dad knows what you've done for the company." She hesitated before continuing. "I probably shouldn't tell you this, but it isn't just Teddy. He and Pauline are really working Dad. They are unmerciful. Pauline is forever drawing comparisons between you and Fiametta with Grandpa. She belittles him by saying that he's going to let the same thing happen to Teddy that happened to Grandpa. Then she calls him an idiot. Teddy picks up from there and goes on about Dad's age and how he doesn't know how to be successful today. It's elder abuse if you ask me."

Kathy paused for a moment and then continued. "So, what can I do to help?"

"Kathy, I just want you to know everything that's going on. I'm afraid getting me out of the company isn't all that Teddy and Pauline are trying to do. When he went so far as to haul me in front of a bank president, I knew then he wanted to destroy my reputation. He has this sinister way of manipulating events. He creates a lie, tells Dad the lie, I deny the lie, and Dad believes the lie even more because to him, it must be true, or I wouldn't deny it! Kathy, I know I'm not making any sense..."

"Oh no, no, unfortunately, you are making perfect sense! Dad doesn't want to believe that there is anything wrong with Teddy. Carrie, Dad sees himself in Teddy. If Teddy fails, Dad fails. His failure is doubled. He fails again as a father, which he never was to us, and he fails as a businessman. Dad will never see Teddy for who he actually is. His ego won't allow him to."

"Kathy, I'm not trying to influence you. I know you still go over there and as long as you are safe, I want you to. I just don't want them pitting us against each other; be careful. The more Dad acknowledges Teddy's brilliance, the more diabolical Teddy gets. I don't know what he is capable of doing. Lonnie truly believes he's a sociopath and could be dangerous."

Kathy wanted to calm Carrie's concerns. "Sis, I love you. I'm not in the thick of it yet, but when they find out that I won't be manipulated by any of them, I'll be right there with you and Lonnie. We'll keep one another posted on anything we hear."

"Exactly! Okay, I'll let you go. I love you, Kathy."

"I love you, too."

CHAPTER SEVENTY-SEVEN
AGE OVER ARROGANCE
JUNE 19, 2017

Madalyn Thomas was Jake's personal secretary. Ben and Teddy entered the offices to her greeting, "Good morning, gentlemen. Jake is on a call right now, but he will be with you in just a few minutes. Can I get you a cup of coffee?".

Ben said he was fine, but Teddy said that he'd like a cup. It surprised Ben. Teddy never drank coffee.

"Do you like that black or with sugar and cream?"

"Just black."

Madalyn walked to a small table situated by a large window that looked over Indianapolis. She was in her mid-forties. Teddy did not miss her figure as she walked to the table and poured a fresh cup of coffee.

"Here you go, sir."

Teddy took a sip and grimaced. "That's terrible coffee; horrible! Here, on second thought, I'll just wait."

Madalyn was taken aback by Teddy's harsh comment. She retrieved the cup from him. "Oh, I'm very sorry, sir. Um, Mr. Bateman will be with you both momentarily."

Madalyn heard Teddy whisper to Ben. "This guy knows we are

here. We have an appointment. How long has he been your attorney? We shouldn't have to wait!"

Ben whispered back, "Ted, she said he'll be right with us."

Jake's door opened, but to Ben's surprise, Jake's father greeted him. It was as if he was welcoming an old friend. Irv was now 91 years of age. He'd long ago retired but happened to be visiting the office that morning.

"Welcome, welcome! I'm glad I'm here to see you both." Irv laughed. "At my age, I'm glad I'm still here to see anyone!" Ben and Irv chuckled. "And you must be Teddy Haughton. I've heard quite a bit about you."

Teddy sternly replied, "It's Ted—TED!"

"My apologies, *Ted*. How have you been?"

Ted replied, "We had a ten o'clock appointment!"

Ben nervously chuckled.

Irv was not the least bit threatened by Teddy's aggression. He'd already determined Teddy would unwittingly become his entertainment for the afternoon. Shuffling ever so slowly, gingerly to Jake's desk, Irv reached into his inside right suit coat pocket. Finding it empty, he glanced at Teddy and gave him a wry smile. Irv then reached into his left suit coat pocket and retrieved his reading glasses. He glanced up only to enjoy Teddy's anger mounting. He set the glass case on the calendar then, straining just a bit to reach into his right back pants pocket—he pulled out a neatly ironed white handkerchief. Teddy's breathing became noticeably heavier. Irv carefully unfolded the handkerchief and opened his glass case. He formed a cloth pocket between his thumb and index finger and began to carefully wipe the lenses. Again, he made eye contact with Teddy and offered a broad smile. Teddy's hands were at his sides, but his fists were clenched so tightly his fingers were turning white. Irv carefully situated his glasses on the tip of his long-pointed nose and slowly ran his finger over the calendar. He couldn't resist reviewing each entry beginning with June 1st to the present, June 6th. He reviewed every square and every hour of each day. Irv was an old pro. Teddy was not going to get under this man's skin.

"Well there it is! Ten o'clock, Tuesday, June 6th!" The old lawyer looked over the top of his glasses directly at Teddy.

"It is the 6th, isn't it?" Teddy gave no response. "Well then, my boy, you are absolutely right! I'm glad you were able to make it!"

Irv turned his attention directly towards Ben as Jake entered the room.

"How is Carrie doing, Ben? Ya know, I've always been very fond of that young lady. I'm sorry she isn't with you today."

"Oh, she's doing fine, Irv, doing fine. Ted here is the one who is going to be running the business. I want him and Jake to get to know one another really well."

Irv looked at Ben and Teddy. He slowly removed his glasses and placed them back in the case. As he was returning them to his inner suit coat pocket, he said, with a chuckle, "Well, there comes a time when we all have to pass the baton to the next generation. I'll let you gentlemen get down to business. It was nice to meet you," Irv paused, "Teddy."

Teddy bristled. It delighted the wise old man.

"Ben, give my regards to Pauline."

Irv shook Ben's hand, nodded to Teddy and without a hint of hesitation or physical restriction sauntered out the door.

"I thought you'd get a kick out of seeing Dad today. He pays a visit every so often. Gosh, I think it was in the early or mid-forties when he started working with your dad and grandfather, Ben." Jake reminisced.

"Yeah, it was a long time ago," Ben replied.

Jake continued. "What are we going to be looking at today?"

"Jake, ya know, I've had Carrie and Ted listed as the co-executors of my Will. Ted is really smart. He takes a long time on the computer learning stuff and he doesn't get off until he fully understands it all. I mean, he can be on a topic all night, but in the morning, he knows everything about it."

Jake sat back in his chair, hands folded at his chin, both index fingers extended and pressed against his lips.

Teddy spoke. "This will needs a lot of work. It was written a long time ago, and it hasn't kept up with today's world. I'm going to be running Haughton Fabrication. If my dad died tomorrow and I'm expected to keep the business going, there aren't enough provisions for me to do it."

Ben added to the conversation.

"Ya know, I think Ted's right, Jake. He works very hard. He has a passion for the business—a passion Carrie doesn't have. She's told me numerous times she just wants to keep her job. That's not the kind of desire it takes to run a corporation. Ted loves this company. He talks about it all the time, all the time. I want to switch Ted to be the sole executor of my will."

Jake spoke. "Now, Ben I'm not a family counselor, I'm your attorney. Have you discussed this with Carrie?"

Teddy sat forward in his chair. "You're right! You are *not* a family counselor. You are currently my attorney, and I'm here to make changes!"

"I see. Well, we can make those changes."

It was obvious, Teddy had an agenda. This would not be their last challenging interaction.

CHAPTER SEVENTY-EIGHT
WHAT'S CHANGED?
JULY 10, 2017

C arrie chuckled to herself as she heard the uproarious applause from downstairs. Glen Haughton, Carrie's cousin and CFO for the packaging division, was the last packaging employee to arrive. Of course, Glen made a dramatic entry. He ran from the car and threw himself into the building as if crossing the finish line of the Boston Marathon. *How wonderful it would be to work in a company with such camaraderie,* she thought.

A few minutes later Asha arrived with a big smile and a beautiful bouquet of Summer Sunflowers for Carrie. Carrie gave Asha a hug. Asha took Carries hand and pulled her into the hallway. The stairwell was packed with all of Haughton packaging division's employees. They immediately cheered when Carrie stepped out of her office. She could not hold back her emotions.

Everyone could see how she was being treated. They all felt badly for Carrie and wanted her to know how much she was loved and appreciated by each one of them.

Glen came up the stairs in mocked anger. "All right, all right. What the heck is going on here? We've got a business to run!"

Janice Rogers, Glen's personal assistant spoke up. "Okay, Glen. Just because you won the round of applause this morning doesn't mean you're someone important!"

Once again everyone laughed and made their ways back to their individual cubicles. Glen remained on the stairs. Carrie knew Glen was behind the show of kindness.

"Thanks, cuz! I really needed that this morning," Carrie admitted.

"Carrie, I don't know everything—I don't want to know. I do know, and everyone else knows, you are the most dedicated and most competent employee in either division. We are blood, Carrie. There is something to be said about that. We are blood! Regardless of what others might say or do, don't ever forget it. You are one of the strongest bands in this family's Sacred Thread!"

It was the answer to prayer Carrie needed. It wouldn't influence Teddy, Pauline, Ben, or the untenable situation she was in—she realized that. Somehow, knowing others recognized her efforts and appreciated her, gave her the strength she needed.

Carrie's phone rang at ten-forty.

"Haughton Fabrication, Carrie Dustin speaking."

"Uh, yeah, Carrie it's Dad."

Carrie's insides began to churn. She paused, took a deep breath and in a very controlled voice replied, "Hello, Dad, what can I do for you?"

"Oh, nothing, nothing. I'm in the field with Ted today. I'm getting all mixed up on our pricing. Do you have the sales sheet there?"

"Dad, I can tell I'm on the speaker. Is Teddy with you?"

"No, no we're taking separate cars. You know that nice sales sheet you and Bud put together a couple of years back?"

"Yes, Dad, I do."

"Why aren't we using that anymore? That was super simple, and it was simple to adjust the pricing when steel prices changed. You just put in one number and all the updates were done. Where is that?"

"Dad, I'm terribly sorry. Teddy changed all of that. He is working his own prices now."

Ben thought a moment before responding. He'd backed himself into a corner. If he pursued the discussion with Carrie, he could be incriminating Teddy. If Carrie was right, and Teddy scrapped the previous process, any concerns he had would be towards Teddy's work, not Carrie's.

"Uh, Okay. Where, where is he getting, where is he getting all the costs?"

"I give him all of the costs for his cost build-up, Dad. It's the same sheet I give to you."

Ben was relieved. He could now direct his questions to Carrie's numbers and not question Teddy.

"Well, where are you getting them? What's changed?"

Carrie could tell Ben was trying to protect Teddy because of something taking place in the field. There was no other reason for him to continue pursuing the possibility she might have done something wrong while totally disregarding the possibility Teddy was in error.

"Dad? Do you remember thirty-four years ago when we established our product costing? Remember how hard we worked through the weekend? Remember how Bud sat in with us as we went through every item? Remember how the auditors said that our system was the best they'd seen, and they were going to use it in their other client's corporations?"

Carrie was becoming more infuriated as she recalled the time and energy she and Bud invested in building their cost system, the system Teddy arbitrarily threw out. It was time to let it all out.

"Remember how happy Bud was that we finally had a means of knowing and controlling every variable from raw material to product delivery? Remember how the sales exploded even though the cost of our product was slightly higher? Remember how our customers appreciated the fact that we could forecast accurately and give great quality? *That's* where I'm getting the numbers!"

Ben was now angry. Carrie was giving him accurate facts—facts that did not fit his world. He continued pressing Carrie, hoping that her responses would incriminate her.

"Well then, tell me why the heck are we losing business?"

Carrie did not respond. Her lack of a response sent Ben into a rage.

"Listen! Teddy and I drove around all day yesterday, all morning. I just wanted to have a friendly visit with clients we've been working with for years. All of the sudden, I'm fighting to keep even our loyal customers! What's going on? They say our prices are changing up and down and up and down. They get a cheap bottle of champagne and a bag of popcorn from Haughton Fabrication, and a letter apologizing for the changes in pricing. They have Asha calling on unpaid invoices when we're late shipping the product to them. What the heck are you two doing to me?"

Carrie was no longer hurt. Carrie was no longer shy. Carrie was no longer fearful of losing her job; in her mind, her job ended during the meeting with the president of Summit Enterprise Bank. Carrie was no longer fearful of losing her father, his love, or his acceptance. Like a heavy curtain coming down on the final act of a play too long in reaching its conclusion, Carrie was through!

"Dad, you cannot sell a product at less than its cost to manufacture, then expect to make money! Teddy gets accurate numbers from me. *Accurate!* I do not set the pricing and I never have. Sales set the price of the product. I suggest you ask Teddy how he sets his pricing and not where he gets his accurate cost buildups. I assure you my numbers are always correct! Oh, and I do go over credit cards, and I do know where *he* purchases the cheap Champagne and popcorn if you would like that recap!"

Ben was shouting over the phone, "We're going to have a meeting when I get in there and we're getting to the bottom of this!"

He hung up. Carrie knew exactly what she would be doing the next four hours.

She stopped what she was doing and cleared her desk. Turning her attention to her computer, she recovered from history every previous cost build-up sheet she and Bud had compiled. She then pulled the corresponding Price List Bud orchestrated for every one of the cost build-up sheets. She pulled the sales for each quarter of those periods and New Business Profiles during those quarters. She began her analysis, ever mindful of the clock on the wall. She expected her dad and Teddy to return by three o'clock.

The results were striking. Even during down-cycles, Haughton maintained a profitable business. The margins were thinner, but they were still in the black. Bud never made a practice of increasing prices every time there was an incremental change in costs. He and Carrie knew the upcoming increases and knew the appropriate sales price to stabilize profitability. Carrie purchased prior to increases, and Bud built a big enough margin in his prices to maintain them while the competition was continually trying to keep their heads above water. Don Malone and the employees in the plant kept production running like a top. Quality product allowed the sales department to control value, while Carrie's accuracy allowed the sales department to control profitability. The philosophy had worked for one hundred eleven years. It had come under criticism only in the past three.

Ben and Teddy finished their last call. It was brutal. Keyton Construction was one of Haughton's most consistent customers. They purchased good quantities of product, not necessarily great quantities, but their consistency was like clockwork. They paid their invoices and always took advantage of the 10% net 30. Most importantly, when Ben and Hal took over Haughton Manufacturing, Keyton Construction was Ben's first sale! To Ben, this was personal.

Ben didn't realize how drastically Keyton's sales had dropped. At lunch, Teddy gave him the numbers Carrie had given him. There was a 70 percent drop in purchases from Keyton! Ben walked into Keyton wanting to know what Haughton Manufacturing could do to assist them. Obviously, something had drastically affected their business. To Ben's surprise, Keyton's business was expanding exponentially.

Haughton Manufacturing was no longer being asked to bid on new business. Ben was losing what little footing he'd previously enjoyed.

"Jack, what happened? Where did we let you down?" Ben asked.

Not willing to put Teddy in an uncomfortable position, Jack simply replied, "Pricing, Ben. Pricing." He then continued, "Ben, when my company is growing like it is, I've got to have confidence in my pricing. Look, I'm a businessman—I sell products. I know how difficult it is to maintain pricing in today's economy, but you have to be able to do it if you ever want to plan for growth!"

"Jack, I totally understand; totally. But why didn't you call me?"

"Gosh, Ben, these are the things Bud and I used to work out. Bud was always confident in pricing. Sometimes you would win, sometimes we would win, but when it was all said and done, we had consistent business and an average pricing schedule everyone could live with. I didn't call you because I could never get through to you. I left messages with Teddy, and he would respond. He shared with me the challenges you are having with your purchasing department. Ben, if your costs are not controlled, there is very little Teddy can do about it. I know you need to make a profit too."

"Jack, will you give me another shot at bidding any questionable business you have? You know, anyone who isn't coming through for you?"

"Ben, if that ever happens, you bet I will. At this time, I am very satisfied with my supply chain."

A dejected Ben left the building. Teddy said, "Let's go grab some lunch."

Ben replied, "I've lost my appetite. We're going back to the office."

They returned earlier than Carrie expected. Ben was first to storm into Carrie's office. Teddy stood behind him in the doorway and smirked.

"I want to know what's going on, and I want to know now!"

A very calm Carrie Dustin looked up from her computer. "Hello, Dad. Hello, Teddy. What would you two gentlemen like to know first?"

"I want to know why we can't keep our customers! I want to know what you are doing! Why aren't we controlling our costs? What have you changed? Obviously, something has changed!"

"Dad, like I told you on the phone-"

Ben interrupted. Teddy, still standing behind Ben, broadening his smirk. "I don't want a review of our conversation. I want to know what is going on and I want to know *now!*"

Carrie stood up, walked past Ben and through the doorway where Teddy was still standing. She made certain her left shoulder came firmly into contact with his as she walked through the doorway and down the hall to the smaller conference room adjacent to Ben's office. Ben and Teddy followed.

Carefully arranged on the conference room table were volumes of papers. These were the backups to Bud's and Carrie's work. These documents, compiled during years of collaboration between Bud and Carrie, were the backbone of Haughton Manufacturing's successes.

Carrie told Ben he and Teddy could either review all the individual quarterly costs and sales or review the single page spreadsheet accurately representing the volumes of work resting on the table.

Assessing volumes of numbers and dates and then compiling spreadsheets efficiently explaining those numbers was one of Carrie's greatest talents. She could create an accurate business profile at a glance. Her analysis left no question where deficiencies were lurking.

Ben looked over the spreadsheet. Carrie gave a copy to Teddy and enjoyed the fact that Teddy had no idea what he was looking at. Teddy intently watched Ben's eyes as Ben was reviewing the sheet. He attempted to mimic Ben's review.

"Well, this sheet tells me nothing has changed in the way you are getting your numbers, Carrie. Am I supposed to believe that?"

For Teddy this was a game of chess. His mind quickly began plotting an immediate response while calculating potential deceptive defensive moves he might have to make later. Before Carrie could concur with Ben's cursory assessment, Teddy spoke up.

"Dad, How many times have I told you? It isn't the sales. I'm doing everything I can out there. It's horrible. It turns my stomach every time I lose another good customer. You heard it; you were with me! One of your original customers—gone! You yourself couldn't even change his mind. If I cannot get consistent pricing from her, how am I supposed to get consistent pricing to them?"

Teddy motioned to the table full of folders and continued his rant.

"It's all there right in front of you; both of us can see it. Carrie put the information together." Teddy let Ben's confusion set in. "I'll tell you when the problem began. It began when Carrie started pulling away from our reliable domestic steel manufacturers. You gave her that authority, Dad. You gave her that authority, and when you did, all control of our pricing was upended. Coils were on the water, and prices were changing before they even landed! Every time we have a problem, Carrie wants to take you back to how it used to be. If this is going to be my company, you need to let me bring it up to date and modernize it. We need technology!"

Although she restrained herself, Carrie was tempted to applaud. Teddy, true to form, true to his character, pulled back truth just enough to stuff it full of lies. She realized beyond any doubt Ben would buy into Teddy's lies. Teddy's lies fit Ben's world better than the truth.

Teddy then turned his attention to Carrie, and in pathetically spurious tones, of affection, said, "Carrie, this is our father. Do you have any idea what you are doing to him? You are hurting him, Carrie. He doesn't deserve this. You may have been good in your day, and I'll admit that. But your day is long past. It's my day, Carrie. I know you don't like me; I'm not asking you to. But you must love *Dad,* don't you?"

Carrie had heard that speech before. It dripped of Pauline's insolence. She chose to ignore Teddy and turn her attention back to Ben.

"Dad, it's your company. I've given you the documentation. I've given both of you the actual numbers, the accurate history supporting profitable adjustments Haughton fabrication made to address market variables. I have nothing more to give."

Carrie left the room, retrieved her car keys and purse, and left the building.

"She's difficult, Dad. I can't work with that."

Teddy left the room and the building. Ben stood alone in the conference room holding a file clearly supporting everything Carrie had said.

"Their right—I am too old for this." Ben turned out the lights and left the building.

CHAPTER SEVENTY-NINE
THE PERFECT MESSAGE
JULY 16, 2017

The following Sunday, Lonnie and Carrie took their regular seats at church. The music ministry team led the congregation of about 450 in a variety of praise and worship songs. Pastor Runyan's message, "Letting God Have His Way" was taken from a passage in the Book of Psalm:

> *"Let me hear in the morning of your steadfast love, for in you I trust. Make me know the way I should go, for you lift up my soul."*

> — PSALM 143:8

The message spoke with clarity to Carrie's heart. She could not change her situation. She could not change the hearts of those who sought to harm her. She could, however, recognize in advance, before it happened, that God would lift her soul. During the closing prayer, Carrie claimed that promise, and it lifted her heart.

When the service was over, Carrie and Lonnie greeted those around them and walked towards the exit at the rear of the building. Gladys Bailey approached Carrie.

"Hi, Carrie, hey, I've got a question for you. This might seem odd, but you work in manufacturing, don't you?"

It was an odd question given the fact that they were at church.

"Yes, I work for Haughton Manufacturing."

"Okay, that's what I thought someone had said. I think your company is one of my husband's clients. He's the CFO for Prescott Profile Extrusions. His controller gave her notice last week, and he is putting out feelers to businesspeople we know to find someone trustworthy and competent to take her place. If you hear of anyone, please let him know."

Carrie looked at her watch, "... *Let me hear in the morning your steadfast love, for in you, I trust...*" It was ten minutes till noon; still morning!

Carrie responded, "If he is here right now and has ten minutes, I know of someone."

"Oh my goodness, yes! Yes, he is right over there. Jim, Jim come over here. Carrie knows of someone who might be interested in interviewing for the position."

Jim Bailey excused himself from the group he was visiting and approached Carrie and Gladys.

"Hi, Carrie! What's this? You might know of someone who would be interested?"

Although Carrie and Lonnie knew Jim and Gladys from numerous church activities, Carrie reached out her hand and in a very pleasant but formal voice said, "Hello, Mr. Bailey, I understand you are looking for an experienced controller. I just happen to be looking for an opening in manufacturing. I'd like to explore the possibility of getting an interview with you for the position."

Jim's jubilation was immediate. He ignored Carrie's outstretched hand and gave her a hug.

"Carrie, you just had one!"

Carrie paused for a moment and then jokingly asked, "Well... how did I do?"

The two couples laughed. Jim said, "Carrie, you would be perfect for Prescott. Do you two have anything planned for lunch?"

Lonnie spoke up, "Jim, we are totally open. What do you have in mind?"

"Have you ever eaten at Weber Grill?"

Lonnie laughed. "As a matter of fact, Jim, yes I have."

"Well if that's okay with you, let's get some lunch together and I will explain what we are doing at Prescott."

Carrie said, "That sounds fantastic. We'll meet you there."

The two couples celebrated with food and fellowship. Jim mentioned they'd canceled a weekend getaway because of the heatwave, otherwise they would not have been at church. Lonnie shared they too had thoughts of getting away for the weekend, but they decided to wait till later. They all agreed, it was a Devine appointment that had brought them together.

CHAPTER EIGHTY

ASHA'S INVITATION
JULY 17, 2017

Carrie composed her letter of resignation and left it on her dad's desk. Jim told her to take whatever time she needed to make the transition to Prescott Profile Extrusions. After thirty-one years of employment, Carrie thought one month would be a gracious transition phase. She would travel to Prescott in the evenings and weekends to prepare for a final transition.

Ben and Teddy came into the office together, which led Carrie to believe they'd been at breakfast.

Carrie waited in her office for her dad to enter with the letter. After fifteen minutes, Carrie heard Teddy's office phone ring and saw on her phone that her dad was placing the internal call. She heard Teddy say, "Okay, I'll be right there."

Thirty minutes later, Asha's telephone rang. Carrie heard Asha give the same response. As Asha passed by Carrie's door, she paused and asked Carrie if she was coming.

"I wasn't invited, Asha," Carrie replied. "Asha, I want to warn you. Be very careful."

Asha was confused and extremely nervous.

Two hours passed. It was now twelve-forty-five. Carrie walked by Ben's office door. The door was shut but there did not appear to be anyone inside. Carrie grabbed her lunch and drove to the park for some quiet time before returning.

After lunch, Carrie returned to the office. Ben's car was gone. Teddy's car was parked in Ben's place. Asha's car was there, so Carrie decided to go up the rear fire exit door adjacent to Asha's office. She wouldn't have to pass by Teddy's office and be interrupted.

Carrie put her key in the exit door and carefully opened it. She quietly let it close and stepped into Asha's office. Asha jumped from her chair and threw her arms around Carrie's neck.

"Oh, Carrie, I am so sorry! I am so sorry, Carrie. Please you have to forgive me. I had no choice. They gave me no choice!"

Before Carrie could ask Asha what had happened, Teddy stood in the doorway.

"This is a business, not a soap-opera. Carrie, come into my office!"

Carrie slowly and deliberately turned around to face Teddy. "I will not go into your office."

"Are you refusing a direct order?"

Carrie thought to herself, *the audacity of this kid!*

"You are in no position to give me an order, consequently, I am not refusing anything."

Teddy glared at Carrie for a moment. He then handed Carrie several forms. It appeared to be a contract. As Carrie reviewed its contents Asha spoke up through tears,

"It's true Carrie, your dad signed the business over to Teddy. Teddy is now the President and CEO!"

Before she could process what she was hearing, what she was holding, Teddy spoke. "I understand you want to submit your resignation. That will be impossible, Ms. Dustin; you're fired! You have ten minutes to remove any personal articles from your office. I will expect your keys to be returned to me. If anything that is not your property is removed or damaged, I will press charges against you. Your last check has been printed. I will escort you out of the office. You are to talk to no one. Ten minutes."

Carrie had no choice but to let Teddy enjoy his bluster. While she was shocked at this latest turn of events, she was completely at peace with taking legal action against the company. Her first call would be to Jake Bateman.

She'd finished packing the few articles she kept personalizing her office when she heard Teddy step into the men's room. Carrie put her office key on his desk. Fortunately, Teddy had left her final check on his desk. Carrie took it and escorted herself out the door and immediately called Jake Bateman.

"Bateman & Bateman Legal Offices, how may I direct your call?"

"Hi, Madalyn, this is Carrie Dustin. Can I please speak with Jake?"

"Hi, Carrie. Just a moment. I think he is between clients."

Moments later, a very warm welcoming voice came over the phone.

"Hello, Carrie. How can I help you today?"

"Jake, I need some personal legal advice. Evidently, my dad signed his business over to Teddy. Teddy took the opportunity to immediately fire me."

"Well, Carrie, you understand that as legal counsel for Haughton Fabrication it would be a conflict of interest for me to advise you."

"Jake, we've known each other a long time. As a friend, can you give me the name of someone I can talk to?"

"Certainly, Carrie. I would be happy to help you."

Carrie was totally confused. "What do you mean?"

Jake explained earlier that morning they'd received a call from a law firm in Leesburg. Teddy Haughton hired a new attorney and requested all Haughton Fabrication files be sent directly to his new counsel. After over fifty years of service, Bateman & Batemen had been unceremoniously fired.

"So, how can I help? I am at your service!"

"Oh, Jake! I am so sorry! I cannot thank you enough for all you and your dad have done for my family. This is just awful, awful!"

"Well, Carrie, what about you? What are you going to do?"

"'I have a position lined up, but I do not want to leave Haughton with a blemish on my reputation. I want my resignation to be recognized and accepted, and I want any reference to my termination expunged."

"I think we can get that done. Is there anything else?"

"After thirty-one years of service, I would expect my dad to give me some kind of severance pay."

"Well Carrie, it doesn't look like he's calling the shots any longer."

"Trust me Jake. I'll make myself very clear to him and it will get done. But I'd like you to add that to your letter."

Jake took a moment to determine how best to persuade Carrie to take another direction.

"Agreeing upon your resignation will not be difficult. Clearing your name will not be difficult. Requesting severance is really a personal matter between you and the corporation. Why don't you talk with your dad first? Getting an attorney involved in something you would be better off handling personally with your dad is not the preferred path to take. Nevertheless, if you cannot negotiate an agreeable settlement, I'm here for you."

"Jake, If I may. I would like this letter to go out certified, overnight directly to my dad's attention."

"Consider it done! Carrie, I want you to be aware of something. They made other changes last week. Please ask your dad about them."

Carrie hung up the phone and called Jim Bailey.

"Prescott Profile Extrusions, how may I direct your call?"

"I'd like to talk to Jim Bailey please. My name is Carrie Dustin."

"OH MY GOSH, CARRIE! WE ARE SO EXCITED TO MEET YOU! I'm Karen Westmoreland. Oh my gosh! Just a moment. I'll get Jim!"

"Hi Carrie! Jim here. Are you ready to get to work?"

"As a matter of fact Jim, I am! I will be available August first if that's convenient for you."

"Convenient? IT'S PERFECT! Listen; Gladys and I are going out of town this weekend. We'll return late Sunday night. I will be happy to give you the cook's tour first thing Monday morning!"

"Thank's Jim, I'll bring my apron! I am really looking forward to it."

Carrie noticed she'd missed a call. It was from her dad. She took a deep breath and returned the call.

"A-low?"

"Hi, Dad, it's Carrie."

"Oh, yeah, yeah, Carrie. Uh, hey look. I know you've had a pretty rough day. I want to let you know that I'm going to take care of you, Yeah, yeah I'm going to take care of you. You've done a super job for the company. Ya know, it's tough out there. It's real tough to do business out there. You've got to have a passion, be willing to get in the trenches and fight. Teddy is tough. He's tough and sharp! He's not afraid to make those tough decisions."

Carrie did not want to be rude, but she'd had enough of Teddy's edification.

"Dad, is there something you wanted to talk with me about other than your son?"

"Well, yeah, yeah. I just want you to know I don't want this to come between us. Ya know, it might be better this way. I mean, you know, it might. But, anyway, I want to make sure you get a nice severance. I'll talk with..." Ben paused. "I'll talk with personnel and have them print out a check." Anticipating Carrie's response, Ben added, "Don't worry. I'll be the one signing it."

"That would be a good idea, Dad. Perhaps we can have lunch and you can let me know what other changes you and Teddy have made."

"Yea, sure, sure. Let's do that. Are you available Friday for lunch?"

"Dad, I have all the time in the world."

"Yeah, well, let's get together Friday. I'll make sure Teddy isn't around. St. Elmo okay with you?"

"St. Elmo is always okay with me, Dad."

"Oh, okay. Well, I love you."

Carrie swallowed hard.

"I love you too, Dad."

CHAPTER EIGHTY-ONE
THE TRUTH!
JULY 21, 2017

Carrie arrived at St. Elmo to find Ben's car parked out front. She walked in and directly to the family table where he was seated. Ben got up from the table to give Carrie a hug. Carrie graciously hugged Ben, but she was void of any feelings.

"Hello, Dad."

"Hi, Carrie. Look, I'm, I'm sorry about what happened. Here, I want to give you your severance check before anything. I made the decision what to give you and I signed the check. I hope you think it's an appropriate recognition for the work you did during your employment. I'm really sorry how this all happened."

Carrie was not going to let Ben get away with a check and hollow words. She wanted to once and for all pry every detail out of him.

"Why, Dad? Why are you sorry?"

"Well, ya know business is tough."

"I'm sorry, Dad. Unemployment is tough. Business is a blessing."

Ben squirmed.

"What I mean is, it's tough to have to make decisions that involve your

family."

"Why, Dad? Why is it tough to make decisions that involve your family?"

This was worse than Ben imagined. He vainly tried to come up with an

explanation.

"When you have to let a family member go to keep the business going, it's a

bold move; it's tough!"

"You are going to have to do better than that, Dad. We had a flat quarter! A

quarter when everyone else in the industry was losing money! Is this really the most difficult time the business has ever had? Was Great-grandpa's working through the Indianapolis Flood, the Streetcar Strike, The Depression, World War II, were those difficult times?"

Ben was not following Carrie's train of thought.

"Well, yeah, sure, those were real tough times."

"Was Grandpa being sent to prison for something he didn't do, was that a

difficult time?"

Ben immediately bristled.

"It was a terrible, terrible time; awful for all of us!"

There was anger in his voice. Carrie's question about her grandfather stirred an emotion foreign to Carrie's memory of her dad.

"Well, if what you say is true and those were all difficult times, why is it that in 114 years, no family member was ever fired during them? No, Dad, NO! You refuse to hear the truth. You refuse to face the truth. You didn't lose the

Sacred Thread of our family. You never took hold of it! You did it your way.

"No, Dad. Not this time. Not in my life. I believe the words my great-grandfather said. I believe the words my grandfather said and my grandma Helen. I believe them, and I will pass them along to Melinda, and she to her children!"

"Look, I didn't want any of this to happen this way, Teddy is aggressive-"

"STOP! Teddy is a loser! Teddy's aggression is a result of something other than dedication and commitment. I think he is sick. I think he is dangerous.

I fear him. I fear him for you. He's not right, Dad, and all you do is cover for him."

"Look, Carrie. I'm the only one he has. Nobody likes him. If he doesn't have me, I don't know what he'd do. He's smart, real smart-"

"STOP! Teddy is spoiled, not smart! He is arrogant. He is unlikeable. You've said it over and over that I just don't like Teddy. Well, now you are absolutely correct! I do not like Teddy. Teddy is unlikable. Teddy doesn't want to be liked; he doesn't care. He only wants control. You've already given him the company you promised to give him after you died. You've given him a car you promised to give him if he graduated. You've given him a new house before he made a significant contribution to Haughton Fabrication. What else have you given him, Dad? What else?"

"I don't want to talk about this anymore!" In Ben's world, the conversation was over. In Carrie's world, it was just beginning. Two Haughton worlds were about to collide.

"Why, Dad? Why don't you want to talk about it? What else are you hiding from me?"

Ben was struggling to change the subject. Carrie could sense the pressure building.

"Look, Teddy's in Chicago for a couple of weeks. He's taking some time off before officially taking over. He's been under a lot of stress. Maybe it will give us some time. You and I should get together for lunch or dinner and, you know, rebuild things."

Carrie looked him in the eye.

"I don't want lunches and dinners. I want the truth! What else have you given him?"

Ben's jaws stiffened. He glared directly into Carrie's eyes. It was a glare she'd only seen in Teddy's eyes.

"I had to make a change. I mean, I mean, Teddy is a man. He's running a business and he's tough. He, he's able to make the tough decisions. You know... I mean, I mean it's just better this way."

"What way, Dad? What are you trying to say?"

It was an explosive moment.

"I made him the sole executor of my will!"

"Another tough decision I suppose? I'm sorry, Dad. I have no appetite, excuse me."

Carrie got up from the table and went directly to the bank to deposit her severance check. She didn't know how much it was, but she didn't need another surprise.

CHAPTER EIGHTY-TWO

REFUSE IT

OCTOBER 2, 2017

New jobs come complete with new learning curves. Carrie's new position was no different. She was concerned about her lack of experience outside the family business. Would she be up to date on the latest terminology and practices?

At Haughton Fabrication she'd partnered with some of the finest accounting agencies in America. Unbeknownst to her at the time, she was also receiving a tremendous education. Carrie discovered that she was far more up to date on processes than she'd been recognized for at Haughton. Prescott Profile Extrusions was ready to upgrade to the programs Carrie had initiated at Haughton. Jim Bailey was ecstatic.

Asha Bakshi was now Haughton Fabrication's controller. She'd been warned. She told Carrie she took the job because the job title would look good on her resume. She hadn't counted the cost. Every week she called Carrie in tears. Teddy was an unethical task master. All Carrie could do was admonish Asha to do what she knew was right; never compromise her integrity. Asha felt it was impossible to have integrity and at the same time work for Teddy Haughton.

On October 18, 275 metric ton of steel arrived. It was the final remnant of Carrie's orders. Don Malone was standing atop the coils which were still on the flatbed trailer. He was reviewing the visible coil tags and spot checking their weight against the BOM. Everything appears to be in order. As Don was preparing to sign the receipt, Teddy walked around the back of the flatbed. His arms were folded. It looked as if he too was inspecting the cargo.

"Don't accept it!"

Don laughed and once again began to sign the receipt.

"YOU HEARD ME! DON'T ACCEPT IT!"

Don realized Teddy was serious. Teddy was refusing the shipment.

"On what grounds?" Don asked.

"Because it's garbage foreign steel. I don't want it! Send it back!"

Teddy turned and walked back into the manufacturing facility. Don told the driver he could not accept the load because of quality issues. The driver didn't care. He was paid to go from point A to point B and then return. He'd be collecting his paycheck regardless.

Don stormed into the production office and directly up to Teddy. "What the devil are you doing? That was perfectly good steel—some of the best quality we've ever run!"

Teddy did not acknowledge Don.

"Ted? Did you hear me? You are going to bring this plant to its knees! I've got two, maybe three months of inventory on hand at the very most! Where are you going to get a replacement of good quality steel in that short of time?"

Teddy slowly looked up at Don as if bored by Don's very existence. "You just keep the plant running."

Teddy smiled, got up from the chair and walked out of the production office. He arrived back at the corporate office and made his way up the stairs. He seemed to be in an unusually good mood—making him even more disarmingly uncomfortable to be around.

"Good morning, Asha, how are you this morning?"

"I-I'm fine, thank you, and how are you?"

"I'm fine too. Thank you for asking. Say, when Ben gets in, have him come to my office."

"Certainly, sir. I will let him know."

Asha preferred Teddy be consistently ugly. Hating him without feeling guilty would be so much easier.

Ben arrived at ten-ten. Asha gave him Teddy's message. Ben immediately went into Teddy's office, which just two months prior had been his. Teddy closed the door. Fifteen minutes later, the two of them exited the office. Ben looked deeply troubled as they passed Asha's office door. Ben returned to his office. Peeking around the corner, Ben said, " Asha. Hold all my calls. We will be at the manufacturing facility."

"All right, sir. I will hold all calls."

She's never seen such sadness. His voice lacked strength and his eyes were empty.

At eleven o'clock Teddy and Ben entered the Haughton Fabrication facility. Teddy walked directly up to Glenda Taylor and asked her to page Don Malone to the office.

"May I have your attention! May I have your attention, please! Don Malone to the front office. Don Malone to the front office, please."

Teddy smiled at Glenda.

"Thank you... uh?"

"My name is Glenda, sir. Glenda Taylor."

"Well, thank you Ms. Taylor. You have a very nice voice."

"Thank you, sir." Glenda blushed.

Don entered the front office. "Hey, Ben, Hi, Ted. I'd shake your hands, but I've got grease on them."

Teddy laughed. "Ah, that's all right, Don. Don't worry about it. Listen, I'd like you to stop production."

A puzzled Don inquired, "When?"

"Right now—this minute. Stop production immediately and have every employee come to the front office."

Don picked up the intercom system. "Let me have your attention! I want all production to immediately stop. Every employee report to the front office."

Teddy returned his attention to Glenda Taylor. "Ms. Taylor, please see to it that no phone calls are received while I talk to production."

"Yes, sir."

The entire day shift now surrounded Teddy and Ben. Teddy spoke while Ben just hung his head.

"Ladies and gentlemen, I am now the single Owner, President, and CEO of Haughton Fabrication. Only I hold that position, and I will not share my authority with anyone. I am immediately releasing Ben Haughton from his employment. Ben, I understand many of these employees have become your personal friends. That's unfortunate. Please say your goodbyes and leave the premises. You are not to enter the manufacturing facilities again without my permission. To do so will be considered trespassing."

On October 18th, Teddy Haughton fired his father, Ben William Haughton.

On Friday, October 20th Teddy took a morning strut through the manufacturing facility. A very concerned Don Malone approached him.

"Ted, you've got to do something! We'll run out of steel in January —January, Ted! There are already customer orders I can't fill because I don't have the right raw material mix on hand. I've run out of materials that meet their specifications. We've got to get some steel in here!"

Teddy smiled. "I want you to run through the weekend. I'll pay the overtime. Keep running through the weekend. I'll give you a detailed forecast on Monday. It will explain everything."

Teddy abruptly turned and went back into the front office. "Where's that young lady, uh, Glenda, I think is her name. Is she here?"

Linda Otterman spoke up.

"She's part-time, Mr. Haughton. She won't be in today."

His raised eyebrow and smirk sent a chill down Linda's spine. He made eye contact with every woman in the room, searching them for any signs of weakness. His gaze was aberrant. After eyeing everyone he returned his attention to Linda.

"That's too bad; that's really too bad. Have a nice weekend everyone."

Teddy left the office. The women took a collective deep breath.

CHAPTER EIGHTY-THREE
PRINT IT
OCTOBER 23, 2017

Teddy arrived early Monday morning and paged Asha to his office. He gave her the forecast he'd promised Don Malone. Teddy told Asha to contact Bob Percelli, Mike Dutro, and Dorthy Falco with the information. From her cursory review, Asha could see it required editing.

"Ted, would you like me to proof this?"

Teddy exploded with anger. "Did I ask you to proof it? DID I? It is perfect the way it is! Perfectly written! PRINT IT! FIFTY COPIES! DO YOU THINK YOU CAN DO THAT WITHOUT CRITICIZING ME?"

Asha shook with fear. There was no answer to his question that wouldn't incriminate her and add to his anger.

"I'll do it right away, sir."

Asha moved quickly. Within minutes she presented Teddy with fifty copies, still warm from the printer.

He abruptly grabbed the copies from her hands. He then drove to the manufacturing facility and requested Glenda to page Don Malone, Rob Steiner, and Tyler Dixon to the front office.

The three men immediately left the manufacturing facility and reported to the office. Teddy handed them the following notification:

Dear United Steelworkers Union 1999 membership,
The Union and Haughton Fabrication Manufacturing was unable to reach
an agreement. In addition, we have concluded that the industry that
Haughton Fabrication Manufacturing is attempting to compete in is too
globalized, competitive, and risky to continue to do business in. The time
allotment for buying steel to remain open past November has come and gone.
The current contract & 90-day closure notice clause is in effect. The plant
will be closed when the steel runs out or approximately November.

Ted Haughton
Haughton Fabrication Manufacturing
10/23/2017

The news was gut-wrenching. It set the three men back on their heels. After 114 consecutive years of a successful family business, an inexperienced adopted son single-handedly severed the final strand of the Haughton Family's Sacred Thread.

Haughton Fabrication was dead.

"Gentlemen, I want that machinery in perfect running order; perfect! I want the line to run like it has never run before. I want everything cleaner than the day it was delivered. Do I make myself clear?"

Don Malone spoke first, "Ted, this is shocking; it's horrible! The steel we needed; it was delivered! You refused the shipment! What is going on?"

Teddy glared at Don.

Rob and Tyler spoke.

"Ted, is there some kind of package for us? A severance plan? How are we going to be protected?"

Teddy continued to glare at the men. "That's all you can do? Think of yourselves? How do you think I feel? I've lost my entire inheritance. I'm younger than all of you. What will I do? Selfish! That's what you are, selfish! I could shut this place down today! I'm being generous. I've given you time to find other places of employment. You want a package? I'll give you a package. You have whatever you've saved! You have whatever my company has generously added to your retirement. Severance? Really? Severance from a company that is forced to shut down? With your attitude it's no wonder we're closing our doors!"

Teddy turned his back on the three men and walked to Glenda Taylor. His disposition immediately transformed. His warm smile was disarming.

"Glenda, dear, would you please hand these out to each of our employees? I need someone I can trust to do this for me."

Glenda's heart was heavy with sadness. She would weather the storm. As a part-time employee, the financial impact was minimal. Her heart ached for those who had been with Haughton Fabrication for many years.

"Certainly, sir. Certainly, I will do that right away."

"Oh, and Glenda, it will take some time for our corporate office to close out all of our books. Asha, our controller, will need your full-time assistance through the remainder of the year. That, I would hope, is good news for you."

Glenda was troubled. "Sir, there are others that work full-time here. They have worked for Haughton Fabrication for many years..."

Teddy smiled.

"I appreciate your concern; I really do. They need to find other places of employment. Glenda, my position requires me to make tough decisions, but my decisions are always good decisions. I want you to come over to the corporate office this afternoon until the end of the year."

Glenda replied, "Yes, sir. I understand."

Teddy turned back to the three men. "You see how easy it is when you have professionals who cooperate? Have a good day, gentleman."

Teddy returned to the corporate office. He walked into Asha's office.

"Hold all of my calls. I want absolutely no interruptions. Oh, I've got an assistant for you. She will be here after lunch. I want you to make a spot for her in the empty office next to mine. Find something for her to do."

Teddy walked into his office, closed his door, and called Preston Edmund. Teddy's excitement was palpable.

"Leesburg Law, Mr. Edmund's office."

"Yes, this is Ted Haughton. Get me Preston."

"I'm sorry, sir. Mr. Edmund is on a call. May I take a message?"

Teddy's exuberance was uncontrollable. "Yes, yes! Tell him Ted Haughton called. It is complete! He will be very excited to get this message. Give it to him as soon as he gets off his call."

"I will certainly do that, Mr. Haughton. Have a nice day."

Teddy turned on his computer. He giggled like a little boy as the desktop picture appeared.

The 2014 Cirrus SR22T was beautiful. Teddy added every avionic upgrade package available to his new aircraft. The plane would cost just over one-million dollars. Not a problem for a young man who'd just concluded the sale and legacy of Haughton Fabrication. Precision Metal Fabrication purchased Haughton's assets and machinery for 18-million dollars.

CHAPTER EIGHTY-FOUR

THANKSGIVING
NOVEMBER 23, 2017

The doorbell rang. Lonnie opened the door to greet Kathy.

"How's my favorite sister-in-law this wonderful Thanksgiving morning? Come on in, babe. The whole family is here!"

Lonnie gave Kathy a hug and a kiss.

Kathy wanted to spend as much time with Lonnie, Carrie, and Melinda as possible. They were family. She followed Carrie into the kitchen to help with the Thanksgiving Brunch. Melinda played the piano which filled the Dustin's home with music.

There were only a few minutes left until the oven timer would signal the completion of Carrie's famous crazy eggs. The homemade hash browned potatoes and smoked ham was ready for serving. Kathy arranged the fresh berry platter filled with strawberries, blueberries, and blackberries. Kathy's presentations always emphasized her artistic flair. It left partakers with a dilemma, should they eat it or just enjoy its beauty? Homemade blueberry muffins, freshly brewed coffee and bottomless mimosas completed the family's epicurean delights!

Good music, good food, laughter, and love. It was the perfect beginning of a magnificent Thanksgiving celebration.

The Dustin's were well aware of Kathy's harried schedule. She'd accepted an invitation from Pauline to have Thanksgiving dinner at their home in Clearwater Pointe. Carrie and Lonnie were grateful she'd spent the morning and early afternoon with them. Kathy excused herself, "Guys, I'd rather be here, but someone's got to try to keep some semblance of connection and peace in this crazy family. Say a prayer for me!" The group enjoyed a Thanksgiving family hug before Kathy left.

Forty-five minutes later, Kathy arrived at the Haughton's home. She walked up the slate pathway towards the beautiful double-door entry. Teddy stood in the doorway with opened arms.

"Hey Kathy! Happy Thanksgiving!" Kathy gave Teddy an awkward hug as she entered her father's home. "I'm so glad you are here. It's good to see you. Mom and Dad are in the family room. Here, let me take your coat."

Kathy thanked Teddy and made her way around the entryway corner into the family room. The fireplace was crackling. Its warmth felt good against Kathy's face.

"Oh, hello sweetie. Dad just went to the garage to get more wood. Can I get you a drink?" Pauline gave Kathy a hug.

"I'll just have some ice-water right now, thanks."

"Ice-water? What's wrong with you? It's Thanksgiving, party time!"

Ben came in with his canvas tote full of cured oak firewood. "Hey, hey, hey! Kathy! Happy Thanksgiving, yeah, it's good to see you, yeah. Did you go over your sister's this morning?"

"Yes, Dad, she sends her love."

Ben took the wood to the fireplace and then returned to Kathy. "Yeah, she called me earlier this morning. Here, let me give you a hug and make this all official." Ben gave Kathy a warm hug. "What can I get you to drink?"

"I'm fine with just water, Dad."

Kathy took a seat in the green leather chair next to the fireplace.

Pauline brought appetizers to the octagonal glass-top coffee table. She could not fight the temptation to start a rift.

"So, you went to your sister's this morning? That's really unfair of her to expect you to make a trip to both places."

Kathy could tell Pauline was egging her on. Pauline wanted to draw a negative comment out of her. Kathy would not have any of her manipulation and stopped her in her tracks.

"Actually, Paul, it was a wonderful morning and afternoon. I thoroughly enjoyed seeing Melinda. She is doing extremely well."

Not to be out done, Pauline said, "Well your brother is the one who is doing well. Tell your sister about your new home and plane."

Teddy beamed with pride. "I sold my house, and I'm building a new home in Leesburg. I bought enough acreage to build my own runway!"

Ben interrupted. "How do they work that up there? I mean, the FAA and having your own runway?"

Teddy took out his cellphone to show Ben the article about private runways, crop dusting, and the laws pertaining to them.

Kathy made the fatal mistake of sharing her opinion. "I think it's sad. All of those devoted employees out of work and we're talking about new homes, airplanes, and runways."

Pauline's jaw tightened. "That's all some people can afford to do sweetie—talk. Teddy made it happen!"

Pauline ran her finger around the rim of her cosmopolitan. Her face became expressionless, except for the vein on the side of her forehead which was just beginning to protrude.

"And how is your little condo, sweetie?"

Kathy did not respond. She realized her comment precluded any possibility she would be included in further Thanksgiving conversation.

At the close of the evening, Pauline retrieved Kathy's coat from the closet. She wanted one last word with her stepdaughter.

"You drive carefully sweetie. And be careful; be very careful."

Kathy sensed a hidden meaning.

Pauline pulled Kathy aside. "Kathy, I'm going to give you some advice, sweetheart. I'm going to warn you. You'll want to stay close to your brother. He's a very powerful man. He does not quit until he has total control, total! Do drive carefully, dear."

Thanksgiving dinner was a success! Carrie and Lonnie were washing dishes and putting the house back in order. It was eleven p.m. when the telephone rang; it was Kathy. Carrie's stomach began to churn as she answered the phone.

"Uh... Hello?

"Hi, Carrie. I'm sorry to be calling so late. I just got home from Dad's place. Carrie, I don't think Teddy and Pauline are finished. I got signals they are going for everything!"

Carrie interrupted. "What do you mean, everything? What did they say?"

"I don't know; it's a feeling. Did you know Teddy made 18-million dollars on the sale of Haughton Fabrication?"

"No! No one ever gave me a final number. Oh my gosh, Kathy! You know he fired Bateman & Bateman, don't you? He's got a new hotshot attorney in Leesburg."

Kathy interjected. "That's the other thing. He's building a house in Leesburg."

Carrie was shocked. "What? He has a new house down here; the house Dad bought for him!"

Kathy continued. "Wait a minute! I'm not through. He is building a new house and a private runway for his new airplane."

"His what?"

Kathy was just getting started. "You heard me right! Teddy bought a new airplane."

Carrie began putting the puzzle together. "Kathy, we're in trouble! Dad made him the executor of his will. Teddy is after everything."

"Exactly! That's what Pauline told me... well, she hinted at it. She said he is powerful and will not stop until he has complete control. I think he is going after our parts of the inheritance."

"Kathy, why would he move closer to the lake? Dad promised that property to you!"

"I'm thinking the same thing. Pauline warned me to stay close to Teddy. Carrie, he's evil! He's repulsive! I'll lose everything before selling my soul to him!"

Carry responded. "We may have already lost everything."

PART SEVEN
PLAYING BEN TO THE END

CHAPTER EIGHTY-FIVE
PRESTON MEETS BEN
JUNE 21, 2018

Ben Haughton lost his first love, Haughton Fabrication. His enthusiasm, his self-esteem, his purpose had been sustained for 56 years by the pounding of the presses, the whirling of the conveyors, and the sounds of forklifts moving materials and product throughout the plant.

Gone were the new ideas, the new designs. Gone was the nine-month incubation of an idea, the engineering and prototyping leading to the birth of a new product line. New customers and new suppliers would now be having lunch or dinner, playing golf, or enjoying a Colts game with another company.

Gone was the reason to wake up at seven o'clock, shower and shave by eight o'clock, grab a quick cup of coffee and an apple pie at McDonalds. Gone was the rush to the plant to greet friends—his family of employees at Haughton Fabrication. It was all gone.

Depression soon filled the voids of fulfillment. When sitting for prolonged periods of time listening to the continual droning of criticism, the mind looks for an escape. The loss, the pain becomes too deep. Ben Haughton was feeling the consequences—he was feeling the consequences in ways he never imagined possible.

Pauline continued her stinging criticisms. The more Ben's heart was pierced, the deeper he recessed into a world of self-imposed deaf numbness.

"What's wrong with you? I can't even reach you anymore. You just sit there daydreaming. I know what your problem is, you've got dementia. Wonderful! Isn't that just great? That's all I need at this point in my life. Taking care of a tired old man with dementia. Come on, Ben. Lighten up!"

In Clearwater Point, every day was the same. Teddy had convinced them to get away from Indianapolis and up to the lake, but it made no difference whether Pauline and Ben were at Clearwater Point or Lake Tippecanoe. Ben was falling deeper and deeper into a cavern of depression.

Teddy called Preston and shared the situation with him. He was tired of hearing his mother's whining and secretly didn't blame Ben for his emotional seclusion. Preston saw this as an opportunity. Teddy needed to convince Pauline and Ben that Ben's mental ability was diminishing too quickly for them to have confidence in his decision-making ability. They had to be convinced that the future stability of what remained of the Haughton Estate was in jeopardy. Teddy alone possessed the mental prowess to make prudent financial decisions.

"Ted, get your dad in here and we can go over the best options for him to protect his desires after he passes."

That evening, Teddy visited Pauline.

"Look, Mom, Dad, this is difficult for me to talk about, but we've got to face facts. Dad, your condition is worsening. You are getting mixed up all the time. It's getting more and more difficult to communicate with you. I know this is putting you and Mom under pressure. I want to help. I've talked it over with my attorney, and there are very important steps we need to take now to protect your estate later. Dad, I'm the only one who can make certain your wishes are followed after you pass."

Ben was puzzled. "Wait a minute, wait a minute. Isn't that why you write a last will? No one can change that."

Pauline broke in. "Shut up, Ben, and listen to your son!"

"Dad, listen. We need to review that Will. Things have drastically changed, and your will was written in very different times under very different circumstances."

"Wait a minute! What the heck has changed? I'm not dead yet! I can still find my way from Indianapolis to the Lake. I know who you are. I get mixed up—okay, I admit that. But I'm not ready to throw in the towel!"

"Ben, if you would shut up long enough for Teddy to explain, you would know what's changed and how you are putting me and my future at risk!" Pauline retorted.

Once again, the duo's tag-team match began. Ben had no one in his corner and no chance of staving off their attack.

"What did you give me, Dad? Huh? What did you give me? You stuck me with a failing company in a losing industry run by people too old to even understand today's business world. I'm young. You took my future away from me! And what do Carrie and Kathy have? You've given them financial help for years! They both have a place to live and jobs to maintain their futures. What do I get? I get an old business you were trying to dump. Oh, by the way. I can't even sell the building and property. The State Health Department took soil samples and found contamination! That's why Precision only purchased the machinery. I started out with a loser, and I am going to lose more money in the cleanup. I had that business for a couple of months. You had it for over fifty years. Whose fault was it, Dad? Whose fault?"

This was the first Ben had heard about contamination. It troubled him deeply. Teddy was masterful. He had a new home, a new airplane, he was constructing a personal runway and twelve million dollars in his bank account. Still, he was able to convince Ben he'd been short-changed.

"Okay, look, we'll go to your attorney tomorrow and reevaluate my will. I don't want any more problems. I want everyone to be treated fairly. No losers! If we have to readjust things, we'll do that. I'm still alive and I don't want your mom or me to be a burden on you kids. If we need care, it gets costly! I need to make certain there is enough liquidity to manage long-term care and allow us to keep our lifestyle."

Teddy backed off the attack. He'd manipulated Ben into the precise position he wanted him.

The following afternoon, Teddy drove Ben into Leesburg to the office of Preston Edmund. Preston made Ben feel like the most important, successful individual he'd ever met. For a moment, Ben felt a surge of self-worth.

"Mr. Haughton, it is an absolute honor to meet you! Sir, you have a very accomplished son! If I might say so, he worships the ground you walk on. Thank you so much for coming here this afternoon."

It only took a moment of recognition, the recognition he never got from Pauline or Teddy, to uplift Ben's outlook on life and living.

"Well, Preston, Ted is smart, he's really smart. I dropped a company on him and put him in a position where the only good business decision was to sell it. Now, I find out that he's going to lose more money because of contamination or some bad stuff the inspectors found. I never wanted any of this. I want to make sure all the kids are treated equally. There is no way the present writing of the will does that. The girls have enjoyed financial gains for a long time. I mean, they are older. Ted hasn't had that. I want to make things right."

Preston glanced over at Teddy, who nodded approval.

"Mr. Haughton, that's admirable, very admirable. Let's look at the will as it currently stands. I'm sure we can adjust it to your satisfaction and to the best interest of your wife and daughters."

CHAPTER EIGHTY-SIX

MORE DECISIONS
JUNE 24, 2017

Ben and Pauline returned to Clearwater Point. He called Carrie and invited her to dinner to review the decisions he'd made. Carrie instantly felt ill. What could possibly happen now?

JUNE 25, 2017, 6:00 PM

Ben and Carrie pulled up to St. Elmo at the same time. There were two parking places on the street. Carrie thought to herself, *positive sign!*

Ben got out of his car and almost ran to hug Carrie.

"Hey, Carrie, it's great to see you! I really missed you up at the Lake. I wish you and Lonnie could get up there more often."

Carrie politely lied, "Well, maybe one day we will both be retired and we can do that together!"

Ben politely agreed although the thought of him being alive when that day came was remote. "Let's get in there and see if our table is available!" Of course, he'd called ahead and reserved the Haughton Table.

"Come in, Mr. Haughton. Ms. Dustin, it is always a pleasure to see you. Please, please, we have your table waiting."

Ben purposely forestalled discussing his meeting with Teddy until after he and Carrie had a couple of glasses of wine and a portion of their main courses.

"Yeah, Carrie. Like I said on the phone, I've made some decisions. I wanted to update my will. Here's what I did; what's going to happen. Ya know, Teddy lived at Clearwater Pointe his whole life; I mean, you know, it's, it's been home to him. The other thing is, with him building his home in Leesburg..."

Ben chuckled. It was a nervous chuckle; it sickened Carrie. Her mind darted from possibility to possibility. What on earth was left to break her heart?

Ben continued talking and nervously chuckling. He was shoveling food in his mouth at an ever-increasing rate.

"...with him living in Leesburg, that's only twenty miles from the Lake House. You and Lon don't go there much at all, and Kathy has never expressed a real interest in it; besides, it's so big. It would be too much work for a single woman to keep up, too much, a lot of work..."

Ben's voice began to trail off. There was a long pause.

"I'm giving the Bahama Beach House to you and Kathy. Teddy will get Clearwater Pointe and Lake Tippecanoe."

Carrie's reaction was spontaneous and involuntary. "Dad! You'd always said you would divide the properties three ways, Teddy would get Clearwater Pointe, Kathy Lake Tippecanoe, and me HBBH."

Ben was firm. "You girls have the properties you already live in and the property your grandma Helen left for you. I want things even and that's what I'm going to do."

"Well, Dad, can I at least comment? The properties we live in, we purchased with our own money."

Ben was unfazed. He'd made his decision.

"Dad? Is there anything else I should know? I mean, I don't want to avoid you because I'm always waiting for another shoe to drop."

"No, there's nothing else. I just wanted you to know so you can call Kathy and-"

"NO, Dad! That's where I draw the line. You tell her or have the executor of your will tell her. No, I will not do that to her."

Ben calmly thought about it. "Yeah; ya, you're probably right. I'll get together with her and let her know. Well, that's that. So, now you know, and we can hope that all of this happens a long time in the future!" Ben chuckled and his shoulders began to bounce. It wasn't charming any longer—it had become annoying.

"Oh, ya know something, there is something else. I want you to do my taxes. You know, handle the money. I'll pay you for your work. I trust you with my bank accounts and would like you to do that."

Carrie thought it would be one last vestige of protection for her dad's wealth.

"Sure, Dad, I'd be happy to do that for you. I'll call the bank tomorrow and begin that process."

"Good, good, well thanks for coming out. Let's make this a regular thing. Now that I'm not working, I'd like to see you more often. I miss that, Carrie; yeah, I miss that."

The next morning Carrie contacted the bank and asked for Blake Williams, Haughton Account Manager.

"Blake Williams, how can I assist you?"

"Hi Blake, it's Carrie Dustin calling."

"Hi, Carrie! I haven't heard from you in a long time. How are you doing? I'm sorry about Haughton Fabrication, we all are. We never saw that coming."

Carrie took a deep breath. "No, Blake, I never saw it coming either. The reason for my call is I had dinner with my dad last night. He's asked me to handle his financial affairs, and I wanted to set that up with you."

There was a long pause; an uncomfortably long pause. Blake seemed uncomfortable as he attempted to formulate what he was about to say.

"Carrie, there's a freeze on that account right now. Your dad has given power of attorney to Theodore Haughton. We have his signature."

Carrie was in shock. She wanted to just leave everyone behind and forget about ever being a part of the Haughton family. Then, it struck her.

"Blake, what was the date of that signing?"

"Well, let's see. Ah, here it is. June 21, 2017."

Just as Carrie thought. Teddy most likely slipped the assignment of power of attorney into the papers Ben signed the day he changed his Will.

"Thank you, Blake. I'm sorry to have interrupted you."

"No problem at all! Don't make yourself so scarce!"

That evening Kathy called Carrie. Kathy was in tears.

"What have they done? What have they done? This is so unfair. It's unfair to you and to me! The Bahamas was always promised to you. I am so sorry, Carrie."

Carrie began to share in the tears. "Kathy, there is nothing we can do. The only thing we can relax in is the fact there is nothing left. That kid has taken it all. No more surprises; it's finished."

"I can't take it anymore. I am over it! Did Dad tell you about the cash he gave Teddy?" Kathy asked.

"What cash?" Carrie asked.

"He's paying for the cleanup of Haughton Fabrication. Teddy convinced him that the contamination had taken place over the years and that it should not be his responsibility to clean it up. Teddy gave him an invoice for four hundred thousand!"

It was surreal.

"Kathy, Teddy has power of attorney! There is nothing I can do about the cash in Dad's accounts."

Kathy gave a mocking laugh. "Ha! Do you think I'm finished? There's more! Carrie, there will never be an end to this story; never! Dad said that Teddy is out of work and needs something to do. Teddy told him he was becoming very successful as a day trader. You know

Dad, he wants so much for Teddy to be successful at something. He gave Teddy two million dollars for the two of them to start a partnership! That's it! There is probably only enough left for Paul and Dad to live on. It's unbelievable. Someone should write a book!"

Carry returned the mocking laugh. "Ha! No one would ever believe it!"

Anger replaced their sense of loss.

Before the next New Year's celebration, Benjamin William Haughton would leave the world he'd created behind.

CHAPTER EIGHTY-SEVEN
THE END OF A CHAPTER

The service was over. Lonnie stepped out from the pew and waited for Carrie, Melinda, Kathy, and the girls to step into the aisle. They walked toward the exit, politely smiling at the family. Former employees, and even Bennet, had taken time off from St. Elmo to pay tribute to a man that meant so much to so many. Kathy walked ahead.

The shout from across the room caused a united gasp. A cold shiver swept over the attendees. It was evil. It deserved no acknowledgment, no attention.

"There was never a place for you as a Haughton. I was chosen! I was chosen every time I walked into the office. I was chosen every time there was a family decision to be made. I was chosen from the day I was born, and I will remain Theodore Haughton, son of Benjamin Haughton and Pauline Haughton; CHOSEN! CHOSEN!"

Teddy's mocking laughter would not subside.

The Dustins never slowed, never turned, never altered their expressions but continued toward the doors.

"You were never going to win! You'll never cease to be a woman and a woman has no business in business! Dad was right, your husband can take care of you; oh, that's right. He was fired from Haughton, too! Losers, losers!"

The mocking laughter continued until, after allowing Teddy's outburst and a moment of her own personal satisfaction, Pauline gently reached up and pulled Teddy's sleeve. She made certain her admonishment was seen by those in attendance. It was an act solely intended to deflect any connection she had with his irreverent show of hatred. His mocking laughter caused an ice-cold chill to fill the chapel as the Dustin's made their exit. Teddy once again took his seat. Pauline patted her son's hand in quiet approval. Her black veil hid a repugnant smile.

Having exited the Chapel, Carrie immediately reflected, "Dad looked peaceful, Lonnie."

"If ever a man deserves to be at peace, it was him," Lonnie replied

"I feel terrible leaving him like that, with the mocking, with the laughter. It wouldn't have been what he wanted." Carrie had maintained a stoic composure throughout the service, but she now wept.

"Honey, you did not leave your dad there. Your dad left three days ago. Today you left evil behind. You left evil, emptiness, and death. It's time for us to start living. That's what Dad would want!"

"Lonnie, Teddy got away with everything. Why does evil seem to win all of the time?"

Lonnie did not answer. Carrie wasn't really looking for an answer. The fact remained, Teddy had been, and would continue to be, the ill-gotten benefactor of all Haughton Fabrication's holdings and the majority of Benjamin William Haughton's Estate.

It appeared there was nothing more Lonnie and Carrie could do.

CHAPTER EIGHTY-EIGHT

THE BEGINNING OF A SAGA
DECEMBER 23, 2021

There was no return address, nothing to identify the package's origin. It required a signature. It was evidently important to the sender—it reached Teddy's hands.

Teddy brought the package into the kitchen and opened it with a knife. The excessive packing tape made it difficult to free its contents.

A book. A book and what appeared to be a contract. The dollars had been blocked out, but the words the sender intended for Teddy to see were very clear:

The Haughtons
Adoption of Evil
Written by: Lonnie Dustin

Teddy had won. He'd manipulated everyone with whom he came in contact. He'd emotionally and unmercifully bludgeoned his father. He'd lied; he'd cheated. Not satisfied with his birthright as an adopted son, he took his sister's promised portions of the inheritance.

Perhaps by documenting the family annals, Lonnie and Carrie could reassemble the fragile strands torn by jealousy and hate. Perhaps those strands could be mended, and the Sacred Thread would continue through Carrie and Melinda. Perhaps by writing this book, its distribution would allow Carrie to regain a portion of what had been taken from her, what was rightfully hers.

Teddy shook with rage. Profanity spewed from his lips like molten lava. He skimmed through the pages and turned to this page:

> *"As for you, you meant evil against me, but God meant it for good, to bring it about that many people should be kept alive, as they are today."*
>
> — GENESIS 50:20

Thanks for everything!

Lonnie Dustin

ACKNOWLEDGMENTS

Writing a novel is a laborious labor of love. It would not be possible without the support of my wife and our daughters. To each individual who unknowingly influenced my character's development, thank you. To my editor, Stacey Smekofske, thank you for your patience, professional direction, and encouragement. Finally, I thank God for every experience, strengthening my character, inspiring my endeavors, fulfilling my dreams, and placing within me a youthful expectation of what He has to offer—new and fresh, every day.

ABOUT THE AUTHOR

Lonnie Dustin's career has included employment with five family businesses. These experiences inspired Lonnie Dustin to write the fictitious Haughton family saga. His observations, blended with a vivid imagination, bring to life a variety of characters—each with very different personalities—each with very different responses to life's challenges.

COMING SOON BY LONNIE DUSTIN

Even in her youth, Pauline Bianchi's craving for acceptance was insatiable-her disguises were abundant. Her deception incurable. At eleven years of age, Pauline Bianchi had already lost intimate contact with herself.

Who was Pauline Bianchi? What turned a child's innocence into demonic retribution? What could have possibly caused such hateful jealousy for Carrie Dustin?

All this and more is revealed in, *PAULINE.*

TEDDY. Victim or victor? Look deep into the mind of a sociopath. Watch how Teddy stealthily maneuvered his way through life— without responsibility or penalty for his actions.

Hated by all who knew him, Teddy wore it as a badge of honor. No one and nothing would get in his way. He was dangerous—but the greatest danger he would cause would ultimately be to himself!

www.ingramcontent.com/pod-product-compliance
Lightning Source LLC
Chambersburg PA
CBHW021603120626
46545CB00001B/38